The Gothic Enterprise

ROBERT A. SCOTT

THE GOTHIC ENTERPRISE

A Guide to Understanding the Medieval Cathedral

UNIVERSITY OF CALIFORNIA PRESS

BERKELEY   LOS ANGELES   LONDON

University of California Press
Berkeley and Los Angeles, California

University of California Press, Ltd.
London, England

First paperback printing 2005
© 2003 by the Regents of the University of California

Title page: Lantern tower of Rouen Cathedral (photo
by Robert Scott).

Library of Congress Cataloging-in-Publication Data

Scott, Robert A.
    The Gothic enterprise : a guide to understanding
    the Medieval cathedral / Robert A. Scott.
        p.   cm.
    Includes bibliographical references and index.
    ISBN 0-520-24680-2 (pbk : alk. paper)
        1. Architecture, Gothic.   2. Cathedrals.   I. Title.
    NA440.S425   2003
    726.6'09'02—dc21   2003007856

Manufactured in the United States of America

13   12   11   10   09   08   07   06   05
10   9   8   7   6   5   4   3   2   1

To Peter Rothwell
with thanks for having made this project possible

Contents

Acknowledgments

It is a pleasure to acknowledge and thank those who have helped make this project possible. I begin with a very special institution, the Center for Advanced Study in the Behavioral Sciences. Known by social scientists everywhere as simply "the Center," it is a fifty-year-old institution that each year brings together forty-eight scholars from as many as fourteen disciplines, from universities all over the United States and around the world. As associate director for eighteen years, I had the opportunity to become acquainted with the work of more than eight hundred of the brightest psychologists, sociologists, economists, anthropologists, historians, and scholars in other disciplines, and to discuss ideas with them. The Center provided me an ideal environment for pursuing a study of Gothic cathedrals. It invites (some would say, compels) those who come under its spell to think broadly, to reach, to transcend the constraining tendencies of traditional disciplinary discourse. Cathedrals belong to no single discipline. Understanding them requires the insights, perspectives, methods, and research techniques of a multitude of fields of inquiry. This is precisely what the Center values, encourages, and makes possible. I would never even have undertaken, much less completed, this project had I remained in a traditional academic department of sociology.

The fellows, staff, and trustees of the Center have contributed to this project in innumerable ways. The scholars who have been

Fellows during my years as associate director have been unfailingly helpful to me in ways too numerous and varied to list here. The Board of Trustees helped facilitate my work by granting time away from the Center so that I could devote time to research and writing. Center directors Phil Converse and Neil Smelser both warmly supported my pursuit of this project and offered extensive, thoughtful reactions to earlier drafts of the manuscript.

I owe a particular debt of gratitude to Douglas McAdam, a former Fellow of the Center and now its director. From the moment he learned about my interest in Gothic cathedrals, Doug conveyed to me his abiding belief in the value of this somewhat unorthodox project. I have especially appreciated his insistent instruction to pay no heed to critics whose skepticism is rooted in narrow, discipline-based concerns over ownership and control of intellectual turf.

Then there are my colleagues on the Center staff. From the start, our assistant director, Nancy Pinkerton, embraced this project and the Sarum Seminar that grew out of it (more about the seminar in a moment) with the same spirit of enthusiasm, joy, energy, and ebullient playfulness that she brings to everything, and I thank her deeply for all that she has done. Leslie Lindzey and Lisa Staton helped prepare successive drafts of this manuscript and devised clever schemes to protect occasional blocks of writing time while I was carrying out my duties as associate director. Jesse Lewis worked his photocopying magic to prepare the illustrations, charts, and graphs. Kathleen Much helped make the manuscript more readable. Finally, Cynthia Moore, Jean Michel, Steve Forte, and Emma Raub were extremely helpful to me in locating books and journal articles, often with only the flimsiest of clues about imagined titles or forgotten authors.

Before beginning this project, I had not realized how many people share an interest in cathedrals. Through conversations with them, talks and seminar presentations I have given, and gatherings I have attended with them, I have been drawn into an extremely interesting circle of people from varied walks of life, people whom I might otherwise never have met. They have helped me in countless ways and added greatly to the excitement of the project.

One group in particular deserves to be singled out for special mention. I began teaching continuing studies courses at Stanford University in 1994, and the next year my wife, Julia Fremon, and I organized our first travel study trip to Salisbury, England, focusing on cathedrals. The alumni of these courses and trips are still together as "The Sarum Seminar," named after the official name of Salisbury Cathedral. The seminar is now in its seventh year and still going strong. Our mailing list includes 150 people, 30 of whom are likely to attend any given monthly meeting. Those who attend the seminar meetings hear presentations by visiting lecturers, give talks based on their own research projects, discuss books, and socialize. A number of the seminar members have undertaken significant projects. Several are writing books, and others have presented papers at the annual International Congress on Medieval Studies and elsewhere.

The courses, trips, and seminar classes rank among the most enjoyable and rewarding teaching experiences of my career, in no small part because of the infectious enthusiasm of those who participate. There may be no greater enthusiast than Cindy Davis, who came on our trip to Salisbury in the summer of 2001. As we traveled around the region to visit cathedrals and abbey churches, stopping in gardens and pubs along the way, Cindy made sketches in a journal to record her memories of the places we visited. The group soon learned that she is a wonderfully talented illustrator, with a charming touch, an amazing eye for detail, and a refreshing sense of humor. Upon seeing her sketches from the trip, I commissioned Cindy to do a series of illustrations for this book, including the "grotesques" that appear throughout. She has been a wonderful collaborator, and her art makes a major contribution to this work. In addition, several friends and fellow travelers have helped enormously by allowing me to use their wonderful photographs of cathedrals: James Boyd, Vicki Fox, Lois Gerber, Virginia Jansen, William Mahrt, Robert Nyden, Nancy Pinkerton, and John Wilkes.

There is also a subset of seminar members to whom I owe a particular debt of gratitude. I will call them "The Gang of St. Gall." They know who they are and why I call them that. To all of them I offer a special word of thanks for their generous gift, and for their abiding interest, support, and friendship over the years.

I have benefited from the help of a number of bona fide medievalists and other specialists. They include George Brown, William Mahrt, Tim Tatton-Brown, Virginia Jansen, Yoshio Kusaba, Barbara Abou-El-Haj, Stephen Murray, Mark Turner, and an anonymous reviewer of an earlier draft of my manuscript. Though each of them has contributed to this project in important ways, I particularly want to thank four of them for their special assistance. Yoshio Kusaba is professor of art history at California State University at Chico. He is extremely knowledgeable about Romanesque and Gothic cathedrals and has shown a generosity of spirit and attentiveness to detail in responding to my unending pleas for help that sets a model for collegiality from which we all can learn. Virginia Jansen is professor of art history at the University of California at Santa Cruz. In addition to having an encyclopedic knowledge of the topic, she brings to her studies a sardonic wit that I have found both refreshing and reassuring. Stephen Murray is professor of art history at Columbia University. His detailed comments on earlier versions of my manuscript have proven invaluable. He has shown a generosity of spirit and tolerance for this neophyte that I will not forget. I have never failed to learn from his comments, and I am extremely grateful to him. Finally, I want to thank Mark Turner, a former fellow of the Center and my successor as associate director. Mark was trained as a humanist with unusually broad interests that extend from literature, philosophy, and linguistics to cognitive neuroscience. He was invaluable in helping me transcend the myriad details about particular cathedrals and focus instead on trying to understand the basic idea of the cathedral and the kind of space and place its builders intended it to be.

I am grateful, as well, for the help of the University of California Press. Jim Clark and Mari Coates patiently shepherded this project through the necessary reviews and approvals, and the manuscript has benefited enormously from the skillful contributions by my editor, Sue Heinemann, and copy editor, Nicholas Murray.

I also wish to acknowledge and thank the dean-emeritus of Salisbury Cathedral, Hugh Dickinson, and his gracious and wise life partner, Jean. Both have been very welcoming to Julia and me and have generously encouraged this project throughout. I have always thought that if, in the end, this book were never to see the light of day, the effort would nonetheless have been worthwhile because Julia and I have gained something from the journey that is far more valuable than a mere publication—the friendship of these two extraordinary, unique, and wonderful human beings.

During our visits to Salisbury, Julia and I have benefited from the companionship of a wide circle of friends who live in that community and who have contributed to my work in ways they may not fully appreciate. They allowed us to become a part of their community, giving us a place within it that made the act of creating this book not only possible but a source of enduring pleasure. The list of our Salisbury friends is long, and I cannot mention all of them here, but I do want to single out a few to whom Julia and I are especially grateful. There is Peter Rothwell, of course, to whom the book is dedicated. His role in the genesis of this project is explained in Chapter 1. I also want to thank Ian and Jane West, their daughter Caroline, and their son Martin, who are among our closest friends in Salisbury. The lovely and talented Kate Shemilt made a special contribution by generously agreeing to shoot the author's portrait, spending a cold January morning in the porch of the cathedral taking hundreds of shots to get just the right one. John Rigiani has been a mainstay of our Salisbury community from the beginning, and we have enjoyed his companionship greatly for all of these years. Added to the list are George and Diana Pelly, Rowena and George Paxton, June Coates, John and Marja Wells, and present and past members of the Sarum College staff: Bruce and Margaret Duncan, Linda Cooper, Sally Litherland, and John Darlington.

Since I did much of the reading and writing for this project while traveling between San Francisco and Salisbury, it seems only fitting that I should thank United Airlines for providing me with so much space in which to work.

Finally, as in our life together, Julia has meant everything to me on this project. She skillfully edited the manuscript and prepared it for publication, including organizing the illustrations. From the very beginning of the project we have shared a common love of Gothic cathedrals. She has provided me with a shoulder to lean on, an ear for listening, a hand for holding, a source of encouragement, support, good judgment, and wisdom. In every respect, she is an ideal partner and companion. The depths of my gratitude for everything she has done to make this project possible, and for the unending pleasure of our life together, cannot be expressed in words.

A Personal Journey

Awe. Inspiration. Humility. These words just hint at the powerful responses evoked by the great Gothic cathedrals of Europe. The visionaries who dreamed them command our admiration and respect, and the audacity of those who actually built them elicits disbelief. How, we may wonder, did ordinary people manage these feats of tremendous physical and creative effort during a time, to quote Thomas Hobbes's *Leviathan* (1651), when life was "nasty, brutish, and short"? Technology in the twelfth to sixteenth centuries was rudimentary, famine and disease were rampant, the climate was often harsh, and communal life was unstable and incessantly violent. Yet communities with only a meager standard of living managed to make the immense investment of capital demanded by the construction of these great edifices. They mobilized the spiritual and civic determination needed to sustain building projects that sometimes spanned centuries. And they created buildings whose exquisite beauty continues to amaze us today.

This is a book about this grand undertaking—the great Gothic enterprise that produced the hundreds of cathedrals and great monastic churches that dot the landscape of Europe. Most other books about cathedrals are devoted to a single building or a set of buildings, and the different styles of columns, vaults, buttresses, altars, and stained glass we find in them. My aim is different: it is to understand the very idea of a cathedral—any cathedral. What did it stand for? What conception did it embody? What sort of a cultural artifact was it? In his classic work, *The Interpretation of Culture*, the American anthropologist Clifford Geertz observes about Chartres cathedral that, although it is made of stone and glass, to understand and see it for what it is, we need to understand the relations among God, man, and architecture that governed its creation and that it embodies.[1] I believe this remark applies as well to all great medieval churches, and his assertion expresses well the fundamental aim of my book.

People who are familiar with my background and training have been surprised to learn that I have undertaken this project. Nothing about my past career as a teacher, researcher, and academic administrator anticipates it. My degree is in sociology, which I taught for seventeen years while on the faculty of Princeton University. My courses there and elsewhere dealt with topics far removed from the subject of this book. Moreover, I have never formally studied medieval history, art, or architecture, nor have books about the medieval period been high on my leisure-time reading list—that is, until about a decade ago, when I began working on this project. Most important, my inspiration did not come via the familiar academic route of a deductive descent from atop some grand theory for which the Gothic cathedral provides a compelling example. It came by the opposite route. I fell in love with one particular cathedral—the Cathedral Church of the Blessed Virgin Mary at Salisbury in England, the building that Samuel Johnson described as "the last perfection in architecture" (Figure 1).[2]

My passion for Salisbury Cathedral compelled me to learn more about it. What I discovered whetted my appetite to learn more about the other cathedrals and great churches of Europe, and by now I have read about many of them. With my wife and partner in this project, Julia Fremon, I have visited several dozen, most of them in England, and a few on the continent. For the past six years we have led travel/study trips for Americans who want to study some of the cathedrals and abbey churches in southern England, so we have gotten to know those particular churches really well.

1. *One of my favorite interior views of Salisbury Cathedral, looking upward from the side aisle.*

Each of the cathedrals and great churches we have visited has its own character, its own beguiling beauty, and that makes it difficult to name a personal favorite. If forced to name just one in England, I suppose Julia and I would say Wells because of its coherence and infectious charm, the carvings on its capitals, and the great scissor arches at the central crossing; however, the mixture of Gothic and Romanesque architecture at Winchester makes it for us a close second. In any case, such ranking in no way diminishes the passion we share for Salisbury.

This immersion in cathedrals led me to ponder and try to answer the three questions that, in our experience, people most often ask about them: Why did people build these great structures? How were they built? What were they used for? Attempting to answer these questions forced me to move beyond the study of any one building and to think instead about the cathedral as an idea, in an effort to understand the fundamental notion embodied in it. This book explains what I have learned.

I have divided my story into five main sections followed by a concluding chapter. Part I, "A Grand Undertaking," describes the great era of cathedral-building in Europe from 1134 to 1550 and explains in a general way what I have learned about how such buildings were actually constructed. Part II, "History," examines the social and economic context of this era to help us understand why this great period of Gothic cathedral-building occurred when it did. Part III, "The Gothic Look," identifies and explains the principal features that make a cathedral Gothic. Part IV, "The Religious Experience," explores how the human search for religion is reflected in the cathedral's form and how that form, in turn, fulfilled its religious function. It includes an examination of the role that dead people, especially saints, played in cathedral-building. Part V, "The Gothic Community," explores how cathedrals both served and shaped the medieval world. The Conclusion draws comparisons between Gothic cathedrals and other monumental building projects that occurred at other times in human history, in an effort to help us understand the fundamental human impulses that produce them.

Before turning to these matters, however, I want to say a few words about how I came to fall in love with Salisbury Cathedral. The story spans my whole adult life, beginning at Stanford University in 1958. As a graduate student in sociology, I began to collaborate with a graduate student in anthropology named Alan Howard, and we coauthored several papers over the years. In 1969 we planned to work together in London for the summer, but before I arrived, Alan moved out of London to the tiny village of Idmiston, near Salisbury. During our three months of work together in Idmiston, Alan and I became good friends with Peter Rothwell, the person to whom this book is dedicated. Peter is a native of Salisbury, where he runs the family business, a chain of fish and chips shops scattered throughout England. Julia first met Peter in 1985, and the following year we spent our entire summer vacation as guests in his house. We have been going back annually ever since, and we now lease a flat four doors from the main gate to the Cathedral Close.

Peter's house is a special place. It sits within the Cathedral Close, just down the street from the eastern entrance at St. Ann's Gate, and literally down the walk from the cathedral and its great surrounding lawn. We could not go to the market, or to the post office, or for a walk or outing without passing the cathedral. At night it is bathed in the glow of huge floodlights, and during the evenings we spent in Peter's sitting room, the tower and spire loomed large through his window. Over a period of years, without our fully realizing it, the building quietly insinuated itself into our souls.

In the beginning, our fascination took the form of observing and admiring its great beauty, particularly its wonderful spire (Figure 2). But in 1986 a major renovation project was begun to replace and restore much of the stone on the tower and spire, stone that had been badly damaged by the elements, including acid rain. Huge steel girders were placed over the central crossing, and on them workers erected ten stories of scaffolding around the entire tower, right up to the base of the spire. (It was estimated that the scaffolding, laid end to end, would span a distance of thirty-three miles!) Over the next few years we followed the progress of teams of workers scampering around the vast corset of scaffolding perched 180 feet or more off the ground, and we found ourselves wondering *how* the cathedral had been built in the first place.

One day in 1991 we were watching the building through binoculars, following the activities of the workers high up at the base of the spire. Work teams and materials were being transported there by means of an elevator mounted on steel runners attached to the side of the scaffold and running all the way to the top of the tower. We could hear the elevator's motor start and stop at each of the levels as work crews and materials were dropped off and collected. As we watched their progress, we began to muse about how teams of masons were brought up to the work site when the tower and spire were originally built, in the late thirteenth and early fourteenth centuries—when there were no mechanical tools or electric-powered elevators to transport workers, stone, and mortar from ground level to the workplace, which at its tallest point is 404 feet above ground. Clearly there would have been a challenging "commute problem" each day as work crews had to ascend the tower and spire and then return to ground level at day's end.

As we pondered this difficulty, we soon found ourselves asking other questions about how the cathedral had been built. Where did the materials to build it come from? How long did it take to complete? Who were the workers, and where did they come from? Who designed it? How was the work organized, and who organized it? How was it paid for, and why did those who built it think it a worthwhile use of scarce resources? How could such a structure have been assembled in a place and time when the population was small, living standards extremely low, life expectancy short, states either nonexistent or weak, and methods of transportation primitive? In short, exactly how did people of the thirteenth century manage to create such a magnificent structure?

2. *Our friend Peter's house lies just a few feet from this corner
of the Salisbury Cathedral green.*

With these and similar questions in mind, I set out to find answers
in published histories of Salisbury Cathedral. It seemed a simple
project for a summer vacation; I would learn the answers to my
questions, and that would be that. But I soon discovered that not
much has been written about the building of Salisbury Cathedral,
and I could find almost nothing about the questions of greatest interest to us. The records and accounts for the period of construction of this cathedral have never been located and are presumed lost.
The few records that have survived pertain only to the decision to
build the cathedral and to the governance of the diocese and the
cathedral during the period of construction.[3] The only way to learn
about how Salisbury Cathedral might have actually been *built* was

to read books about similar cathedrals that were under construction at the same time. Initially, I turned to literature about other Gothic cathedrals in England and quickly learned about the close connections between them and the great churches on the continent, particularly those in France. As I absorbed these materials, my eyes were opened to a new range of questions that went far beyond the somewhat narrow engineering and organizational matters that had first attracted my attention. In addition to asking "how," I was drawn to the other questions that animate this book, namely, "why," and "for what purposes."

To answer them I began reading tomes about medieval theology, music, and philosophy. I learned about the political economy of medieval society and the role cathedrals played in stimulating economic development. I read books about religious fervor, about relic cults and the pilgrimages they spawned. I studied the demography of thirteenth-century England. I read about the organization of building trades there and in continental Europe, about the systems of medieval agriculture from which the labor to build cathedrals was drawn, and numerous other topics as well. After a while I offered a series of courses through Stanford University's Continuing Studies Program, and Julia and I began to lead trips to Salisbury and to sponsor an ongoing seminar for adult enthusiasts who have contributed their own original research.

Though I have learned a great deal, I still have a long way to go. Even so, I believe that I have learned enough about Gothic cathedrals to enable me to "read" them more intelligently than I previously could. My hope is that this work will enable you to feel the same. I warmly welcome you to join me in the quest to comprehend these awesome, mysterious, and magnificent works of humankind.

PART I

A GRAND UNDERTAKING

CHAPTER I

What Is the Gothic Enterprise?

 The movement I call the Gothic enterprise began in the first half of the twelfth century in the Greater Paris Basin. In fits and starts, it continued for the next four hundred years throughout Europe. By the mid-fifteenth century Gothic cathedrals could be found from Scandinavia in the north to the Iberian Peninsula in the south, and from Wales in the west to the far reaches of Central Europe in the east. I know of no comprehensive list of medieval Gothic cathedrals, but the total would surely be in the hundreds. In addition, thousands of abbey churches were built during this period (more than five hundred just in France), plus tens of thousands of small parish churches. One authority, Jean Gimpel, estimates that between 1050 and 1350, more stone was cut in France alone than at any period in the entire history of Egypt. Gimpel also reckons that there was one church for every 200 inhabitants of France and England, and that the English cities of Norwich, Lincoln, and York, with populations in the range of 5,000 to 10,000, each had forty to fifty churches. Another authority, Richard Morris, estimates that of the nearly 19,000 ecclesiastical buildings in existence in England and Wales today, nearly half date to the medieval period.[1] Imagine all the quarrying, carving, and laying of stone, the harvesting of timber, the mining of lead, and the assembling of

Map 1. *A few of the Gothic cathedrals
in the Greater Paris Basin.*

other materials required to build these structures. This was clearly the greatest, most sustained ecclesiastical building campaign in the history of Christendom.

The earliest Gothic great church was the Abbey Church of St. Denis, located seven miles north of Paris. Under the direction of St. Denis's famous and influential Abbot Suger, work on erecting a Gothic-style west front began in 1137, quickly followed by the renovation of its choir to the new style in 1141. Though St. Denis was not a cathedral (see box), the work there appears to have stimulated renovation to the new Gothic style of a large number of Romanesque cathedrals in the surrounding Greater Paris Basin (see Map 1). These included the cathedral churches at Sens (1140s), Senlis (1151), Reims (1150s), Laon (1160), Noyon (1160), Notre Dame of Paris (1160), Chartres (1194), Amiens (1220), Troyes (1220), and Beauvais (1226), to name just a few.

The Greater Paris Basin proved fertile ground for Gothic cathedral-building for good reason. Unlike other regions of France, such as Flanders, Burgundy, and Champagne, where powerful counts supported the construction of monasteries and cathedrals, the vicinity of Paris had seen precious little church-building during the previous century because of the general weakness and financial impoverishment of the monarchy. But once the monarchy began to gain strength (see Chapter 5), the absence of a recent regional style, combined with the fact that most abbeys and cathedrals in the Greater Paris Basin were old and in disrepair, created an opportunity for wholesale renewal of churches that could not have arisen elsewhere.[2]

The new style of the west front and choir of St. Denis was not an abrupt departure from the earlier style; rather, it involved a liberal borrowing of the most advanced features of the Romanesque great churches that were being built in adjacent provinces of northern France. But even if none of its constituent elements was novel, the elements were employed and coordinated in fresh ways. The renovation of St. Denis in turn jump-started great-church-building

---

WHAT ARE GREAT CHURCHES?

The term *great church* includes both cathedrals and large abbey churches. A cathedral is the seat of the bishop, who is charged with the care of souls within a designated area (the diocese). An abbey church is at the center of a group of buildings housing a monastery or convent and under the direction of an abbot or abbess. In effect, the abbey is the seat of the abbot or abbess, the leader of a religious house belonging to an established religious order.
(For more on terminology, see the Appendix.)

campaigns throughout northern France and elsewhere, although considerable time elapsed before the Gothic style emerged as predominant. Moreover, what appeared were not carbon copies of the west front, choir, and planned nave of St. Denis, but projects that explored the implications of Abbot Suger's ideas. Over time, the Gothic style transformed the earlier Romanesque into something new, a style that would become the antithesis of Romanesque architecture. (See Chapters 7 and 8 for a detailing of the Gothic style and its differences from Romanesque architecture.)

Initially, the new style received its warmest reception in northern France and, slightly later, in England. This pairing should not surprise us because the cultural, political, economic, and ecclesiastical ties between England and France ran deep. A great many of the leading prelates of twelfth-century England were French, and those who were English by birth had been educated at the great cathedral schools of France, such as Chartres and Notre Dame. By 1140 English kings had greater influence in certain regions of France than did the nominal suzerains of the French monarchy, and French had been the first language of English elites since the Norman Conquest of 1066. It seems natural that the new style of architecture being developed in and around Paris inspired the building of great churches in England—especially as the timing was right. The burst of cathedral- and great-church-building after the Norman Conquest had lulled by the mid-1100s, creating an opportunity for a new style to take root.[3]

Elements of Gothic design appeared in widely dispersed places throughout England. One was in the great Cistercian abbeys of the north, such as those in Ripon (1160), Byland (1170), and York Minster (1150). Another was in the southeast, where the pivotal development was the rebuilding of the choir at Canterbury following its destruction by fire in 1174. As seat of the head of the Church of England, Canterbury Cathedral galvanized the Gothic church-building movement in England. Its immediate progeny included cathedral churches at Rochester (c. 1179) and Wells (1180), the great abbey church at Glastonbury (1184), and cathedrals at Chichester (c. 1187), Winchester (c. 1190), Lincoln (c. 1192), and Llandaff, Wales (c. 1193).[4]

The new style quickly found its way to other parts of Europe. In Sweden, work on Uppsala Cathedral began in the 1230s, and in Germany cathedrals were begun at Strasburg and Cologne in 1240 and 1248 respectively. In Germany, initially, the use of Gothic elements in cathedral design was generally cautious; such elements were insinuated into preexisting Romanesque structures in such a way as to preserve the integrity and harmony of the early style rather than to modify or contrast with it. In this sense, Gothic architecture was being adapted in Germany to the well-established Romanesque style rather than being used as an alternative to it. (By the late Gothic period, however, some of Europe's most interesting and beautiful examples of Gothic architecture appear in the great urban churches of Germany.)[5]

Gothic architecture also came to Italy in the early thirteenth century. If any single building project can be termed responsible for introducing the Gothic style into Italy, it was the great church of St. Francesco at Assisi (1228). This Franciscan church, which was greatly influenced by the evolving Gothic style in France, was the order's mother church and thus became a model for other abbeys of the order. Even so, regional and local influences predominated, and nothing like an official Gothic style was uniformly adopted throughout Italy. Most of the other Italian examples of Gothic architecture were constructed relatively late in the Gothic period.[6]

In Spain, the influence of the Romanesque pilgrimage church of Santiago de Compostela was overwhelming, creating at first an environment that was not particularly congenial to the Gothic departure from traditional styles. The first evidence of Gothic influence in Spain appeared in the cathedral at Ávila late in the twelfth century, which served as the model for such thirteenth-century Spanish cathedrals as those at Lérida (1203), Burgos (1221), Toledo (1222), and León (1255). The more clearly Gothic cathedrals of

Spain, such as Barcelona Cathedral, Palma de Mallorca, Gerona, and Santa María del Mar in Barcelona, and those at Seville, Castile, Granada, Salamanca, and Segovia all were built much later. The earliest of these was Barcelona Cathedral (1298), and the latest was Segovia Cathedral (1525); dates for the others are scattered through the fourteenth and fifteenth centuries.[7]

Gothic cathedrals did not appear in the Low Countries until the fourteenth century, with beginning dates of construction concentrated most heavily in the years 1330 to 1440. In Central Europe, examples of Gothic cathedrals appear at about the same time, most notably the Prague Cathedral, whose construction began in 1344. Its design blended elements of English and German Gothic styles and served as the model for Kutna Hora, a major collegiate church in Bohemia, which was started in 1388. But most of the church-building activity in Central Europe, as in Germany, produced large urban parish churches rather than towering cathedrals and great churches, because by now church-building had become the measure of civic standing and pride in the emerging towns of the region.

Even this brief account shows clearly that the Gothic enterprise was anything but smooth and linear.[8] Taken in its entirety, the movement arose from a series of very complicated building campaigns marked by discontinuities, fits and starts, diversions, and side-tracked initiatives of every kind. What propelled and sustained it was the realization by bishops, abbots, kings, and others that the Gothic cathedral was a powerful theological and political symbol—symbolism we will explore in this book.

CHAPTER 2

How Were the Cathedrals Built?

What feats of human ingenuity and perseverance enabled ordinary human beings, using rudimentary tools and technologies and working under extremely difficult circumstances, to transform blocks of stone, lengths of timber, ingots of lead, pieces of iron, mountains of sand and quicklime, and other commonplace materials into majestic works of art?[1] The process was enormously complex. Before work could begin, an overall plan was needed, identifying the component parts and specifying their appearance and the means of assembling them to form the whole (Figure 3 shows a typical cathedral "footprint"). The builders had to envision the sequence of actions allowing them to combine the parts at appropriate stages, including how, step by step, to gather the necessary materials and workmen, and how to acquire the revenue to pay for everything. Next, a site had to be found and cleared so the foundations could be marked out, trenched, and laid. Building materials then had to be located, delivered to the site, and assembled there. To do all of this, a workforce with the necessary skills had to be found and hired, and a sufficient number of ordinary laborers engaged to carry, load and unload, mix, and lift the construction materials. This workforce had to be instructed, supervised, and paid, and the work checked for quality. In addition, because a main aim of the Gothic style was to flood the interior with

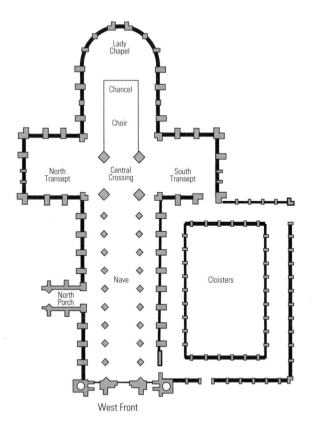

Lady
Chapel

Chancel

Choir

North
Transept

Central
Crossing

South
Transept

Nave

Cloisters

North
Porch

West Front

3. *This floor plan of a typical medieval cathedral shows
the standard "cruciform" footprint, the orientation of
the building west to east, and spaces for many altars.*

light, builders had to devise new ways of constructing vaults, buttresses, and arches that would allow them to open the side walls for windows.

Salisbury Cathedral as an Example

A brief look at how Salisbury Cathedral (Figure 4) was constructed offers some insights into the challenges that cathedral builders faced in transforming their vision into material reality. It took approximately one hundred years to build Salisbury Cathedral. Most accounts I have read give the starting date for its construction as 1220. On April 28 of that year a ceremony was held at the eastern end of the Cathedral Close to mark the laying of the first foundation stones. A good deal of preparation, however, had to be done before the first foundation stones could be laid, suggesting that the work began several years earlier. The construction program that began in 1220 seems to have proceeded more or less continuously for forty-six years, by which time most of the main vessel of the building was complete. This was immediately followed by a second building campaign, which produced the present tower and spire, as well as a freestanding bell tower, which was later demolished. This second campaign probably began about 1266 and was completed by 1320.[2]

Salisbury Cathedral was constructed on a virgin site, built to a uniform design, and was the result of a single, more or less continuous building campaign. These three features distinguish it from most other Gothic cathedrals, which involved elaborate renovations of preexisting Romanesque structures or a series of distinct building campaigns strung out over long periods, during which new architectural styles and building techniques were introduced into the original design.

Much of what is known about the building of Salisbury Cathedral has been pieced together from fragments of historical records and findings of modern archeological studies of the building. The site chosen for the new cathedral was a seventy-acre plot of land owned by the bishop, Herbert Poore, on a water meadow near the River Avon (see p. vi). A water meadow is a plot of low, flat land adjacent to a stream. Although water meadows are subject to periodic flooding—and Salisbury Cathedral itself has been flooded a number of times in its eight-hundred-year history—this site is underlain with a thick bed of chalk that provides a firm, even ground for the foundations of the building.

The design of the building has been attributed to a canon of the chapter, Elias de Dereham, who was also affiliated with Canterbury Cathedral. The master mason, who took responsibility for execut-

4. *Salisbury's expansive cathedral green, surrounded by walkways and the houses of the Cathedral Close, provides a majestic setting for the building.*

ing Elias's grand design, was Nicholas of Ely. His first task would have been to clear the site so that foundations could be trenched out and laid. Presumably he first located and laid out the central crossing, which measured thirty-nine feet by thirty-nine feet and was to serve as a guide for defining other dimensions of the building (see Chapter 7). From the crossing it was then possible to plot out the foundation for the remainder of the building.

Once the outline had been measured off, a four-foot-wide foundation was trenched, establishing the entire perimeter of the building. As with any large building, the foundation had to be laid in a single, continuous process, because foundations laid in separate sections over time are prone to uneven settlement, which can lead to later catastrophic collapse. Because the water table in Salisbury is extremely close to the surface, the foundation trench could be excavated only to a depth of perhaps four feet. The trench was filled with flint gravel and chunks of chalk mixed with straw. (Retired Clerk of the Works Roy Spring reminds us that the gravel and chalk pieces had to be flat rather than round, or else the foundation would act like a bed of ball bearings!)[3] The foundation stones laid at the ceremony of dedication in April 1220 were placed on this bed. The entire foundation was then built up above ground level to a height of twenty or twenty-five feet. Once it was finished, construction on the rest of the building could proceed.

Construction moved from east to west. (You may find it helpful to refer to the footprint of Salisbury shown in Figure 5 as we go along.) The first segment to be completed was the easternmost Lady Chapel, here known as the Trinity Chapel. It was dedicated on September 28, 1225, five years and five months after the first foundation stones were laid. The cathedral chapter moved from a temporary wooden chapel that had been assembled at the eastern end of the present site to the Trinity Chapel, which it immediately began to use as a formal place of worship. The next twenty years (1226–1246) were devoted to building the chancel, choir, and transepts, up to the end of the first bay of the nave. Twelve more years were required

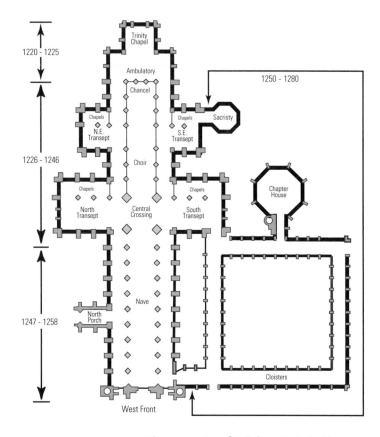

5. *The construction of Salisbury Cathedral began at the eastern end in 1220 and proceeded west. Note that Salisbury has double transepts, allowing for a greater number of eastern-facing altars.*

to complete the nave and the west front up to the top level of the roof (1247–1258). Finally, the next eight years (1259–1266) were devoted to roofing and vaulting the nave, vaulting the aisles, and finishing the exterior facade of the west front.

This work, of course, required massive quantities of stone and other building materials. Once the foundations had been trenched and the foundation itself built, the work of laying stone walls began. The walls of Salisbury cathedral are not formed by solid blocks of stone from inside to out. Instead, they are constructed in three parts: an outer layer of stone that has been evenly cut on the outward facing side and roughly hewn on the side facing in; an inside-facing layer of stone similarly carved and laid; and a rubble core between the two visible faces. Each layer of stone is twelve to fifteen inches thick, and the rubble core, consisting of pieces of chalk mixed with mortar, is of an equal thickness.

The courses of stone that form the walls and pillars of Salisbury Cathedral are bound together with lime mortar. This mortar was produced by adding water to a mixture of sand and quicklime, which was a by-product of firing ordinary chalk. The water and lime combined to produce "slaked," or hydrated, lime, which eventually set as the surplus water in it evaporated. In the early stage of curing, the slaked lime reacted with carbon dioxide in the air to form a new compound, calcium carbonate, which is the hardened mortar found in medieval buildings today. The rate at which the mortar hardened depended on atmospheric conditions such as cold, sunshine, rain, and humidity. Two or three years, or even more, could pass before the mortar became strong enough to support further construction. As I explain in more detail in Chapter 9, the curing process could be a significant factor for cathedral builders, dictating the pace at which their work could proceed.

An enormous quantity of stone was required to build Salisbury Cathedral. Roy Spring has estimated that there are 60,000 tons of stone in the main building, 6,400 tons of which are in the tower and spire. Much of it is limestone (called "Chilmark stone") taken from quarries at Tisbury and Chilmark some twelve miles away. An additional 12,000 tons of Purbeck marble were taken from a quarry at Downshay in Dorset and used to build the decorative stone shafts that adorn the Chilmark stone columns of the interior.[4]

The Chilmark stone was probably transported by oxcart, each cart carrying about a ton of stone, enough to make up to ten of the blocks used to construct the straight-line courses that form the exterior and interior walls. Transporting stone was one of the most expensive and aggravating tasks of medieval cathedral-building. According to historian L. F. Salzman, the cost of transporting a load of stone by cart from a quarry to a work site twelve miles away, as was done for Salisbury, was equal to the purchase price of the stone itself. To reduce these costs, it was customary to dispatch stonecutters to the quarries in order to trim and prefabricate the stones before transporting them.[5]

It was always cheaper and easier to transport stone by water than by land. Salzman has estimated that the cost of transporting a load of stone several hundred miles by ship or barge compared favorably with the price of an overland journey of only thirty miles (it was cheaper, that is, so long as the cargo did not have to be loaded and unloaded more than twice).[6] For this reason, the stone in cathedrals near navigable bodies of water often came from quarries located long distances away. Canterbury Cathedral, for example, was built from stone that came from Caen in Normandy and was shipped across the English Channel to a port from which it was transported to Canterbury, presumably by oxcart. Using landlocked quarries, which were certainly closer than Caen to Canterbury, would have required carting stone on roads of very poor quality and across the hilly countryside of Kent.

One of the few existing accounts of transporting stone for great-church-building projects pertains to the Cistercian abbey at Vale Royal in Cheshire,[7] founded by Edward I of England in 1277. In a period of three years (from 1278 to 1281), 35,448 cartloads of stone, each weighing a ton, were transported from the quarry to the workshop five miles away. To accomplish this, carts had to have left the quarry every fifteen minutes of each working day for three years.[8] At the quarry, stone masons worked in groups of eight, each group under the command of a master quarryman.

Stone, of course, was not the only material that posed mammoth logistical problems of transportation. Timber was another. Roy Spring estimates that there are 2,800 tons of timber in the roofs of

Salisbury Cathedral, much of it hewn from trees in local forests.[9] Trees would have been sawn and roughly squared where they were felled and then carted by oxen or horse teams to the building site, where the precision work of prefabricating the roof frames could take place. The size of some of these timbers staggers the imagination. In a presentation to our seminar group, Roy Spring recounted the dimensions of a single piece of timber that spanned the central crossing of Salisbury Cathedral. Termed the "rood beam" because it supported the cathedral's great cross, the timber was four feet thick and eighty feet long![10] The imagination strains to visualize felling the giant oak from which this single piece of timber was taken, rough-hewing it on the site, and attaching great wheels to it, front and back, so that teams of draft animals could pull it from its home in the forest across the hilly terrain of the Wiltshire Downs to the cathedral site.

Similar challenges were involved in locating, transporting, and refining other materials needed to build Salisbury Cathedral. Four hundred tons of lead were required to cover the roofs and build the gutters and spouts to carry off rainwater. The building needed thirty-two thousand square feet of glass, hundreds of tons of chalk and sand for making mortar, paint for the expansive interior and exterior surfaces, reeds for constructing scaffolds, and so on.[11] Tremendous effort was expended merely to locate, transport, and prepare the materials for finishing by the skilled artisans whose fine work we admire today—the stonecutters, marblers, layers, carpenters, carvers, painters, plasterers, polishers, smiths, glaziers, and plumbers who converted these raw materials into great works of art.[12]

The technological challenges that faced the builders of Salisbury Cathedral are illustrated by the construction of the tower and spire. When the main vessel of the building was completed, it had only a small, squat, eight-foot tower topped with a skylight, or "lantern." Shortly after the end of the first building campaign, probably in the late 1260s (the exact date is still a matter of debate), a decision was

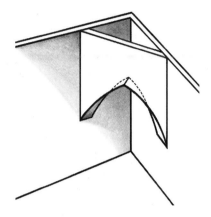

6. *A "squinch" arch was used to fit the octagonal spire of Salisbury Cathedral onto the square tower.*

made to add the present tower and spire. The best guess is that it was finished by about the beginning of the fourteenth century. The total height of the building from pavement to the top of the spire is 404 feet. The tower is 110 feet high, and the spire adds an additional 180 feet of height to the building. The tower, of course, is square, but the spire forms an octagon, so the builders began by adding four "squinch" arches across the corners of the square (see Figure 6), forming an eight-sided base that made it possible to begin building the spire.

The first twenty feet of the spire uses stone that is twenty-four inches thick, but after that the spire begins to taper to a thickness of only nine inches. To lay this stone, workmen built a wooden framework inside the emerging shell of the structure, providing a platform from which to lay each course of stone. The stones are joined to one another with iron cramps frozen in place with molten lead. The work proceeded in this way until the workmen reached a height fifty feet from the top. Because of its taper, the space inside the spire could no longer accommodate interior scaffolding. The alternative strategy was to erect scaffolding on the outside, attaching it to holes drilled into the topmost course of stone. When the top was reached, a capstone measuring five and one-half feet in diameter was added. This was built in sections consisting of four courses of stone, each course composed of several stones cramped together in the same

7. *To change the aircraft warning light at the top of the Salisbury spire, a worker must hold onto iron rungs and climb, leaning backward over the capstone almost 400 feet above the ground.*

way that stones of the spire were joined. Finally, a tall iron cross was fitted atop the capstone (see Figure 7).

The interior scaffolding (Figure 8) remains intact and is used by workmen today who must climb the spire periodically to make repairs or to replace the red signal light that sits atop the capstone. They do this by climbing the scaffolding to a small door some forty feet or so from the top, called "the weather door." They must exit through this door and climb to the very top using a series of iron rungs attached to the outside of the spire. The final thrill comes when they must lean outward and backward in order to pull themselves over the massive capstone. Such a feat is not for the faint of heart—but, of course, visitors are not permitted to climb to the top of the spire!

Materials to build the tower and spire (as well as the roof) were brought up from ground level by means of a giant windlass mea-

8. *The tower and spire of Salisbury were built with the help of wooden scaffolding made of great timbers. The scaffolding remains in place today and is still used to climb to the top of the spire.*

suring almost eleven feet in diameter. It was made of wood and operated by two or more persons who pulled and stepped on the twenty-four one-foot-wide handles attached to the exterior of the machine (see Figure 9). Their work caused a giant wooden axle to rotate, to which was attached a large rope that lifted materials from ground level to the roof.

Given the demanding nature of the tasks involved in building a Gothic cathedral, and the absence of equations for structural engineering, it should come as no surprise that many cathedrals suffered structural failure. Towers and spires collapsed, walls fell over, buttressing systems gave way, and roofs fell in. The tower and spire of Salisbury Cathedral were originally supported only

9. *Building materials were lifted from ground level by means of a windlass powered by workers.*

by the four columns that mark the central crossing. As construction progressed and more and more weight was added, these columns began to develop an unhealthy bulge of nine inches. In response, 112 wooden and stone buttresses were added to the interior and exterior of the building in an effort to redistribute the crushing weight. Moreover, the spire developed a worrying tilt of twenty-seven and one-half inches to the south and east, which required inserting strainer arches in the central crossing and southwest choir aisle. (J. M. W. Turner depicted these arches in the lovely 1802 painting shown in Figure 10.)

Salisbury has been lucky. Beauvais Cathedral, which is the tallest Gothic cathedral ever built, suffered a catastrophic collapse of a portion of the choir in 1282. In addition, a 291-foot stone crossing tower with a wooden steeple that was added in 1569 collapsed four years later. The Norman central tower of Winchester Cathedral fell in 1107, and there are recorded collapses and failures at other cathedrals such as Gloucester (late twelfth century), Worcester (in 1175), Lincoln (in 1240), Ely (in 1321), Norwich (in 1361), and Hereford (in 1786), to mention but a few. One source estimates that at least 17 percent of all cathedrals built during the medieval period,

10. *An 1802 painting of Salisbury Cathedral by J. M. W. Turner shows one of the "strainer" arches added to stabilize the tower and spire. It also shows the stone choir screen that separated the clergy in the choir from the laypeople in the nave. The screen was later removed to open up the vista from end to end.*

Romanesque as well as Gothic, ultimately suffered catastrophic damage and collapse![13]

One detailed report of the collapse of a cathedral spire has survived. In 1861 the 270-foot spire of Chichester Cathedral collapsed, and the event was described in detail by the great nineteenth-century cathedral archeologist, the Rev. Robert Willis. The history of Chichester Cathedral from the thirteenth to the nineteenth century is littered with accounts of concerns about its deteriorating and unstable condition. By 1860 the situation was becoming critical, as Willis explains:

> On the south side of the choir [the] stone had given way, having been propped up by one upright and two raking shores of oak now in a rotten state. In the northwest pier fissures were discovered . . . wide enough to admit a man's arm, and so deep that a five-foot rod could be pushed in for its full length. . . . Iron ramps and straps had been applied from time to time to stay the progress of the settlement, while other cracks had crippled the eastern bays of the nave, and caused a most unsightly breach in the rich pointed arch opening from the south aisle of the nave into the south transept.[14]

Desperate measures were taken to shore up the structure, but to no avail. Repairs and reinforcements at one location in the building merely produced failure at another location. As Willis reports,

> On Wednesday [February 20th, 1861], crushed mortar began to pour from the old fissures, flakes of the facing stone fell, and the braces began to bend. Yet the workmen continued to add shoring until three hours and a half past midnight, notwithstanding the violent storm of wind which arose in the evening and beat first on the north-east side of the church, but as night advanced, came with unabated force from the south-west.
>
> On Thursday, the 21st, before daylight, the work was resumed. Seventy men, working with most commendable enthusiasm and courage, under great personal risk, made strenuous efforts to increase the number of shores, under and around the tower; for those applied only the night before were bent, and the danger became more and more imminent. The workmen were only induced to quit the building by the

inevitable dinner hour of noon. But by this time, the continual failing of the shores, showed, too plainly, that the fall was inevitable. Warning was given the inhabitants near the building, on the southwest, and the workmen, returning at one, were prevented from re-entering it. Anxious groups, outside the cathedral enclosure, stood gazing at the tower, and in less than half-an-hour, the spire was seen to incline slightly to the south-west, and then to descend perpendicularly into the church, as one telescope tube slides into another, the mass of the tower crumbling beneath it. The fall was an affair of a few seconds, and was complete at half-past one. No person was injured, in life and limb; neither was the property of any one of the neighbours damaged in the least.[15]

The Workforce

What kind of a workforce was needed to construct a cathedral like Salisbury? Where did the workmen come from, and how were they organized? Because few records for Salisbury Cathedral have survived, no precise answers are possible. There are, however, fragments of building accounts for a few other Gothic great churches that allow us to speculate about the labor force that built Salisbury.

We begin with the question of size. Judging from the amount of material required to erect a Gothic cathedral, one might imagine that a huge labor force would have been needed. In fact, the relatively small amount of information that has survived pertaining to cathedral workforces suggests that, although it could be large, it hardly amounted to an army. A famous account survives for the year 1253, which records the number of workers of various kinds on the Westminster Abbey site, week by week, for three-quarters of that year's building season. This frequently cited set of accounts is one of the few surviving documents that enable us to estimate the probable size and composition of the workforce required for a Gothic cathedral. One of our seminar members, A. Richard Jones, has done a masterful job of reformatting the information from the medieval scroll into a spreadsheet database, rendering it, perhaps for the first time, readily usable for detailed study and analysis.[16]

Jones's analysis of the Westminster Abbey accounts shows that during the year 1253 the largest number of workers employed on the site at any given time during the peak building season, from April 27 to November 30, was 435 and the smallest was 119, that the modal size of the weekly workforce was 331 and the average size was 309.[17] These figures do not include either quarriers and their assistants or vendors and their assistants, who provided stone, lime mortar, lead, timber for roofs, wood for scaffolds, glass, iron, and other construction materials. Also excluded are task workers, who probably composed, Jones has estimated, about one-quarter of the total labor force.

Another set of accounts that has survived tells us about the workforce at the Cistercian abbey at Vale Royal in Cheshire. Vale Royal was built between 1277 and 1330; the years covered by the surviving accounts are 1278, 1279, and 1280. During this three-year period, the largest number of workers listed on the books was 321 in June 1278, but the next largest was 160 in July 1280.[18]

Both Westminster Abbey and Vale Royal Abbey were built with royal patronage. This usually allowed a generous level of guaranteed funding and, equally important, the right to impress laborers to complete the job quickly.[19] Therefore labor force figures for structures under royal patronage probably overstate the likely size of the labor forces used elsewhere in the same period. Their true value is in helping us construct a rough picture of the likely maximum size of workforce needed to build structures of this magnitude.

What kind of workforce was it? The most complete and careful description I have found appears in Jones's analysis of the Westminster account book for 1253. Jones identifies fifteen categories of workers. Not surprisingly, common laborers outnumbered skilled workers, but the ratio could vary. Vale Royal Abbey has been studied by Douglas Knoop and G. P. Jones, who list the total number of workers on the account books by category, aggregated and averaged for the entire thirty-six-month period. Their data suggest a ratio of approximately two common laborers for every skilled worker. Roy Spring has estimated that for the construction of Salisbury Cathedral, five or six unskilled laborers would have been required to support the work of a single skilled craftsman. Knoop and Jones estimate that in quarries the ratio was more on the order of twenty to one. In considering this matter, we need to remember that cathedrals and other types of great churches that were built during the High Gothic period required larger numbers of highly skilled artisans to complete the ornate carving of capitals, statuary, plinths, and so on. During the earlier period, when building in the Gothic style was just beginning, less emphasis was placed on ornateness, and therefore the ratio of unskilled to skilled laborers was probably larger. The same would have been true for the later, much simpler and plainer Perpendicular style that came into favor after the Black Death had severely depleted the population.[20]

How many hours per week did they work, how was the work organized seasonally, what were they paid, and where did they come from? The work year was divided into two periods: the most active period, when outdoor building was done, roughly spanned April through September, and the less active period of indoor work, October through March.[21] During the cold winter months, the laying of masonry had to stop because the lime mortar hardened slowly, and the remaining moisture in it might freeze in cold weather, causing it to crumble at the time of the spring thaw. Toward the end of September, then, workmen would close the site down, covering and bandaging the raw edges of laid masonry with either straw or dung.[22]

A second reason for stopping construction during the winter months was the dramatic decline in the number of hours of daylight, particularly in northern Europe. In his paper about Westminster Abbey, Jones has calculated the number of hours of daylight month by month for the year 1253. The variation is remarkable, from a low of less than 8 hours in December to a high of 16.5 hours in June. Eight hours of daylight were not sufficient to keep a work site up and running efficiently. To the degree that any work continued, it seems to have involved a small number of skilled masons and carpenters who could work on carving and other detail work inside their workshops and lodges. Even for them, the basic wage rate was reduced. Others might go to work in quarries, and many rejoined their families and worked on their small farms during the winter.[23]

Where did the workmen come from? At Vale Royal, only 5–10 percent of the masons were locals, whereas half the carpenters and smiths and 85–90 percent of the common laborers lived nearby. This evidence supports the view that most skilled craftsmen were itinerants, many of whom traveled great distances, going from one job site to another in search of work.[24] Most of the small army of common laborers was probably recruited locally. From their wages and work schedules, I can only conclude that they were peasant farmers first and foremost, who supplemented their incomes by working at cathedral construction sites. The pace and timing of cathedral-building would then have had to accommodate the demands of the annual agricultural cycle.[25]

During the active building season, the typical workday began shortly after sunup and ended just before sundown, probably with regular breaks for meals. In a week with no feast days on the liturgical calendar, the workweek began on Monday morning and ended early Saturday afternoon. When feast days came up, all work ceased the afternoon of the day before the celebration. Jones's study of the accounts for Westminster Abbey indicates that the master mason, accountants, and certain other categories of workers were paid for holidays, that stone layers were paid for half of them, but that laborers were paid for none. In his study of the accounts for Vale Royal Abbey, Jean Gimpel identified a total of twenty-nine feast days and concluded that since each feast day meant a holiday of a day and a half, the typical medieval man worked for an average of only four or five days a week.[26]

What do we know about wage rates? It is misleading to try to translate medieval monetary values to modern ones, because the medieval economy depended so heavily on barter and the currencies that were in use were local. The surviving records do allow us to learn something about the relative pay of various levels of workers at each site.

The highest-paid was the master mason, whose salary could reach as much as 24 pence per day. Next in grade was the skilled worker, whose rate of pay was based on whether he chose to include meals and lodging as part of his pay or provided them for himself. The fifty-one masons who worked at Vale Royal during the summer of 1280 were paid a weekly wage equivalent to 2.2 to 6.5 pence per day. At the bottom of the scale, ordinary laborers were paid meager wages and worked irregular hours. At both Vale Royal and Salisbury, their daily wage amounted to only 1 to 1.5 pence per day.[27]

Cost and Duration

The sketchy details we have leave no doubt that vast sums of money were required to build a cathedral or other type of great church in the Gothic style. For instance, the new eastern arm of Westminster Abbey, built between 1246 and 1272 by Henry III, cost £45,000 in the currency of that day, and the cost of building the main part of Salisbury Cathedral is estimated to have been £28,000. Although, as I have said, no reliable method exists to express these sums in modern equivalents, using as a crude index the average pay of hod carriers then and now, I calculate the cost to be staggering. Medieval hod carriers probably earned no more than 2.5 pence per day. I have been told by local contractors in Salisbury that hod carriers today in England probably earn £6.50 per hour, or £52 per eight-hour day. On the basis of these wage rates, the cost of each Gothic cathedral or other type of great church would work out to hundreds of millions of pounds in modern currency.

Whatever the actual figure might turn out to be, it would, by any standard, be amazing. Henry III's twenty-five-year project at Westminster Abbey (Figure 11) cost £45,000 in a period when the entire income for his whole realm was only £35,000 *per year*. This one building project consumed 5 percent of the total wealth available to the king for a quarter-century.

Not only were costs high, but, by modern standards, Gothic cathedrals took a very long time to complete. Even if conditions were

11. *King Henry III invested a substantial share of his treasury in reconstructing the eastern arm of Westminster Abbey. The Gothic west front, shown here, was added later.*

ideal—that is, capital was adequate, the weather was good, there were no devastating outbreaks of plague, famine, civil unrest or war, and so on—it could take a good half-century or more to build such a structure. Salisbury Cathedral was completed at what is generally considered to be lightning speed, and it took forty-six years to erect the building's main body. Similarly, Chartres Cathedral took sixty-six years to complete, and Westminster Abbey, which enjoyed generous royal patronage during a third of its renovation period, took approximately seventy-five years to complete.

In the history of Gothic cathedral-building, however, it was not unusual for two centuries or more to elapse between the start of the initial building campaign and the completion of all or most of its component parts. The materials compiled by another member of my seminar on Gothic cathedrals, James Boyd, enable us to piece together rough estimates for the time required to build the typical Gothic great church. His study is based on data from 217 building projects, including Gothic cathedrals and other great churches such as abbeys and monasteries. Because few building records have survived, it is difficult to verify the precise dates when construction began and ended for many of the churches in his sample, but the data are often good enough to permit a close estimate of the elapsed time from start to finish. In this context, the word "finish" is misleading, because many projects were never actually completed. Rather, at a certain point the ambitious building campaigns simply stopped. What I am referring to, then, is the time span between the beginning of renovations in the new Gothic style and the effective end of new building campaigns.

Some cathedrals were built quickly. Examples in France include Auxerre, Coutances, and LeMans, all of which appear to have been built in four decades or less. In England, one of the most rapidly built great churches was Glastonbury Abbey, which was destroyed by fire in 1184 and rebuilt to the Gothic style in a span of just 17 years (1184–1200). Among cathedrals, we have already seen that Salisbury was built fairly quickly. Others, however, seem to have taken an eternity to build. Canterbury is an example. Even if we discount the nineteenth-century northwest tower of Canterbury, construction of the rest of the cathedral as we see it today spanned 343 years, from 1175 to 1517. The French cathedrals at Amiens, Beauvais, Bourges, Evreux, Lyon, and Rouen took more than three centuries to complete, and others, such as Narbonne, Sens, Orleans, and Senlis, took even longer. In England, Bristol Cathedral appears to hold the record: construction began in 1218 and did not end until 1905, a period of 688 years!

These examples represent the extremes. My own analysis of Boyd's data indicates that, *on average*, construction of the Gothic cathedrals in England took between 250 and 300 years from the estimated time when construction or renovation in the Gothic style began until the point at which major new building campaigns ceased.[28] For certain English cathedrals, information is complete enough to paint a rough picture of what transpired during these centuries of building. Except for places such as Glastonbury Abbey and possibly Salisbury, building seldom proceeded without interruption. Rather, we usually see a series of more or less discrete building campaigns interspersed with intervals of little or no construction. This pattern is illustrated by the various building campaigns at Canterbury Cathedral (see Table 1).

During the late eleventh and early twelfth centuries, a great Romanesque cathedral was erected at Canterbury near the site of the original cathedral built by Augustine starting in the sixth century. It is believed to have been finished by 1130. In 1174, four years after Thomas Becket's murder in the cathedral, the great Norman-style choir known as "the Glorious Choir" was destroyed by fire. Renovation of this choir marks the introduction of Gothic architecture into the building. Between 1175 and 1184 work proceeded on rebuilding the choir as well as adding a trinity chapel and corona, which was to serve as Becket's shrine. It was completed in 1184. At this point major construction projects ceased for a period of almost 50 years. In 1236 work began again, this time on a 3-year project to build a new cloister in the Gothic style. Another period of relative inactivity ensued from 1239 to 1303. Then in 1304 work

TABLE 1. *The Building of Canterbury Cathedral (1175–1517)*

DURATION	YEARS	EVENT
	1174	Fire burns Anselm's "Glorious Choir" (Romanesque)
10	1175–1184	Choir, Trinity Chapel, Corona
33	1185–1217	Inactivity
3	1218–1220	Becket's shrine finished, Prior's Chapel
15	1221–1235	Inactivity
3	1236–1238	Cloister and refectory rebuilt
65	1239–1303	Inactivity
17	1304–1320	Choir screen and Chapter House rebuilt
15	1321–1335	Inactivity
1	1336	Window, St. Anselm's Chapel
4	1337–1340	Inactivity
3	1341–1343	Infirmary, Table Hall rebuilt
19	1344–1362	Inactivity
4	1363–1366	Black Prince's Chantry and Chapel of Our Lady in Crypt
10	1367–1376	Inactivity
92	1377–1468	Crypt, nave, transept, cloisters, Chapter House, Pulpitum, St. Michael's Chapel, south transept vault, southwest tower, Henry IV's Chantry, north transept, Lady Chapel vault, tabernacle arch, southwest tower
21	1469–1489	Inactivity
28	1490–1517	Central tower, strainer arch, Christ Church Gateway

TOTAL SPAN IN YEARS = 343
YEARS OF ACTIVITY = 161 (47%)
YEARS OF INACTIVITY = 182 (53%)

12. *Canterbury Cathedral as it appeared in 1799,*
before the Norman-style northwest tower was replaced
with a tower in the Gothic style.

began on the cathedral's great choir screen. This project took 17
years to complete. Another gap of 15 years followed (1321–1335),
at which point there was a burst of building activity involving the
creation of a window in St. Anselm's Chapel and, after another brief
lull, the erection of an infirmary hall. Together these two projects
took 8 years to complete. A gap of 18 years ensued, followed by 3
years of building and then 9 more years of inactivity. In 1377 building resumed until 1468. The period 1469 to 1489 saw no real building activity, but then in 1490, and throughout the next 27 years, work
was done on the central tower, on the gateway, and on erecting a
strainer arch. In short, of the 343 years from 1175 to 1517, building
occurred in only 161 years, with gaps totaling 182 years. A 1799
painting of the cathedral (Figure 12) shows how it looked for 314

years, before a 3-year project was undertaken (1832–1834) to replace the original Norman northwest tower of the west front.

Not every Gothic cathedral and great church followed as complex a route to completion as Canterbury, but with few exceptions they experienced the same pattern of stops and starts. No armies of workers descended on a cathedral-building site and labored day in and day out, decade after decade, until the work of building it was complete. Funding was the crucial factor. When funds were available, progress usually proceeded apace; when they faltered, inactivity followed until another fund-raising appeal could be mounted.

Cathedral-Building in Context

No matter how we choose to look at it, cathedral-building was an impressive undertaking. To appreciate what it encompassed, imagine what it would involve today. Consider the case of England. In total land mass England is slightly smaller than the state of Alabama (approximately 50,000 square miles). Its population during the greatest period of building was roughly equal to the population of Georgia (about 6 million people). One-third of these people were young—the largest proportion of them under five—and another 7 percent were old or otherwise unproductive.[29] Planting, tending, and harvesting crops represented the primary occupation of up to 95 percent of the population, whose survival literally depended on their crops. The average life expectancy for those fortunate enough to survive to the age of twenty was only twenty-five to thirty years more. During the most active period of cathedral-building, England was afflicted by the worst famine to occur during the entire Middle Ages, recurrent epidemics swept the country, including outbreaks of plague, and there were significant periods of war and incessant civil unrest. No more than 5 percent of the population could read, and no more than 2 percent could write.

Yet England managed to build some twenty-seven Gothic cathedrals, hundreds of abbeys and monasteries, and thousands of parish churches, at enormous cost, over many years. For the sake of illustration, if this effort had taken place in the lifetime of our own country, an average Gothic cathedral begun in 1776 would be under construction until 2033! I do not exaggerate when I say that this four-century-long period of Gothic cathedral-building counts as one of the most impressive accomplishments in all of Western history.

PART II

HISTORY

CHAPTER 3

Kings, Feudal Lords, and Great Monasteries

Of the many common questions about Gothic cathedrals, the most difficult to answer is, "Why did it happen?" Identifying, much less understanding, the panoply of factors—political, economic, religious, demographic, technological, cultural, and social—involved in producing Europe's great Gothic cathedrals is a daunting task. Medieval societies were fragmented, disorganized, and chaotic, making it difficult to identify and trace the connections between the constituent elements of these societies and the cathedrals they built.

To grapple with this question, I organized my reading around two issues. First, building any cathedral requires the basic wherewithal to do so. There must be enough liquid financial capital to support enormous start-up costs; an ability to locate, transport, refine, and process the necessary raw materials; a large labor force sufficiently free of other obligations; workers skilled in the necessary crafts and an adequate supply of semiskilled and unskilled laborers to support them; and an ability to organize and coordinate the design and construction over a very long period of time. How, I wondered, did the basic wherewithal for the Gothic enterprise come to exist? A large part of the answer, I believe, lies in the system of feudalism, especially its later stages, which preceded the era of Gothic cathedral-building.

Second, I wanted to understand the forces that motivated bishops to want to build such cathedrals. I discovered that one of the most important factors was a growing challenge of heresy that confronted the established church at the end of the eleventh century and beginning of the twelfth (see Chapter 4). Another was the quest by kings in France and elsewhere to strengthen the monarchy and engage in expansive programs of nation building (see Chapter 5).

What I found was that Gothic cathedrals were the outcome of a complicated, often disjointed process that is best described as "a bit of this, a bit of that, and a bit of the other." In a sense, this conclusion is disappointing because it results in an untidy account that somehow seems inadequate to the phenomena it purports to explain. There seems to be a mismatch between the singular elegance, grandeur, uniformity, and beauty of the buildings and the messy, confusing, and chaotic world that produced them. That such a world could have produced such works of art is but one of the fascinations Gothic cathedrals will always hold.

The Rise of Kings

An understanding of the medieval institution of kingship is fundamental to understanding cathedral-building. After the Roman Empire collapsed in the fifth century, kings drawn from regional tribes began to emerge in Western Europe. After a time, a position of clear dominance was assumed by the Carolingians, a line originating in a Frankish family that succeeded in creating, at least for a time, an empire in which German, Roman, and Christian elements were fused into a common way of life. Its most famous and greatest member was, of course, Charlemagne. The Carolingian monarchs inherited from their ancestors a conception of kingship that dictated basic forms of economics and commerce throughout the medieval period. It defined the duties that those who aspired to rule were expected to fulfill, and also defined how wealth was accumulated, how it was transferred, and how it was spent. In particular, it helps us to understand why so much wealth was invested in building monumental churches.

Georges Duby quotes an unnamed source as saying, "In the kingdom of heaven, there is but one who reigns and that is he who hurls thunderbolts. It is only natural that on earth as well there be only one who reigns, under him." Embedded in this grand conception of kingship were two broad functions. One was to exercise control over secular affairs by providing for one's subjects, protecting them, ensuring the peace, and administering justice. The other function was sacerdotal or priestly, and involved responsibility for managing relations among the monarch, his people, and God. In this respect, the king played the role of a mediator, aiming to win the favor of the deity for himself and his people.[1]

Enacting these functions in turn dictated two main forms of economic activity: pillage and sacrifice, or, in the words of medievalist Georges Duby, "to despoil and to proffer."[2] These complementary actions governed the exchange of goods, resulting in a pervasive circulation of gifts and ceremonial offerings that permeated the entire society. Some of the offerings the king was required to make came from the labors of his subjects, but the most important source of wealth by far was pillage. The king led raiding parties against neighboring tribes and principalities to seize property and people and bring them back to the homeland. Each spring the king would gather his princes, counts, and dukes, along with their warriors, and organize them as an army under his banner to conduct plundering raids. Great gatherings held on the eve of such expeditions were overseen by the principal bishops and abbots of the realm, who administered blessings to the army, hoping to ensure a productive foray and safe return. During such raids, kings and their agents seized anything they could transport—jewels, coins, weapons, agricultural equipment, food, and animals. In addition, they kidnapped able-bodied members of neighboring tribes to sell as slaves or hold for ransom.

In principle, all of the booty gained from pillaging belonged to the king; he could do with it as he pleased. In practice, the king used the spoils of war in three ways: some he kept for himself, some he gave to the men who had joined him on raids, and some he used for sacrifice. The share kept for his own use was an entitlement that went with kingship. Duby writes, "The sovereign was he-who-gives—who gives to God and who gives to man." Distributing plunder to his war band was viewed as a natural part of the king's obligations to his allies—indeed, gifts were considered an entitlement by the *comitatus* (the band of companions). The same sense of obligation that governed the relationship of a king to his princes, counts, and earls in turn governed their relationships to their underlings. Direct beneficiaries of a king's largesse were expected to use a portion of the goods they received to help petitioners, peasants, slaves, and others in their care and to help support people affiliated with the household estates they ruled.[3]

That the king reserved a share of the booty for sacrifice reflected the prevailing beliefs of the time. People viewed the happiness and well-being of the realm as depending on the king's gifts to God, and they expected these acts of sacrifice to be opulent. Lavish sacrifice, they believed, conveyed to God the high regard in which the king and his people held Him. Conspicuous sacrifice was essential if soils were to remain fertile and harvests abundant, plagues kept at bay, and the people protected against raids, shielded from the perils of weather, and guarded against natural catastrophes of every kind.[4]

The links between art and sovereignty were multilayered. For one thing, it was important to a king's persona and fitting for his role as gift-giver, whether to God or humans, that beautiful works should flow from him. As we have seen, this act of sacrifice required lavishness because the intent was to overwhelm the recipient, with the hope of enhancing the giver's influence. The splendor of these gifts publicly displayed a king's ability to ensure a benevolent and protective divine presence within his kingdom. The greater the sacrifice to God, the more powerful a sovereign seemed in the eyes of his subjects. The artistry employed in sacrificial gifts had to be grand.

Another link between art and sovereignty had to do with the king's quasi-sacred status. Because kings represented themselves as earthly embodiments of God, they were expected to be arrayed in splendor as well. Kings required collections of valuable ornaments, and the longer these were held and passed through a bloodline, the greater was the power attributed to them. Valuable works of art, especially heirlooms, added to a king's charisma. To serve this function, the valuable metals and stones the king had accumulated could not be left as raw materials. They had to be incorporated into various adornments, and for this reason, the treasuries affiliated with the royal households created workshops employing the very best craftsmen in the realm.[5]

In these and other ways, art and artists became vitally important instruments for promoting the power and legitimacy of the monarchy. Men who acquired power took a keen interest in developing new artistic styles that would identify them and distinguish them from those over whom they had triumphed. As new groups came to power, they tended to develop and embrace artistic styles of their own, including, most especially, distinctive styles of architecture.

The new practices of sacrifice I have described had profound economic consequences. In the pre-Christian period the act of sacrifice had usually entailed destroying or burying the valuables offered to the gods, thus permanently removing them from circulation. Some goods, of course, found their way back into circulation through grave-robbing or recapture by opposing tribes, but most were permanently lost. From an economic standpoint, this pattern of "consumption" of goods created a significant drag on an already precarious economy.

With the introduction and gradual spread of Christianity throughout the West, the form of sacrifice began to change. As Christianity took hold, a class of specialists—priests—emerged who proclaimed themselves "masters of the sacred."[6] Increasingly they challenged the hold of kings on this role, first sharing it, but ultimately preempting it for themselves. They taught that the portion of the king's wealth reserved for sacrifice should be turned over to them, so that they could use it more appropriately to venerate God. In their minds, wealth was best spent for "the Glory of God"—

which, among other things, meant building grand basilicas appropriate for enacting their rounds of prayers and liturgical worship. In this way, priests eventually managed to capture for the Church the "dead man's share," a practice that in the long run kept the wealth in circulation. Duby believes that this change in the way sacrifice was enacted may have been one of the most important contributions of early Christianity to long-term economic growth and development throughout western Europe during the Middle Ages.[7] Another significant consequence was that it freed priests from having to engage either in warfare or in the drudgery of manual labor for their livelihood. They became consummate consumers who produced little or nothing in the way of tangible goods.

The Rise of Feudal Lords and Great Monasteries

The system of governance just described was the ideal to which early medieval kings aspired, but in reality the rule of sovereigns was fraught with tremendous difficulties. One reason was that pillage could not sustain the appetite for spending indefinitely. By the early ninth century, the supply of obvious, easy, geographically proximate targets had been exhausted or annexed into the kingdom. The search for new booty required longer, costlier, more challenging expeditions. Louis the Pious, who succeeded Charlemagne as emperor in 814, found plundering scarcely worth the effort. To his north and east lay a world that was too poor and untamed to yield much booty, and potential targets to his south were well organized and able to resist his acts of aggression.[8] Pillage, in short, was no longer a dependable method for amassing wealth.

Moreover, kings encountered problems in retaining and exercising control over the people they ostensibly ruled. To govern, kings had to keep tabs on their subjects, which required incessant traveling around their kingdoms. Even the strongest monarchs found it impossible to keep watch on everyone, and the problem grew in direct proportion to the expansion of the empire. As a result, kings had to cede a certain amount of their power to their nobles, charging them with responsibility for keeping the peace in subdomains of the kingdom. Naturally, this created opportunities for strong underlings to establish their own independent bases of power.[9]

Every kingdom was also under the continual threat of foreign invasion. In the eighth century, western Europe became the target of repeated, devastating raids by hordes from the Islamic regions to the south and Vikings from the north and west. The kingdoms of France and England, parts of Germany, the Low Countries, and Spain came under siege, and their populations were generally defenseless. In responding to these raids, a king's army was at a significant disadvantage. It could not be everywhere at once, and in any case it had been created and trained not for defense but for invasive forays. Such a fighting force took a long time to mobilize and deploy. Local lords, on the other hand, were somewhat better positioned to provide protection, if only because the territory they had to defend was smaller. They could build and defend fortresses to which subjects could retreat during raids. A defensive force could also be much smaller, more quickly mobilized, and more easily trained. Increasingly, therefore, defense of the lands passed into the hands of local magnates. Gradually the political structure of a strong monarchy that conquest had made possible began to crumble. Thus, by the first millennium, though the basic functions of governance that had characterized the Carolingian period remained as vital as ever, the manner in which they were carried out had changed.[10]

As the great kingdoms established by eighth- and ninth-century monarchs unraveled, the disintegration they set in motion went beyond just the relationship of kings to their princes and nobles. A similar process, driven by the same logic, began to affect the relationship of princes and nobles to overlords of the middle rank who were ostensibly under their control. Political units became smaller and smaller in response to the practicalities of defense and the effective exercise of authority in this largely rural, increasingly hostile world. As the tenth century dawned, western Europe was dissolving into a thousand small territories, each ruled by a single overlord

who tried to administer justice, defend the people under his immediate control, protect his wealth, and, in support of these efforts,
pillage his immediate neighbors. Under this system of feudalism,
kings did not disappear. Throughout the tenth and eleventh centuries and into the twelfth, kings remained an important force in the
social, political, and economic life of medieval Europe. Nevertheless, under feudalism, they no longer dominated as they once had;
instead, they became part of the unstable and complex mix of secular and ecclesiastic figures aspiring to gain control over a particular territorial domain.[11]

As society broke into smaller and smaller units, anarchy and devastation threatened, and in due course a new and different version
of the social contract emerged. Proposed and enforced by powerful ecclesiastics, mainly bishops from the south of Gaul, it was
known as the "Peace of God."[12] The Peace of God incorporated
the same functions of governance as kingship did in the Carolingian era. But instead of combining them in a single office and therefore a single figure—the king—it differentiated three orders: those
who fought, those who prayed, and those who worked. Responsibility for conducting warfare, including raids to acquire booty to
support oneself and others, fell to feudal lords and their warrior-
knights. Bishops and other ecclesiastics assumed the religious leadership role that had previously belonged to kings, and they were also
responsible for keeping the peace. The role of peasants remained
the same as before, to toil on behalf of those who fought and those
who prayed.

Those who fought—princes, counts, earls, dukes, knights, and
warriors—had managed to gain and retain control over the thousands of small territorial units that had formed as the Carolingian
empire disintegrated. With pillage less lucrative, rulers gathered
their wealth by exploiting those who worked. They spent their
wealth in three ways, each derived from the conception of governance they inherited from the Carolingians. First, they made contributions to great religious houses, thereby enabling prelates to

fulfill the sacred obligation of a community to offer sacrifices to God. Second, they prepared for and waged war. Feudal lords spent vast sums trying to discover and develop better ways to fight and train for war, better battle equipment, and so on. They bred new lines of warhorses, studied new battle strategies and tactics, and supported technological innovations in weaponry. The trebuchet, for example, had evolved by the thirteenth century into a monstrous slingshot. Invented in the eleventh century, early versions of this war machine worked by means of twisted ropes, but early-thirteenth-century models employed a system of pivots and counterweights that could hurl twenty-five-pound stones a distance of two hundred yards. The machine was used to batter the walls and towers of hill forts, towns, and castles and to terrify those who were under siege.[13]

Feudal lords also spent lavishly on military equipment for their battle companions. Duby reports that by the end of the eleventh century, the price of a richly adorned chain-mail shirt equaled the purchase price of a good farm.[14] In addition, they demonstrated their success as leaders by inviting their peers to orgies of conspicuous consumption. They engaged in endless rounds of hospitality, sponsoring great feasts for friends and allies. Reckless, wasteful spending of accumulated goods was a way of proving one's wealth and power. Indeed, in their world one of the main purposes for amassing wealth was to spend it conspicuously. The scope of their lavishness is suggested by the grocery list for a Christmas feast in 1240 under the auspices of Henry III. Though a king's feast was no doubt more elaborate than those given by lesser nobles, the list nevertheless illustrates the dimensions such events were expected to assume:

> In 1240 the king ordered officials throughout the realm to supply what seems to be an amazing amount of flesh, fowl, and fish. The meat consisted of five bulls, eighty porkers, fifty-eight boars, forty roe deer, 1,500 lambs, 200 kids, 1,000 hares, and 500 rabbits. The poultry and birds requested were 7,000 hens, 1,100 partridges, 312 pheasants, 100 peacocks,

twenty swans from Cambridgeshire and Huntingdonshire, ten from Buckinghamshire and Bedfordshire, and as many as possible from the lands of the Bishop of Winchester and of the late Earl of Surrey, together with 20 herons and bitterns, and if possible, in excess of 50 cranes. Finally orders were placed for 300 shad, 120 salmon (to be turned into 300 pies and the remainder salted), thirty lampreys and an unspecified amount of herring.[15]

The material needs of those who fought, as well as of those who prayed, had to be met by those who worked. A peasant's place in life was to supply the labor, services, and goods that would feed the insatiable appetites of the other two orders for self-indulgent consumption or for lavish sacrifices to God. Under feudalism, at least initially, the peasant classes sank into virtual slavery.[16]

But what exactly was the function of those who prayed? As I have indicated, they claimed that their role was to ensure the peace and to act as spiritual mediators between their communities and God. Initially, the bishops asserted their spiritual guidance, but in time more and more of the responsibility for this fell to abbots and monks. One reason for this was that the bishops' role as peacekeepers drew them more deeply into the secular realm. The monastic orders took the opportunity to gain ascendancy as spiritual mediators.[17]

Feudal lords found allies in the great monastic orders. In order to govern, feudal lords needed to assert their independence from kings yet still present themselves as carrying out the functions of governance embodied in the Carolingian concept of kingship. They soon discovered that monastic orders were a vital asset, providing the special link to transcendental forces that kings had once enjoyed and symbolizing the quality of divine anointment that feudal lords lacked. Great monasteries thus provided feudal lords with a way to secure their grasp on all the functions of governance that kings before them had held.[18]

By separating responsibilities for sacred from secular affairs, monks freed themselves to devote their full attention to venerating

God and sacrificing on behalf of the communities that supported them. Believing that the welfare of a community depended upon the devoutness and piety of those who worshipped God on its behalf, communities of monks withdrew from the secular world. At the great French monastic church of Cluny, which had been established in 910, monks now went beyond a mere recitation of the daily offices and found ways to pray around the clock by spelling one another through each twenty-four-hour cycle. This elevated their order to new heights of spiritual devotion, and they could assure their growing list of feudal sponsors that the sacerdotal function of leadership was being executed in exemplary fashion. This was a claim that bishops and canons who, with their new responsibility for secular affairs under the Peace of God, could not possibly match. At the same time it left feudal lords free to devote their full energies to secular matters.

The monastic existence demanded a communal effort in which music and liturgy, performed in unison, enabled each member to find his way to God. The holy life meant exegesis, interpreting the scriptures in an effort to move past the visible to the invisible and so to God. Every monk labored over the scriptures, and grammar and memory systems (see "Meditation as a Communal Activity" in Chapter 11) prepared him to progress from the oral to the spiritual and so to penetrate the meaning of every syllable. The monks' aim was to transcend the limits imposed on humans by their senses and by ordinary ways of knowing. Monasticism was a continuous effort to surmount sense perception and intellectual understanding to achieve knowledge of God, to experience communion with God, and by so doing to reveal the divine mystery and achieve special favor in the eyes of God.

To confirm their legitimacy as masters of the sacred, monks aspired to become models of Christian virtue. Fine food, drink, money, precious metals, and luxuries of every kind were anathema to them. Their ideal was a life of fasting, chastity, and poverty, denying themselves all luxuries and serving only God. The sacerdotal functions of ensuring God's benevolence toward the community and oneself, taming God's wrath, and ensuring advocacy on one's behalf in heaven became increasingly urgent amid the disorder, uncertainty, and fear that accompanied the weakening and collapse of the Carolingian monarchy. A fragmented society required within it a group of people perceived as capable of holding back the forces of disarray and strengthening order, peace, and safety. Priests had always claimed that function, but monks, for a time at least, succeeded in partially monopolizing it.

If monastic life was intended to be austere, great monastic churches were quite the opposite. No expense was spared on building and decorating the sacred places in which monks worshipped. To do otherwise, it was thought, would be to demean God and thereby diminish the influence monks might gain in His eyes. The same logic that had led kings to engage in opulent sacrificial practices led to similar ones under monasticism. Monastic communities felt compelled to spend for the glory of God. Grandeur was required in all things. The architecture had to incorporate all forms of human creative expression in a unified fashion. The design of the basilica could not be separated from music or isolated from ritual, costume, or movement. All were part of a whole in which each element blended with the others to form a single, unitary spectacle honoring a single God. In this world, veneration of God through sacrifice was an umbrella under which all forms of human enterprise and creativity were harnessed to a single grand purpose. Above all, the style of the building had to be distinctive, separate from the style favored by kings. It was in this context that the Romanesque style of church architecture flourished (see Figure 13).

The role of monks and monasteries in the feudal system eventually came to encompass an additional function of vital importance to the feudal lords, namely, providing links with ancestors. Feudal society was built on kinship ties traced primarily through the male line. Kinship issues were vital to feudal lords because dukes, counts, and masters of castles, who were not directly anointed by God as

13. *Romsey Abbey is perhaps my favorite monastic church. Its solid, regular, soaring spaces provide a haven from the outside world.*

kings were supposed to be, often tried to establish their legitimacy by claiming descent from royalty (and hence from God) by a tangled, often highly tenuous network of distant blood relationships.[19] One way to express and make tangible the connections of a feudal lord to an earlier king and thus to God was worship of the ancestors who provided the imagined bridge between the living and the higher reaches of the hereafter. For this reason, efforts to claim and display links between feudal lords and the dead became matters of great importance. As I will explain in Chapter 12, commemoration of the dead was elevated to a central place in feudal society, and religious life increasingly focused on tombs, masses for the dead, and other acts of remembrance.

The alliance between feudal lords and monastics produced a flood of donations to religious houses. The faithful were instructed that gift-giving to religious houses could redeem their sins and earn the good will of a guardian saint who might intercede with God on their behalf in this world and ensure favorable placement in the next. The major religious orders began to accumulate immense wealth. The pious donations that flowed into religious houses exceeded anything previously experienced in the history of the Christian Church and peaked in the period surrounding the first millennium. Most of these gifts took the form of land, considered to be the most valuable of all forms of wealth, particularly when the gift included peasants who could farm the land on behalf of the landowner. By far the greatest beneficiaries of the transfer of land were monasteries, of which the Benedictines were the most prominent example. Under this system, however, bishops and the episcopal hierarchy did not disappear. Though weakened as an institution, the episcopate also received support from feudal lords and continued to benefit from gifts made by kings. Yet in comparison to monastic orders, the episcopate ran a distant second. The transfer of wealth from secular to religious institutions firmly established the Western Christian Church in a position of paramount importance and represented, without doubt, the most dynamic change affecting the economy of eleventh-century Europe.

Changing Sources of Wealth

How was all this lavish and conspicuous spending by ecclesiastics and feudal lords financed? Although we've identified three social orders, from the viewpoint of economic production and consumption, there were only two classes: those who owned land and those who did not. Land was the main source of wealth, and that wealth was obtained through the exploitation of the peasants who farmed it.

In time, great landowners of every rank encountered an almost grotesque mismatch between their desire for economic resources and genuine limits to the yield that could be realized from ruthless exploitation of peasant labor. In the early feudal period, most great landowners simply bilked their peasants shamelessly, but they eventually discovered that this situation could not last. Excessive extraction merely diminished productivity and invited civil unrest. As this realization dawned, the more enlightened ecclesiastical magnates and feudal lords began to search for ways of improving agricultural productivity.

One of the most important new approaches was adopting a more lenient attitude toward peasants. Some landowners began to let peasants keep a larger share of what they produced and also to cultivate previously unused, often marginal, tracts of land known as *assarts*. Peasants were encouraged to relocate and develop assarts by offers of money and supplies to cover start-up costs and being permitted to keep a larger share of the yield from crops than had been customary. In addition, some feudal lords and ecclesiastics allowed peasants to sell the surplus they produced at market; as long as the lord retained the right of taxation, he could continue to prosper by levying a tax on the peasant's profits. This new system of assarting preserved and even expanded the basis of wealth; it also allowed landlords to count on a more regular, steady flow of money, throughout the year. The benefits to the peasants, of course, were enormous. Over time, their standard of living improved markedly, accompanied by an increase in fertility rates. Their newfound economic independence also improved their morale. Most importantly, the profit motive was introduced among at least some of the peasantry.[20]

Another common strategy that feudal lords adopted to increase their income was to find more rational methods of administrating their lands. Previously, when wealth came from pillage, the oversight of the lands owned by feudal lords and monastic orders had been largely neglected, left to estate managers who only loosely and often carelessly supervised the work. As reliance on pillage died out and the attention of landowners turned to increasing the income from their own estates, they discovered that they could generate more wealth by reclaiming the responsibility for managing the land. Interest grew in developing better methods of farming and in studying the crop yields associated with different practices. Landowners quantified results, introduced accounting systems, tried new methods of crop rotation, and experimented with other growing methods. Landowners also began to support new agricultural technologies. These included developing new breeds of farm animals, new types of plows, better harnesses, and better systems for irrigating farm lands, milling grains, storing and preserving food, and so forth.[21]

These agricultural changes were introduced gradually and rather unevenly, and they took a long time to implement. But as the changes took hold during the eleventh and early twelfth centuries, they began to transform the economy of medieval society. For one thing, the newly increased wealth of landowners—kings, aristocratic families, and monastic orders alike—enabled them to mobilize the economic resources, materials, and workforces necessary to build great palaces and cathedrals.[22] Such building projects created a demand for skilled craftsmen, day laborers, and vendors of stone, lumber, lead, paint, plaster, and lime.

In addition, the lavish lifestyles of great land magnates required bakers, winemakers, cellarers, cooks, cloth makers, tailors, grooms, and vendors of every sort, as well as domestic workers, all of whom settled in or near the places where great land magnates lived. Though their primary obligation was to provide goods and services for the landowners, vendors soon found that they had surplus goods. To sell their own surplus and to purchase goods for themselves, landowners developed markets and fairs as well as centralized warehouses for the storage of goods. Towns often formed around places where markets and fairs were held, and a new urban class of merchants and traders began to populate them. All of this economic activity contributed to the accumulation of capital, an increased money supply, and the beginnings of wage labor. Cluny provides an instructive example. By the late eleventh century, Cluny had built the largest basilica in all of Latin Christendom. By 1122 this grand monastic church derived only one quarter of its food supplies from its own land. The remainder had to be bought from local vendors at a cost, Duby tells us, of 240,000 silver coins a year. The result was a huge infusion of liquid capital into the hands of local bakers, vintners, gold and silver smiths, butchers, blacksmiths, carpenters, dyers, woolers, millers, weavers, and other tradesmen and specialists. This in turn gave rise to the creation of mints to produce the local currency.[23]

The growing use of money introduced all sorts of new skills, abilities, and ways of thinking into the culture, particularly in the hundreds of towns all over Europe where markets flourished. For example, those who had to use money had to learn to count. They had to learn to estimate the monetary value of material goods and to translate the value of services they offered or purchased into basic monetary units. These accounting skills enabled them to grasp the idea of profit and instilled in them a way of thinking that encouraged the manipulation of money for financial gain.[24]

Town growth in particular was closely bound up with the vitality of the great ecclesiastical and secular courts.[25] Larger settlements in the early Middle Ages provided shelter for the headquarters of important lordships: bishops, cathedral chapters, and abbots among ecclesiastics, and counts, whose warriors guarded the town. Not only did these towns, with their markets and fairs, become the hubs of commerce, but they also served as centers for collecting taxes and minting money. The more liquid capital accumulated in these hubs, the more an entirely new class of citizens arose—tradesmen, merchants, and members of craft guilds—to provide and sell goods to consumers. In this way, towns became an engine of economic growth.

Towns also contributed to new political divisions and new forms of social conflict. Those whose livelihoods were rooted in the new urban centers were acquiring wealth in a form that was different from and to some extent independent of the wealth of great landowners. Instead of being based on land, the wealth of city dwellers tended to be in the form of consumer goods and liquid capital. Feudal lords wished to control the growth of the new merchant classes, to regulate their activities, and to tax their profits, but merchants needed freedom from exploitation to ply their trades. As they accumulated capital, they struggled to free themselves from the constraints imposed by the lords and bishops—ironically, the very lords whose lavish spending had made the merchant class possible in the first place. (This conflict is discussed further in Chapter 6.)[26]

A further development was the need of the great feudal lords to borrow in order to support their spending habits. As already noted, the standing of feudal lords, abbots, bishops, and kings rested on conspicuous consumption, driven to extremes of extravagance by competition among them. Thus, although greater wealth was being created by the changes mentioned above, even this was not sufficient to underwrite their profligate spending. The great land magnates increasingly resorted to borrowing from people who were amassing liquid capital.

All these developments were gradual, unevenly distributed throughout Europe, and in most respects discontinuous. But in the end, slowly yet surely, urban vitality came to prevail over the countryside. Eventually technological developments, population growth, increasing commerce, the emergence of a money economy, urbanization, and new forms of rational organization came together to create a new, capital-based economy, which made cathedral-building, among other things, possible.

CHAPTER 4

The Age of Cathedral-Building

 During the height of feudalism, when local lords and abbots of great monastic orders were in the ascendancy, kings and bishops had not simply dropped out of sight. Both remained important actors in the medieval social drama and survived intact enough to be able to challenge those who had preempted their authority. In fact, as feudalism began to wane during the twelfth and early thirteenth centuries, the monarchy and the episcopate found themselves strategically positioned.

The gradual weakening of the power of great feudal lords had many causes, but two in particular stand out. First, given their relentless spending, they were forced to borrow more and more money, and in the end their financial situations became precarious. As a result, they were no longer able to protect those under their care as effectively as they once had. Second, as we have seen, liquid capital began to compete with land as a form of wealth. The combined effects of growing indebtedness and dependence on nontransportable wealth compromised the lords' ability to rule. Meanwhile, a turbulent political situation arose in France, with the threat of invasion by the German emperor and the English king (see

Chapter 5). Citizens turned to the king as the only one who could establish and maintain order, and protect them from invading forces.

Monastic orders were also undergoing upheavals for many reasons, none more important than the insidious and corrupting effects of opulent spending by the monks on the settings and adornments for worship. The Cluniacs provide an instructive example. The monks of Cluny believed their solemn duty was to magnify God's glory by celebrating the liturgy with the greatest possible splendor. To do this required a lavish basilica lavishly decorated. The same logic soon led them to feel that those who performed the liturgy needed attire befitting the setting, and this attitude ultimately extended to the food the monks ate and the wines they drank. In the end, Cluniac monks came to enjoy a lifestyle not unlike that of the feudal lords.[1] Such extravagance stood in stark contrast to the original idea of austerity at the founding of monasticism.

Monastic orders were further weakened by their dependence on the feudal lords, whose standing and power were being eroded by changes in the society. As they became less able to rule, the monastery as an institution became less secure. Monasticism did not simply fade, to be replaced by cathedral chapters. Rather, there was a transition period during which a series of reform movements took place, all of them intended to uphold the monastic ideal of holiness. The spiritual movement embodied in monasticism, which preached salvation by removal from this world, had not yet run its full course.[2] New monastic orders were emerging whose notions about the Christian mission were radically different from those held by the Benedictine and Cistercian orders. Some reform orders, such as the Franciscans (founded by St. Francis in 1209) and the Dominicans (founded by St. Dominic in 1215), began to turn away from the seclusion and isolation of the monastery and to live and preach in the newly developing urban settings throughout western Europe. They loathed ostentation and ornamentation, they argued for a return to simpler forms of worship, and, above all, they stressed the importance of living as witnesses to Christ among the people by adopting vows of poverty. To practice as they preached, they deliberately chose to live among the poor to whom they ministered. Penniless, homeless, and defenseless, they begged for their daily food and labored at menial tasks alongside other members of the order assigned to work.

Both of these new religious orders posed a radical challenge to monasticism as originally conceived, for they were not tied to land. They established places of living and working inside the town walls. They believed their mission was to spread the true doctrine of Christ; to succeed, they needed to enter the secular world armed only with the scriptures. As Duby explains,

> A Dominican Friar owned nothing—except his books. His books were his tools. His mission was to spread the true doctrine . . . to this end he had to practice, hone his intelligence, read, study, learn to wield reason as a weapon. . . . The Dominicans lived together in religious communities . . . but not for the purpose of singing the Lord's praises in unison at every hour of the day, as the Benedictines did. . . . The Dominican monasteries were set up in the heart of the urban masses they were supposed to enlighten. . . . A Dominican monastery offered physical shelter; once the friars had accomplished their given tasks, they came back to sleep and to share the food for which they had gone begging.[3]

These reform movements played a vital role in changing the mission of Christianity. The Church began to turn its attention away from exquisitely enacted and demanding performances of esoteric liturgy aimed at transporting the suppliant from this world into the next. Reformers had different concerns. They asked why God had returned to mankind in human form. They wished to know why the divine essence deigned to lower itself to become flesh. This new emphasis led to preaching a way of life in which people did not try to imitate the glory of angels, but aimed instead to follow in Christ's footsteps and become apostles. In place of splendor, reform monastics preached austerity, but now in an urban setting. The powerful questions that lay behind the newly emerging movement helped to frame the context in which cathedrals came to supplant great monastic churches as the premier ecclesiastical structures.

Because this new religious sensibility emphasized good works in this life as a necessity for entry into the next, it unleashed a torrent of activities rooted in affairs of this world. They included the mounting of the Crusades to liberate the Holy Land from the control of infidels, as well as bringing the Christian message to ordinary people, alleviating their suffering, and working for their salvation. The reform movements also focused on God manifest in the human form, that is, the body of Christ. This idea is at the core of the theology that came to be practiced and preached in Gothic cathedrals. Through Christ, depicted in majesty at the pinnacle of the great west doors of Gothic cathedrals, humans gained entrance to the light-filled sanctuaries that held God and promised to lead people to him.

The Christ of the Gothic cathedral was depicted as God incarnate, the living Christ. He connected living human beings with the notion of God the eternal. Cathedrals became, so to speak, vectors through which God, Christ as God incarnate, kings, bishops, other clergy, merchants, tradespeople, and peasants were all portrayed as linked together in one grand scheme. As Duby describes it, "At the junction . . . where the created and the uncreated, the natural and the supernatural, the eternal and the historical came together, is where Christ was situated, as God made man. He was 'light born of light,' yet was made of solid flesh. Ever since the building of Saint-Denis, Gothic art had strained to express the incarnation."[4]

Given this redefinition of the Christian mission, it was natural that the great basilicas in which people would worship should be located in towns and cities where they lived. Cathedrals were the churches of bishops, who now lived in cities, and cathedrals thus became intimately connected with cities. As cathedrals flourished, so did the chapters of canons that governed them. Cathedrals were truly urban institutions. They symbolized the new urban vitality. Chartres Cathedral was the seat of the bishop of Chartres, but it was also the

14. *In contrast to monasteries, which were purposely located in the countryside away from the temptations of urban life, cathedrals— such as Burgos, shown here—typically sit in the center of the city.*

church of the city of Chartres; Salisbury cathedral defined and symbolized the city of Salisbury—indeed, the city and the cathedral were founded together. In this sense, the art of cathedrals connoted the birth of cities (see Figure 14).

As cities became more prosperous, cathedrals benefited from the gifts of the new urban elite. Traders and others gave alms to the cathedral chapters because profit was still synonymous with sin— some merchants had a bad conscience that bishops helped assuage by securing contributions for building cathedrals. Cathedrals also became sources of civic pride and stood as beacons that drew people from the countryside to the center of the city.

All these developments combined to make Gothic cathedral-building possible. But why did their construction occur when it did? What happened to activate the basic wherewithal? One answer lies in the alarming problem of heresy that began to plague the church during the eleventh and twelfth centuries.

The Problem of Heresy

As conflicts arose between orthodox belief and notable deviations from it, heresy became a worry to established prelates of every stripe, regardless of whether they were members of monastic orders or of secular cathedral chapters. Because the opulent lifestyles of the monastic communities had compromised their status, however, these religious orders were poorly positioned to respond to the growing threat. For the reasons already discussed, bishops—allied with a series of powerful popes—were now in a stronger position to meet the challenge of heresy. In the process, they could reclaim a dominant position for the previously weakened institution of the episcopate. Bishops spearheaded the assault on heresy, and the new cathedrals were critical in the attempt to stamp it out.

The problem had two aspects: political and religious. Though feudalism was dying out in the north of France, south of the Loire, in Aquitaine, a version of feudalism survived that nourished the seeds of both rebellion and heresy. Historically, Aquitaine had never accepted the basis of Carolingian authority. The princes of Aquitaine never quite believed that their power came from sacred sources, and they did not concern themselves with liturgy. They believed in ruling by sheer force and hoped that by paying monks to pray for them, they could ensure their good standing before God. They simply went on enjoying life largely unconcerned about salvation.[5]

Eleanor of Aquitaine married the very pious French monarch Louis VII (1137–1180), but because he was so devout and committed to orthodox beliefs, he could not accept what he saw as her errant ways. The monks around him, including Abbot Suger, convinced the king to repudiate Eleanor. She quickly married Henry Plantagenet, King of England (1154–1189), who had already inherited Anjou and Normandy. His marriage to Eleanor extended his control over half of modern-day France. He rejected the Gothic aesthetic associated with French monarchy and the political and theological orthodoxy it symbolized. His opposition made events in Aquitaine a matter of great urgency to the French king.[6]

To add to the problem, throughout the cities of southern France, itinerant preachers belonging to the Albigensian sect insisted on the necessity of reforming the Roman Church. (The name Albigensian is derived from the city of Albi in the Languedoc region where the group was centered. They were also known as Cathars, from the Greek word for *purified*.) The Albigensians asserted that because monks, canons, and bishops were corrupt, the Church must rid itself of the lot of them. Albigensian preachers extolled the life of poverty and preached that anyone who touched money was automatically corrupted by it. Only those who were poor, abstinent, and free of any practice created by Satan to tempt humans could be spiritual mediators. Because they were themselves poor and ascetic, they were extremely effective in persuading people to follow them and cede to them the sacerdotal function.

Their challenge to the established church was truly radical. As the movement gathered steam, members preached forgoing the services of the bishop entirely and even denied that priests were required. A state of grace, they taught, simply came to the worshipper without any need for rituals such as the Eucharist, baptism, and absolution, all of which were dismissed as useless. They derided priests as no more than magicians and gave no credence to miracles and alleged powers of healing attributed to kings and saints. The order they established was socially egalitarian, and for perhaps the first time since the earliest days of Christianity, women were welcomed as full-fledged members of the sect.

From the point of view of bishops, the Albigensians' destabilizing ideas could not have come at a worse time. By the end of the twelfth century, when the bishops were attempting to disseminate a new religious orthodoxy that sought to unify all of Christianity under the firm control of the pope and his episcopal allies, the Albigensian heresy was attempting to completely undermine the foundations on which the Church was built. The Church, the pope, and his bishops, who by the eleventh century had come to believe that their most important duty was to root out infidels in Jerusalem, now had to divert their efforts from crusades and instead attack heresy in their own backyard.

As the year 1200 dawned, the Church of Rome found itself under siege. The monastic ideal of withdrawal would no longer suffice; the Church stiffened and adopted a rigid, totalitarian stance, centered on the pope. For the next two hundred years a succession of popes instituted policies aimed at systematically eradicating heresy. They now claimed full moral jurisdiction over the entire earth. They sent an endless stream of legates to visit bishops to ensure their obedience to papal rule. Georges Duby quotes from the sermon delivered by Pope Innocent III (1198–1216) at his installation, in which the new pope declared that he was not only successor to St. Peter, but "Christ's lieutenant, king of kings, who stood above all princes of this world and passed judgment on them. . . . Halfway between God and man, smaller than God, greater than man."[7]

Initially, in the late twelfth century, the church sent Cistercian monks to debate the Albigensian preachers. Not only did the Cistercians embody the qualities of abstinence, self-denial, austerity, and poverty that the Albigensians praised, they were well trained in the use of logic and reason, and they used these skills to argue against Albigensian theology in public debates and sermons. In their rhetoric, the Cistercians easily outclassed the Cathar preachers, who knew what they believed but could not defend it against the rigors of logical attack. But in the end the campaign failed, because so many Cathars were friends, relatives, and neighbors of the citizens of Languedoc, who had no wish to reject them or cause them trouble merely because of their beliefs.[8]

With the election of Innocent III as Pope in 1198, the campaign took on a new and sinister tone. It begin with a brutal crusade followed by an equally brutal Inquisition launched against real and suspected members of the sect. Knights who might earlier have gone on crusade to the Holy Land were deployed against the heretics in southern France. In 1209 Innocent III summoned the knights of Ile-de-France and gave them his blessing to invade Languedoc with orders to exterminate the heretics. Jonathan Sumption and Stephen O'Shea recount the extreme brutality of the crusade against the Albigensians. The siege and massacre in the town of Béziers in 1209, near Narbonne, illustrates the savagery of the assault. Only a portion of the population of Béziers were actually Cathars. Most citizens were orthodox Christians who felt it their duty to shelter members of the dissident sect whom they knew as friends, neighbors, and relatives. As the crusaders stormed the city gates, they sought instruction from their leader, a Cistercian monk named Arnold Amaury, about which of the citizens to attack. He is reputed to have replied, "Kill them all, God will know his own." In a single morning all twenty thousand citizens of the town were slaughtered.[9]

The brutality continued unabated. Another grotesque incident occurred in April, 1210, in the town of Cabaret, an estate built on the slope of a mountain northeast of Carcassonne and a famous place of Cathar pilgrimage. The citizens of Cabaret awoke one morning to the spectacle of a procession of nearly a hundred men stumbling toward their city. The men were defeated defenders of the nearby town of Bram. All had had their eyes gouged out and their noses and upper lips sliced off. They were led by one hapless soldier who was spared one eye so that he could lead the procession. The men were sent to Cabaret to remind those who harbored Cathars of the terrible fate that awaited them.[10]

The crusade against the Cathars was followed by an equally repressive Inquisition, led by Dominican monks. Cathars and their sympathizers were rounded up and given an opportunity to confess their affiliation or their sympathies. Confessed Cathars were given an opportunity to swear allegiance to the orthodox faith. If they did not, they were burned at the stake. Sympathizers were questioned until they named names. Sometimes they named people who had already died, thereby sparing the living, but this tactic was soon foiled by the Inquisitors. who ordered the graves of those named to be dug up, their remains burned, and their property seized.[11]

Meanwhile, to shore up and strengthen the foundations of Christian doctrine, the Church of Rome introduced surveillance measures throughout Europe, even in areas where heresy was not particularly apparent. The parish as a central location for ordinary people was once again strengthened. Each peasant was designated as a parishioner of a specific place, and strictly forbidden to receive sacraments in any church other than his or her own. Through the offices of the local priest, attempts were made to compel everyone to practice religion regularly; lay people were told that they had to make confession and receive communion at least once a year. Surveillance duty made the village priest little more than a petty tyrant who continuously pried into and monitored the affairs of his parishioners.[12]

Presiding over the local priests were the bishops, who, as heads of dioceses, were charged with the ultimate responsibility for care of the souls of everyone who lived and worshipped in their domain. Bishops had two special missions—to police heretics and to enlighten ordinary parishioners by instructing them in proper dogma. And at the center of the diocese stood *the cathedral*, the nexus of the bishop's moral authority and the monument to his role. Cathedrals were the centers from which bishops taught the correct and true message of the Church. They stood squarely in the middle of the elaborate, closely organized, hierarchical network of parishes and dioceses, all headed by the pope.

As works of art, cathedrals became powerful instruments of propaganda in aid of the Church's great struggle against heresy. As we shall see, each new cathedral was a concrete display and representation of orthodox Catholic theology. This theology portrayed God as light and the universe as a luminous sphere that radiated outward from God, infusing the body of Christ, who as both God and man linked ordinary humans and the divine.[13] Cathedrals were the vectors through which this process worked, and bishops, whose seats were housed in these great buildings, were the spiritual masters of the orthodoxy.

Duby has even suggested that the Gothic cathedral became an instrument—possibly the most effective one of all—of repression by the Catholic Church.[14] I would say instead that the Gothic cathedral stood for a great many things and reflected a variety of interests. Cathedrals were products of the episcopate's efforts to reassert control over religious matters; of the Church's crusade against heresy; of the bishops' desire to express, assert, and celebrate their place in Christendom; of the king's efforts to regain supremacy over feudal lords; of the pride of local merchants, tradesmen, craftsmen, and vendors in the cities they helped to found and run. All these forces interacted to produce the great enterprise of Gothic cathedral-building.

The Initial Vision

Though Gothic cathedrals may have come into being partly to avert heresy, the first Gothic church was not a cathedral, nor was it built with heresy in mind. It was an abbey church, and its aim was state-building. The Gothic enterprise began with the Abbey Church of St. Denis and its famous leader, Abbot Suger. Until recently, most medievalists attributed to Abbot Suger the leading role in inventing and introducing Gothic architecture into Europe. Recent studies and interpretations assign him a more modest role.[1] All agree, however, that Abbot Suger was at the center of the development of the Gothic style, and that his abbey church was where the elements of Gothic design first came together.

The Abbey Church of St. Denis dates to the late fifth century. It was originally built to house the relics of a martyred third-century saint, variously referred to as Denis, Denys, and Dionysius. Denis was one of seven bishops sent to convert the people of Gaul during the reign of the third-century Roman emperor Decius, and he became the first Bishop of Paris. He was subsequently martyred during a persecution of Christians, and in 626 his remains were moved to a Benedictine abbey known today as the Abbey Church of St. Denis. According to a legend concocted by a ninth-century abbot of the Church of St. Denis, Denis's decapitated corpse, led by an angel, walked from the site of the martyrdom at Montmartre to the site of the abbey church.[2] Because of his sacrifice and the purpose of his mission, Denis was eventually adopted as the patron saint of France. His relics, and the abbey's other prize relics—a nail and a thorn from the crown of thorns of the Crucifixion, said to have been brought back from Constantinople by Charlemagne—made it one of the most famous churches in all of France. It gained renown as a major shrine and became an important place of pilgrimage.

Adding to its luster was its selection as the final resting place for a string of French monarchs. Royal burials there are believed to have begun during the late sixth century, and by the tenth century there were more royal tombs at St. Denis than in any other place in France. In addition, from Merovingian times (up to 751), copies of royal documents were deposited at the abbey, and subsequent official histories of France were based on these materials. Over the centuries, French monarchs showered the abbey with gifts, including land, money, precious jewels, and, equally important, licenses to hold a series of important fairs, whose proceeds greatly benefited the abbey. The first fair was founded in 635. Known as "Foire de Saint-Denis," it was held each October concurrently with the celebration of the saint's feast day and apparently functioned as a great market for winter provisions. A second fair, called the "Foire du Lendit," lasted up to sixteen days each June, during which all of the contents of the various reliquaries housed at the abbey were displayed.[3] Other royal concessions previously made, including granting the abbey independence from the jurisdiction of the bishop of Paris, effectively freed the monastery from what would otherwise have been onerous feudal obligations. These privileges were renewed and extended periodically by the Carolingian and early Capetian kings.

By the twelfth century, St. Denis's place as the premier royal abbey of France had become firmly established. The historical ties between the abbey and numerous French monarchs were extremely close, and St. Denis's importance within the French realm seems beyond dispute. One sign of its close tie to the monarchy is that the abbey became the repository of various pieces of regalia that symbolized the king's authority, items of treasure used during coronation ceremonies. Because St. Denis was a royal abbey, in a certain sense its fate and the fate of the monarchy were linked. If French kings prospered, so too did the abbey church, and if the monarchy faltered, the fortunes of the abbey church were correspondingly threatened.

Suger was the Abbot of St. Denis for almost thirty years. Born in 1081, he was appointed Abbot of St. Denis by King Louis VI in 1122 and remained in that post until his death in 1151. Although scholars differ in their interpretation of his political importance, he is known to have been an advisor of some kind to the two monarchs who ruled during his lifetime, Louis VI (1108–1137) and Louis VII (1137–1180).[4]

For the French monarchy, politically, these were precarious times, characterized by confusion, anarchy, and a lack of political legitimacy and authority. Kings Louis VI and Louis VII traced their ancestry back to the tenth-century king Hugh Capet (987–996) and his descendants Robert II the Pious (996–1031), Henry I (1031–1060), and Philip I (1060–1108). All of them ostensibly led France, but in reality they barely managed to control their immediate domain in Ile-de-France, much less the distant provinces of the kingdom, most of which were ruled by princes whose systems of government were more advanced, more stable, and stronger than those of the nominal suzerain. One authority, Lindy Grant, describes these Capetian monarchs inelegantly as "squashed, like the filling in a sandwich," between realms controlled by princes and feudal lords who governed the surrounding provinces of Poitou, Anjou, Blois-Chartres, Champagne, and Flanders.[5] In this precarious state, this whole region of France operated as little more than a protection racket, with the king the biggest villain of all. Louis

VI was the first Capetian king to succeed in significantly strengthening the royal government, and apparently he was greatly aided by Abbot Suger.[6]

The eleventh century was marked by bitter struggle between the Church and the Holy Roman Emperor over a variety of issues, especially over the investiture of bishops.[7] At the heart of this dispute lay the issue of who held the right to appoint bishops: kings or popes. Behind this question lurked another, even more basic one: Who among all living humans was entitled to claim first place in the eyes of God? The French and English kings managed an accommodation with the Church, so that by the first decade of the twelfth century, the central issue had pretty much been resolved. Kings agreed to permit popes to appoint bishops, but retained the right to invest them with ring and staff. In return for this, bishops swore homage and fidelity to the king in secular matters.

Although England and France had made peace with the pope, the German emperors remained locked in bitter, sustained disputes with a succession of popes. Because of their alliance with the Capetian monarchs, the popes considered France to be friendly territory; indeed, several popes of the late eleventh and early twelfth centuries were granted haven in France when they were pursued and threatened by German monarchs. One of these popes, Calixtus, was forced to take refuge in France in 1119 to escape the German Emperor Henry V (1106–1125). Once there, Calixtus convened a council in October 1119 at Reims—as close to the doorstep of the Empire as he dared go—in order to push his views of episcopal investiture. At Reims, Calixtus declared the German emperor excommunicated. The price of absolution he set was Henry's acceptance of the pope's right of investiture. The pope's action made it virtually impossible for Henry to rule effectively, and he finally made a temporary settlement with the Church. But in August 1124 Henry V, in league with his father-in-law, Henry I of England (1100–1135), formed an alliance for the purpose of invading France in retaliation for the pope's actions at Reims. The intent of the invasion was to deny the pope his haven and thus enable the German emperor to gain the upper hand in the investiture dispute.[8]

Facing grave peril, King Louis VI convened a national assembly of French feudal lords and bishops at the Abbey Church of St. Denis. The issues at stake for the king and for France amounted to nothing less than forging sufficient unity among the warring factions within France to repel the threats from east and west. In one version of the story, Suger was the master strategist who orchestrated the occasion to save the monarchy, strengthen it, and extend its grip on all of France. Another version portrays Suger as simply capitalizing on a moment of regal weakness to gain advantage for his abbey. In either case, there is little disagreement about what actually happened.[9]

Suger, as convener, began the assembly by reminding all who had gathered of St. Denis's role as special patron of France, declaring him to be the saint who, "after God was the singular protector of the French realm." In a solemn procession St. Denis's relics were brought from the crypt to the choir, where the king, kneeling, prayed to him to intercede with God on behalf of France and save the realm. The king declared that if, through St. Denis's intercessions, God saw fit to spare France, he would personally show his gratitude to the saint by making great gifts to the abbey that honored him. His prayers completed, the king then rose and walked in solemn procession from the choir to the high altar, where Abbot Suger presented him with the banner of St. Denis. Holding the banner high, the king declared his intention to go into battle in the saint's name and in the saint's personal cause, described as preserving France itself. The banner of St. Denis would protect the king and his followers from harm and in the end bring victory. The king then appealed to those assembled to join him in defense of the realm.[10]

As we might imagine, the response was tremendous. Princes, feudal lords, and bishops came forward to stand with the king in defense of France under the protective banner of her patron saint. No doubt they were partly motivated by the fear of falling under the rule of the German emperor. Though many of them considered the French king their political enemy, they must have realized that it would be better to unite in his defense than to face the prospect of domination by a German monarch.

For a week the newly united French army, which had assembled at Reims, awaited the German attack. It never came. On August 14 the German emperor retreated. The French king had won a bloodless victory. France had apparently been saved by a miracle granted by God through the intercession of her patron saint. Now more than ever, France, its monarch, its patron saint, the Abbey Church of St. Denis, and Suger were inseparably linked. Indeed, henceforth, the banner of St. Denis served as the king's battle standard and came to be identified as the *oriflamme*, the legendary banner of Charlemagne. "Montjoie Saint Denis" became the war cry of French armies. The spiritual and temporal powers in France, which had always been present to some extent, had been vigorously renewed, and from 1124 onward the Abbey Church of St. Denis became the religious and, in an important sense, the political capital of France.

Some historians see Suger as nothing more than an opportunist, but others argue that he was genuinely motivated by a grand theological vision that influenced virtually everything he did.[11] The vision comprised three basic truths. The first was that any king, but most especially the king of France, was, to use Suger's own words, a "Vicar of God . . . bearing God's image in his person and bringing it to life." The second was that any king of France had not only the right but also the sacred duty to "subdue all forces conducive to internal strife and obstruction to his central authority." The third was that the Abbey Church of St. Denis, as haven to the relics of the patron saint of France, who was "after God, unique protector of the realm," symbolized and embodied the central authority of the monarchy and therefore the unity of France.[12] From this perspective, Suger's two main objectives—strengthening the monarchy and aggrandizing his own abbey church—were harmonious parts of a single vision, two facets of the same fundamental theological ideal.

On the heels of France's triumph over the Germans, Suger undertook two more projects. The first was to aggressively pursue the writing of an official history of France, which came to be known as the *Chronicle Tradition of St. Denis*. Medieval historian Gabrielle Spiegel argues that through this project the monks of St. Denis became the historical voice of France and her first national historians. Under Suger's guidance, they compiled an archive on the French monarchy, an enterprise that made St. Denis "the official custodian of the royal myth."[13]

The *Chronicle Tradition of St. Denis* attempted to synthesize in a single text all that was known about the history of France, focusing on the guidance and governance of her monarchs. According to Spiegel, "The chroniclers . . . [described] French history as a coherent evolution and used the past to legitimate contemporary political life. They furnished an interpretive strategy for understanding the basic character and dynamic of French kingship, and treated royal action as part of an eternal pattern of behavior which was rooted in the spiritual nature of political society as established by God."[14] For good measure, they published their works in French as well as in Latin, presumably to make them accessible to a wider audience.

Suger's second great project was rebuilding the abbey church (see Figure 15). Some historians view this as his attempt to embody in stone, wood, and glass his vision of the alliance of the monarchy to the abbey church and of the abbey church to its saint, and thus to God. These are the relationships that Suger, presumably with the king's approval, had sought to articulate in the great assembly and which he now sought to explicate in the chronicles. One proponent goes so far as to describe Suger as an "architect who built theology."[15]

At the National Assembly of 1124, when the king prayed to St. Denis to spare France, he promised that if his plea was answered,

15. *The west front of the Abbey Church of St. Denis shows the very early Gothic style.*

great gifts would follow. In the end, two gifts were given. The first consisted of priceless jewels. What is interesting here is not only the value of the gift itself, but the specification of its recipient. The jewels were represented as gifts given personally and directly to the saint himself, not to the abbot or the abbey church. Indeed, the abbey church seems to have been represented as little more than a depository, a depot where items meant for the saint could be dropped off. Putting the matter in this way implied that future donations to the abbey church would be similarly interpreted and understood; that is, because the saint had granted the king a miracle, others giving gifts to the saint might reasonably expect St. Denis to intercede on their behalf as well. Expressions of piety toward the saint soon became, in effect, a continuing source of revenue for the abbey, which kept and used the gifts for its own purposes.

The king's second gift was the return of all the precious relics claimed to be associated with the Passion of Christ. These relics had been given to the abbey in the ninth century by King Charles the Bald (843–877), who had also granted the abbey church an annual feast in honor of the relics, which eventually led to the establishment, in 1048, of the fair called Lendit. Lendit was an extremely important source of revenue not only to the abbey but also to the monarch, who received a portion of the profits from the sale of licenses and goods. In 1109 King Louis VI had transferred some of the relics from St. Denis to the cathedral church of Notre Dame de Paris, along with a license to hold a second fair, called Outer Lendit. The king's 1124 gift reversed his earlier decision. He ordered that the relics be returned to St. Denis together with the right to sponsor Outer Lendit. In making this second gift, the king explained that the miracle that had rescued France from the grasp of the German and English kings was evidence that Christ had "deigned to ennoble the entire French realm"; thus, it was only fitting that the relics of his Passion should be returned to the site where the miracle had occurred.[16] The gift enhanced St. Denis's role as the greatest pilgrimage site in all of France and positioned it as a potential rival of the three premier sites for Christian pilgrimage during the Middle Ages: the Church of Santiago de Compostela, and the tombs of St. Peter and Christ.

The gifts gave Suger both the resources and the rationale to proceed with his ambitious architectural project. His abbey church was in a decrepit state. It was a slightly renovated version of a structure built three and a half centuries earlier that was not adequate to serve as a major place of pilgrimage. Suger's writings note that it was too small to accommodate the huge crowds now drawn to it to venerate the relics and participate in Lendit. In one often-quoted passage, Suger speaks of "gaping fissures in the walls, of damaged columns and of towers 'threatening ruin'; of lamps and other furnishings falling to pieces for want of repair; of valuable ivories 'moldering away under the chests of the treasury;' [and] of altar vessels 'lost as pawns.'" In another place he explains,

> Often, on a feast day completely filled, the church disgorged through all its doors the excess of the crowds as they moved in opposite directions, and the outward pressure of the foremost ones not only prevented those attempting to enter from entering but also expelled those who had already entered. At times one could see, a marvel to behold, that the crowded multitude offered so much resistance to those who strove to flock in to worship and kiss the holy relics, the Nail and Crown of the Lord, that no one among the countless thousands of people because of their very density could move a foot. . . . The distress of the women, however, was so great and so intolerable that you could see with horror how they, squeezed in by the mass of strong men as in a winepress, exhibited bloodless faces as in imagining death; how they cried out horribly as though in labor; how several of them, miserably trodden underfoot [but then] lifted by the pious assistance of men above the heads of the crowd, marched forward as though upon a pavement.

And he comments, "More than once, the friars who were showing visitors evidence of Our Lord's Passion were overcome by the anger and quarreling of the crowds and, having no other way out, escaped through the windows with the relics."[17] Suger felt not only that his dilapidated abbey church was inadequate to accommodate the crowds, but that it was actually *demeaning* to its relics and its newly enhanced place in the French realm. Great relics, he believed, should have a great basilica. A new abbey church must therefore be built.

But work did not begin for nearly thirteen years. Suger's attention and energy were diverted by other matters. One of these was his position as counselor to Louis VI, which he held until the king's death in 1137. A second was a project to improve the administration of his own abbey. For some time he had recognized that the lands owned by the abbey were poorly administered and that their proceeds were therefore inadequate. During these interim years, Suger devoted some of his time to improving his cash flow. Third, to impose a new style on the building, Suger had to find the materials and the craftsmen who could execute the planned renovation. He meant this monument in honor of kings to be a summing up of all of the aesthetic innovations he had admired in his travels on behalf of Louis VI. He had to cast a wide net to gather craftsmen from distant places with the skills to execute the work he wanted done.

When work finally began, first on a new west front in 1137 and then on the choir in 1141, it proceeded quickly. The choir took just three years and three months to complete and was ready for dedication in 1144 (see Figure 16). The renovations were paid for from three sources: revenues derived from property owned by the abbey church, which according to Suger's own account contributed one-quarter of the required sum; gifts made by pilgrims who came to venerate the sacred relics; and profits from Lendit, which together provided the other three-quarters of the funds.

The design for the new basilica reflected the abbot's and the monarch's shared vision of linking the monarchy, through the abbey church and its saint, to God, as articulated in the great assembly of 1124 as well as the new *Chronicles of St. Denis.* According to the art historian Otto von Simson, "St. Denis . . . was to be the capital of the realm, the place where the different and antagonistic factions within France were to be reconciled and where they could rally around the patron saint and the king."[18] It was intended to be an architectural statement of the alliance between sacred and secular power that Suger and the king wanted to promote.

The person who actually drew up the design of the building is unknown, but it seems clear that Suger provided the inspiration. Borrowing innovations in building design from Sens and elsewhere in the provinces of northern France, Suger worked with his master mason to create a design that would embody his theological and political vision. The theological vision was of an interior space where people could glimpse heaven. Consistent with his view of heaven, his great church was to be geometrically regular, orderly, coherent, enduring, and filled with light. It would symbolize a place where

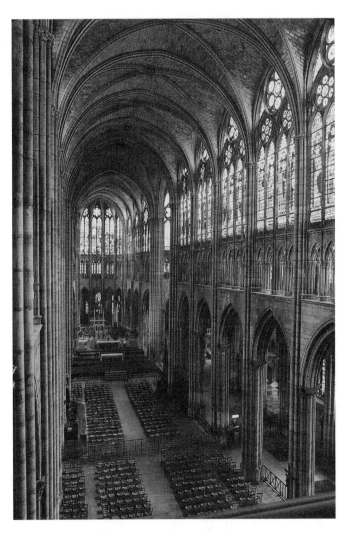

16. *The nave of the Abbey Church of St. Denis continues the Gothic style that was pioneered in the choir.*

diverse and seemingly contradictory forces and elements could be reconciled under one all-embracing canopy. The structure would provide a place for all things, bringing into ultimate harmony discordant forms and elements, as he imagined Divine Order did, subsuming them neatly within a single, overarching geometrical order. In Georges Duby's apt phrase, it was to be a "monument of applied theology."[19] As the ceremony of dedication would imply, Suger envisioned a monument in stone embodying the close ties between the abbey church and the French monarchy. His design can also be seen as reflecting an effort to reconcile the antagonistic factions of France under a single roof, providing a place where all of France could rally round its patron saint and king. The intended line of descent portrayed was from God to king and abbey church and thus to France.

In keeping with the abbot's genius for ceremony, the dedication of the choir in 1144 was an impressive dramatic and liturgical enactment embodying central aspects of the theological and political vision reflected in the overall design. To ensure great crowds, the ceremony was scheduled for June 11, 1144, three days before the convening of Lendit. The list of invited guests was truly grand; as Suger noted,

> We sent invitations by many messengers, also by couriers and envoys, through almost all the districts of Gaul and urgently requested the archbishops and bishops, in the name of the Saints and as a debt to their apostolate, to be present at so great a solemnity. Numerous and different ones of these [we welcomed] joyfully to this celebration. . . . Our Lord King Louis [VII] himself and his spouse Queen Eleanor [of Aquitaine], as well as his mother, and the peers of the realm arrived. . . . Of the diverse counts and nobles from many regions and dominions, of the ordinary troops of knights and soldiers there is no count. But of the archbishops and bishops who were present the names are placed on record as follows . . . [20]

and he goes on to name the bishops of Reims, Rouen, Sens, Canterbury, Chartres, Soissons, Noyon, Orleans, Beauvais, Auxerre, Arras, Chalons, Coutances, Evreux, Terouanne, Meaux, and Senlis.

To entice these distinguished prelates to the dedication ceremony, Suger offered them places of prominence and honor, assigning each one the duty of conducting a dedication service for one of the altars in the renovated choir. This offer was irresistible to many of them, because it underscored their place of significance within the French realm. At the same time it demonstrated to all those in attendance their subservience to the monarchy and, by implication, to the abbey church as well. It seems to me that the ceremony was a dramatic enactment of Suger's quest to bring together under one system of royal and ecclesiastical authority every element in the realm.

To express the grand theological and political vision inherent in the liturgy of the dedication ceremony, Suger cleverly employed every device he could conjure. For example, during the procession of relics, the king outranked all ecclesiastical dignitaries and personally carried the sacred relics of Christ's Passion and of St. Denis for display at the high altar. Thus, when those in attendance prayed to the relics, as custom bound them to do, they were in effect also bowing and praying to the king. Repeatedly during the ceremony the king was linked to God. In his sermon Suger described Christ as "The True Governor of the world" and the king as "his earthly agent." He proclaimed, "The King bears in his person the living image of God . . . a vicar of God . . . bearing God's image in his person and bringing it to life."[21]

The bishops and feudal lords of France who attended could not fail to be impressed with the potential of the new architectural style. Though Suger was a spiritual son of Saint Benedict, and therefore someone who should have been committed to rural, small-scale enterprises, he had built what was arguably the most urban of monastery churches. Subsequently, the bishops who presided over the newly emerging cities of the French realm and elsewhere carried on his work. Whether by deliberate design or not, Suger's brilliant manipulation of powerful religious and cultural symbols had a tremendous influence that ultimately consolidated and strengthened the monarchy and secured its position of ascendancy in French history, a role that would last for 650 years. At the same time, it led to the development and dispersion of a new style of architecture with obvious potential for aiding in the achievement of both secular and religious ends, whatever they might be.

CHAPTER 6

"The Cathedral Crusade"

On the heels of the renovation of the Abbey Church of St. Denis, work began on renovating and rebuilding in the new Gothic style dozens of cathedrals and great monastic churches throughout the greater Paris Basin. The great Gothic enterprise had been launched. Good evidence suggests that St. Denis strongly influenced these subsequent developments. The guest list of prelates from northern France and elsewhere who attended the dedication of the choir at St. Denis includes seventeen leading bishops and archbishops. If we correlate their names with the starting dates for construction of Gothic portions of the cathedrals and other great churches of northern France, a strong relationship appears. One student of the topic, Christopher Wilson, refers to Suger's guest list as a "roll-call of the cathedrals which would be rebuilt in the next 100 years."[1] Specifically, renovations of existing Romanesque churches in the Gothic style immediately got under way at Sens in the late 1140s, Senlis in 1151, Reims in the early 1150s, and at Noyon and Notre Dame de Paris in 1160. Most of these projects involved interior renovations, principally of the choir areas, but there were also significant examples of new Gothic exterior facades like the one erected at St. Denis in 1140, including new west fronts at Chartres (1140s), Senlis (c. 1170), and Laon (1190). The work at St. Denis seems to have initiated the Gothic cathedral-building movement that would continue for more than four hundred years (see Figure 17).[2]

What was the character and spirit of this movement? German historian and sociologist Martin Warnke has termed it "a great cultural competition." Former Chancellor of Salisbury Cathedral Ian Dunlop describes it as "the cathedrals' crusade."[3] Without question, the movement was a status competition of staggering proportions involving bishops, kings, and abbots who vied with one another to erect Gothic cathedrals and abbey churches of grander and grander design. Georges Duby imparts a sense of its character when he writes, "The bishop was a great lord, a prince, and as such, demanded that people take notice of him. For him, a new cathedral was a feat, a victory, a battle won by a military leader. . . . It was this urge to acquire personal prestige that accounts for the wave of emulation which, in the space of a quarter century, swept over each and every bishop of the royal [French] domain." Duby recounts an episode involving the archbishop of Reims, who not only had his own image created in his cathedral's stained glass windows, complete with an entourage of suffragan bishops worshipping at his feet, but actually arranged to have a recently completed entry porch demolished and rebuilt to make it larger and grander than one that had just been built by his great rival, the bishop of Amiens.[4]

Bishops thus compared what they had built or planned to build with what other bishops had done or planned to do. It became a sign of one's place in the church and society to claim that the height of the nave of one's cathedral, the magnificence of its tower or spire, the grandeur and beauty of its stained glass, the length of its nave, its overall mass—whatever—was greater, bigger, better, more audacious than any that had preceded it. Indeed, as a practical matter, it would have been impossible to raise the money needed to undertake building a new cathedral unless it was to be more impressive than any already planned, under construction, or completed.

To call this competition a mere status contest diminishes its true nature. As later chapters explain, Gothic cathedrals and great mo-

17. *The new style first developed at St. Denis quickly inspired the redesign of great churches all over northern France, including here at the Cathedral of Notre Dame, Paris.*

nastic churches were vital elements in the larger social project of managing the relations between the society and the sacred. Questions of a cathedral's grandeur were central to the most fundamental issues of social power. A particularly revealing example of the character of this cultural competition comes from a contemporary chronicler's account of the building of the cathedral at Auxerre, southeast of Paris:

> Seeing that his church was suffering from the age of its construction and badly put together . . . whereas all the bishops around him were raising cathedrals of a new and most splendid beauty, [the bishop] did resolve to order a new edifice with the help of specialists skilled in the art of building, so that it might not be so wholly different from the others in its appearance.[5]

The initial plan called for renovating the original cathedral, but apparently the project was not going well. The attempt to merge the newly fashionable Gothic style with the older Romanesque style was not succeeding, and signs of structural failure began to appear. The Bishop of Auxerre despaired that his renovations would ever result in a structure of any note. And then, the chronicler tells us, "fate intervened." On May 6, 1210, the Feast Day of St. John, the old cathedral caught fire and burned, leading one observer to describe the fire as "timely, not to say opportune." Immediately, the bishop set out to build a new cathedral along far more ambitious lines, using new Gothic forms. One year to the day after the fire, the first stone was laid.[6]

In cathedrals and other kinds of great churches being built in France during this period, the quest was to achieve ever greater interior height. Table 2 shows the increasing interior nave height for selected French cathedrals and the date when construction began. In England the competition more often took the form of building interior spaces of astonishing length. Salisbury achieved an overall length of 452 feet, 8 inches; Canterbury, 540 feet; Winchester, 554 feet; and St. Paul's, London (destroyed by fire in 1666), 600 feet. Not everyone approved of the competition to erect buildings of

TABLE 2. *Beginning Dates of Construction of Selected Cathedrals in France and Their Nave Height*

CATHEDRAL	START DATE	NAVE HEIGHT
Sens	1130	80 feet
Notre Dame	1163	108 feet
Chartres	1193	121 feet
Bourges	1195	123 feet
Reims	1212	124 feet, 9 inches
Amiens	1220	138 feet, 10 inches
Beauvais	1230	157 feet, 6 inches

SOURCE: Compiled by the author from data presented in Jean Gimpel, *The Cathedral Builders.*

greater and greater ostentation. Outraged, the Cistercian Abbot Bernard of Clairvaux exclaimed: "The church clothes her stones with Gold but lets her sons go naked. . . . The eyes are fed with gold-bedecked reliquaries . . . and they [the faithful] look more at the beauty than venerate the sacred."[7] But it was Abbot Suger who expressed the prevailing view. In describing a vision he had for building a jewel-bedecked Gothic choir, he said, "It was as if they [the holy martyrs] wished to tell us through their own mouths, 'Whether you wish it or not, we want only the very best.' "[8]

Given the nature of this cultural competition, building Gothic great churches also caused a tremendous amount of friction and even violence between those who built them and those who had to supply the resources and labor. No balanced account can ignore the terrible violence and civic unrest produced by the Gothic enterprise.

In a book entitled *The Medieval Cult of Saints*, the historian Barbara Abou-El-Haj recounts in fascinating detail how major places of pilgrimage often became sites of pitched battle where violence, bloodshed, and murder occurred. In speaking about Santiago de

18. *Early in its history the Cathedral of Santiago de Compostela was the scene of rioting against the power of the bishop.*

Compostela (Figure 18), the site of the tomb of Saint James and one of the most important places of pilgrimage during medieval times (and still today), she reports the conflict-ridden relations between prelates and townspeople. Discussing a famous history of the shrine, she states,

> About the town it tells quite a different story from the *Pilgrim's Guide:* how townsmen and a group of canons rioted in 1116–17, how for a year the burghers seized the town of Santiago and dismantled the bishop's power (established a commune), how they set fire to the nearly finished church in an attempt to assassinate Gelmirez [the bishop] so that the restored cathedral roof had to be fortified with defensive crenellations still visible in a c. 1600 drawing.[9]

One cause of violence was that the burghers wanted autonomy within the urban markets where they sold their goods, which was denied them because monarchs granted monopolies to local bishops in conjunction with pilgrimage. Instead, they had to rent their market stalls from canons of the cathedral chapter. Worse yet, the canons had stalls set up to sell goods manufactured by their own craftsmen, directly competing with the local burghers.

The same pattern was repeated at another great place of pilgrimage, Vézelay, site of the tomb of Mary Magdalen. At Vézelay a lucrative pilgrimage trade developed that profited the clergy but greatly burdened the town, resulting in communal violence on several occasions. Locals clashed with the prelates at every phase of building Vézelay's great pilgrimage church. Abou-El-Haj writes, "The abbot and the town haggled over everything: the quotas of vines, the dean's servants picking his quota of grapes, fishing and forest rights, pasturages, the number of bushels owed to the seigneurial mill, and prompt payment, as well as payment in coins. Nothing was trivial in a marginal economy stretched to the limit to pay professional masons and carvers to build and decorate on such a scale."[10]

Vézelay was the scene of at least four significant crises during the twelfth century, each engendered by a climate of unrest fed by the complicated and uneasy relationships among the abbot and his monks; the abbey and the local count; the abbot, the local count, and the townspeople, most especially members of the mercantile class; and the abbey and the bishop of Autun. The first crisis culminated in the murder of the abbot of Vézelay, and the third with outbursts of extreme violence that eventually required both the king and the pope to intervene. The fourth was marked by a long period of scheming and violent maneuvering by the local count and his henchmen that came to a head when the monks of the abbey were exiled from their own church.[11]

The same themes of civic unrest, rioting, violence, and bloodshed appear in almost every major historical study of the building of Europe's great Gothic churches. For example, two studies by the art historian Stephen Murray, one about Troyes and the other about Beauvais, show how conflict-ridden major cathedral-building campaigns could be. In describing Beauvais, he writes, "The construction of Beauvais cathedral as a historical process involved the agency of four overlapping institutions: the monarchy, the bishops, the chapter, and the commune. The relative power of each of these four institutions was in the process of changes, and these adjustments were liable to produce interludes of violent conflict." He recounts the urban riots of 1232–33, caused by the insistence of the bishop, Miles of Nanteuil, on collecting the full range of tolls and taxes due him from the bourgeois. The bishop's demands were urgent because he was going bankrupt from the enormous costs of the grand cathedral he sought to build. In the end, there was a chain reaction of unpleasantness and conflict:

> Oppressive taxation coupled with the confusing system for the election of the mayors led to royal intervention and the imposition of a foreign mayor. This led to urban rioting, which led to renewed royal intervention. The protest of the bishop was met with retaliation on the part of the king, which provoked excommunication of the king's agents, finally leading to the confiscation of the bishop's revenues. The construction of the cathedral was almost certainly brought to a temporary halt.

About Troyes, Murray explains that the power and standing of the bishop were challenged by a powerful rival, the Count of Champagne. Armed conflict erupted between the two, and the count's forces prevailed. In the end the bishop managed to resume his spiritual and ecclesiastical powers, but secular authority was retained by the count.[12]

In a similar vein, art historian Jane Williams's study of the windows of the trades at Chartres Cathedral reveals the deep antagonisms that existed between the various social groups in Chartres. (These windows depict various kinds of tradesmen making, transporting, and selling their wares.) She recounts in detail the enduring, complex patterns of strife that pitted the bishop against the cathedral chapter, the bishop and canons against local counts and countesses, and all of these against local tradesmen and peasants. Disputes periodically erupted in the form of riots, one in 1210 and the other in 1215, both in the midst of the major building campaign.[13]

Given the key role that cathedrals played in the process of monarchy-building, these recurrent episodes of civic unrest, conflict, even murder, should not surprise us. They are as much a part of the story as the communitarian impulses that generated the collective will to build such monuments. Both modern scholars who see cathedrals as great monuments to community-building and those who see them as instruments of exploitation, oppression, and violence are probably right in the sense that both are pointing to important truths. Neither perspective by itself tells the entire story.

To me, it seems clear that only a persistent determination, verging on stubbornness, and a willingness to engage in back-breaking labor over long periods, never giving up, made the creation of these wondrous cathedrals possible. The work had to be organized communally and accomplished by sustained, collective effort. The dynamics of organizing a community and its members for such an effort must be understood in the context of the larger cultural and existential projects of which Gothic cathedrals were a part. The Gothic enterprise was intimately bound up with the political and social dynamics of the medieval world, and with the role played in that world by the enduring effort to bring the sacred into secular human life as a resource in coping with the daunting daily challenges of that life.

PART III

THE GOTHIC LOOK

CHAPTER 7

What Is the Gothic Look?

Cathedrals have been part of Christianity from the time of Constantine (306–337). Their design and architectural styles have varied from one historical era to another, but in one important respect they are alike: all cathedrals display a distinctive geometric regularity in their design. This quality reached a high point in the Gothic style, reflecting an effort to achieve a rational, harmonious, and proportional result. Appreciating the role of geometry in their design is fundamental to understanding Gothic cathedrals.

In Salisbury Cathedral, for instance, the total height from ground level to the tip of the spire approximates the overall length from west to east. Inside, the central crossing (the point of intersection of the principal transept with the east-west axis) measures 39 feet by 39 feet (actually, 39 feet 2 inches by 39 feet 6 inches, as slight deviations are inevitable in a building of this magnitude). Virtually every other dimension of the building is directly related to this core dimension (see Figure 19). For example, the length of each of the ten bays of the nave is 19 feet 6 inches, or precisely one-half that of the central crossing, and each bay's width is also 19 feet 6 inches (give or take a fraction of an inch). The entire nave is composed of twenty identical spaces, each measuring 19 feet 6 inches square, plus ten identical spaces that each measure 19 feet 6 inches

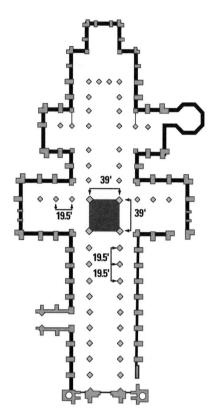

19. The design of Salisbury Cathedral is geometrically derived from a square 39 by 39 feet.

by 39 feet. Taking into account 2 feet of interior cladding, the nave is almost precisely as wide as it is high, and the two transepts and the presbytery also display an affinity to the core dimensions of the main crossing.

The cathedral church at Sens provides a second illustration. As Otto von Simson describes it, "The ground plan of Sens being designed *ad quadratum,* the square bays of the nave are twice as wide as those of the side aisles; owing to the tripartite elevation, it was possible to give the same proportions to the relative height of nave and aisle." The elevation of the nave is also subdivided so that "the octave ratio of 1:2 permeates the entire edifice."[1]

In his book about Amiens Cathedral, Stephen Murray provides

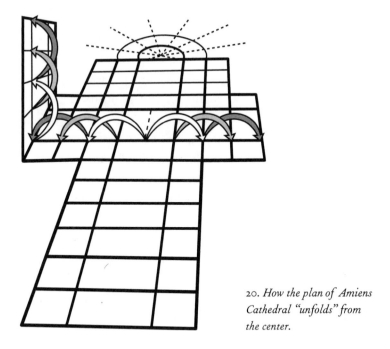

20. *How the plan of Amiens Cathedral "unfolds" from the center.*

a third illustration of the way geometry enables us to derive the basic overall design of Gothic great churches. Murray says, "The design begins with the square of the crossing. . . . Peripheral spaces will be, in a sense, unfolded from the central square." He shows how each dimension of the nave, choir, and double aisles of Amiens can be drawn by rotating diagonal lines from the central crossing (see Figure 20). He notes further that "the designer is obviously also concerned with allowing numbers to express proportions—hence, the repetition of 3's and 5's; of 5's and 7's."[2] A similar proportionality has been found repeatedly in other Gothic cathedrals and great monastic churches, including ones built well before the Gothic style appeared. Clearly, regular proportions and modular arrangements of repeated volumes were important to medieval architects.

Not all cathedrals, Gothic or otherwise, of course, are constructed according to the same measurements in feet and inches that one finds at Salisbury or Amiens. Renovations had to accommodate the dimensions of the existing buildings. In any case, no uniform standard measure of length yet existed. Yet what these spaces do have in common is a quest for geometric precision regardless of any specific measure of length. It is as if geometry were functioning as the "genetic code" for each building, in the sense that each has its own characteristic proportionality based on variations of a single length from which all, or nearly all, other features of the building's design derive. As Victor Hugo said of the design of Notre Dame Cathedral in Paris, "To measure the toe is to measure the giant."[3]

The quest for geometric uniformity, when followed consistently, gives Gothic cathedrals their characteristic organic unity. Every part of the building is linked logically, harmoniously, and proportionally to the whole. Looking again at the floor plan of Salisbury Cathedral shown in Figure 19, we see that the easternmost bay of the nave is essentially duplicated nine times. This duplicative quality applies not only to the broad dimensions of a bay space, but down to the finest detail. The art historian Erwin Panofsky calls this facet of design the principle of "progressive divisibility." According to this principle, he explains, "supports were divided and subdivided into main piers, major shafts, minor shafts, and still more minor shafts; the tracery of windows, triforia, and blind arcades into primary, secondary, and tertiary mullions and profiles; ribs and arches into a series of moldings."[4] The phrase "progressive divisibility" conveys the idea of a "visual logic" in which the subordinate members of a structure are related to one another to form a coherent whole. One hallmark of the Gothic style is the manner in which this principle is expressed visually, often even in the smallest details of individual shafts and moldings. The piers, shafts, and vaulting of Amiens Cathedral (Figures 21 and 22) exemplify this quality.

The design of a great church, then, reflects a desire to achieve a series of precise, geometrically related components, each part

21. *The piers and shafts in Amiens Cathedral show what Erwin Panofsky terms "progressive divisibility," a characteristic of Gothic design.*

22. *"Progressive divisibility" is also
a feature of Gothic ceiling vaults.*

deriving its definition from the building as a whole, each subpart deriving its measurements from the element to which it belongs. One practical result is that the components of the building are more or less identical repetitions of each other. Once segment A has been built, let's say the first bay of a nave, that bay serves as a template for the second bay, the second a template for the third, and so on. Having built one primary module, such as a bay span or width, the master mason could generate all other elements in the scheme by applying numerical rules, learned by rote through steps of con-structive geometry. In other words, all the principal elements of a design could be automatically indicated and interrelated without re-course to calculation.

If geometric regularity is a feature of all great churches, what, then, distinguishes Gothic cathedrals from others? The key to answering this question is understanding the central defining ele-ment of the Gothic style—light. All of the features we associate

23. *Light reaches the highest points in a Gothic building, as shown here in the side aisle of Canterbury Cathedral.*

with Gothic architecture—pointed arches, flying buttresses, ribbed vaults, soaring ceilings, stained glass windows, pinnacles and turrets—were developed in the service of the desire to flood the interior space with as much light as possible.

The interiors of Romanesque great churches are characteristically somber. As originally built, they were dimly lit, and it is not unusual to discover areas of the interior that are barely touched by light. Moreover, the walls are ponderous, solid, and somber. In dramatic contrast to this style, the walls of Gothic cathedrals appear almost porous. Light permeates the interior and merges with every aspect of it, as though no segment of inner space should be allowed to remain in darkness, undefined by light (see Figure 23).

Today visitors to Gothic cathedrals, especially in England, often find clear glass in the windows, but this was the result of later renovations. The medieval builders' ideal is exemplified by the interior of Chartres or Canterbury Cathedral, where the glass is colored in deep primary tones. As a result, even though the interiors are filled with light, the spaces acquire deep and rich color tones. The attempt to combine these two things—increased light and deep color—impelled the builders to reach for greater and greater heights. The aim was to transform the interior spaces into a semblance of the Heavenly Jerusalem.

Flying buttresses, ribbed vaults, and pointed arches—the characteristic elements of the Gothic style—all worked together to permit larger windows and to open up the interior spaces, allowing the increased light to penetrate the building more completely. But how exactly did they do this? What, for example, was the advantage of the Gothic ribbed vaults over the earlier barrel, or tunnel, vaults? A barrel vault—the simplest kind of vault—is just a longitudinally extended arch. It must be supported along its entire length by thick walls. If the objective is to achieve interior illumination, the barrel vault cannot help, because it encloses space rather than opening it, and it cannot be penetrated to permit light to enter from above without risking collapse. The ribbed vault was developed to overcome these limitations (see Figure 24).

The ribbed vault replaced the "groin" that occurs at the point where two tunnel vaults intersect with newly invented "ribs," as shown in Figure 24. By articulating the lines of the groin, the ribs can rest on a few specific "springing points," which themselves rest on round pillars, or "piers." The spaces between the ribs can then become "webbing," or sculpted surfaces that open up, heighten, and give delicacy to the vaulted unit. The spaces between the piers can be left entirely open or become a thin wall pierced with windows. This technique of ribbed vaulting is used not only at the intersection of two narrow aisles or walkways, where the tunnel vault would use groins, but also along the full length of each aisle, and ribbed vaults can even form the ceiling of huge spaces in the cathedral, including the choir and the nave (see Figure 25).

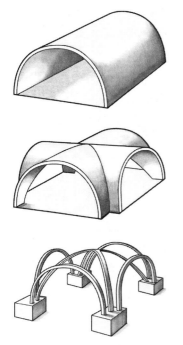

24. *A barrel vault and a ribbed vault.*
The barrel vault must be supported along
its entire length by thick walls, whereas
the ribbed vault can rest on a just few
"springing points."

Ribbed vaults are stronger than barrel vaults, and they require less material to build. In addition, ribbed vaults are actually easier to build, because the ribs and webs can be built separately, while a barrel vault must be built and supported as a single unit. Ribbed vaults are more flexible and adaptable to different architectural styles than groin vaults are, and they permit more variations, including spanning greater distances without the danger of collapse.

The pointed arch also has many architectural advantages. One problem with the rounded arch is that its height is dictated by its width. This is not true of the pointed arch, which can span varying distances while the crowns of all the arches in a building remain more or less even. Pointed arches are sturdier, by a factor of 20 to 25 percent, than rounded arches. And the thrust generated by a pointed arch is directed more effectively toward the supporting piers and walls than is the case for a rounded arch.[5]

Figure 26 is a drawing of three sections of the nave of Win-

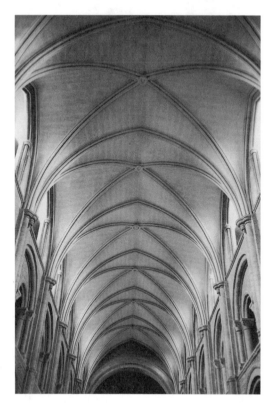

25. *Another of my personal favorites is Christchurch Priory. This picture of the nave reveals how ribbed vaults can span wide spaces as well as narrow ones, leaving every part of the church open to light.*

chester Cathedral. The bay on the left shows us what the original Romanesque bay looked like; the middle bay shows how it was carved back; and the right bay shows what it looked like after the masons had transformed it into the Gothic style by refacing the existing stone and installing pointed arches. Like ribbed vaults, pointed arches require less material, are stronger, and open up the interior space to light, promoting skeletal building. Builders can go higher while using more wall space for windows. Nowhere have I seen the contrast of styles demonstrated as dramatically as at Winchester, with its Romanesque transepts (Figure 27) and Gothic nave (Figure 28).

Light generally requires height, and to get it, designers had to find ways to siphon off the weight of the roof and high vaults, other than onto interior walls, which had been opened up and "thinned out" by the extensive use of pointed arches. The transfer of stress was achieved by the third component we associate with the Gothic design, the flying buttress. Romanesque churches used "quadrant arches" (quarter-circles) to buttress the pressure, or thrust, generated by their high barrel vaults. To achieve the Gothic aim of a light-filled interior, buildings had to become taller—too tall to be supported by traditional quadrant arches. The supporting arches had to be raised above the aisle roofs to abut the high vaults, as if they were flying over them; hence the expression "flying buttresses." Flying buttresses shifted the weight of the roof and vaults away from the supporting walls to side structures that in turn carried it down to the ground (see Figure 29).

Examples of ribbed vaults and pointed arches can be found in pre-Gothic churches. A leading student of French Gothic architecture of the twelfth and thirteenth centuries, Jean Bony, suggests that pointed arches were introduced into western Europe from Islamic architecture by crusaders or, in some still unknown manner, via northern Italy.[6] Another expert on Gothic architecture, Paul Frankl, asserts that the introduction of diagonal ribs to a groin vault is traceable to the vaults of the choir aisle of Durham Cathedral in England, which were constructed between 1093 and 1096.[7] Although the flying buttress is a unique creation of Gothic architecture, its antecedents are traceable to the Romanesque quadrant arch. In other words, all three principal elements associated with Gothic architecture arose out of church-building activity during the Romanesque period.

Beyond these three elements, Gothic architecture introduced wall arches, built over the tops of walls to create a system of ribs anchored on the lateral surfaces of the walls. These wall arches, together with transverse arches and diagonal ribs, were met by the flying buttresses about one-third of the way up from their springing to counter pressure and thrust. Wall arches were necessary be-

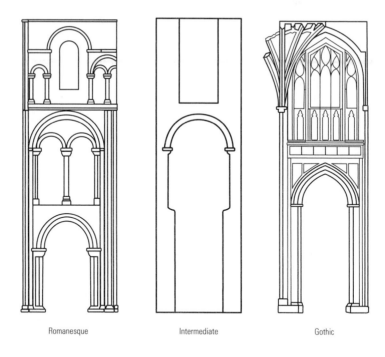

Romanesque   Intermediate   Gothic

26. The nave of Winchester Cathedral was transformed
from the Romanesque to the Gothic style by cutting
back the original Romanesque bays.

cause ribs alone could not reduce the amount of weight exerted on
the walls. They enabled the builders to concentrate the forces of
thrust down toward the area from the springing point to a point
about one-third up the vaults (the "haunch"), which was then coun-
terbalanced by the flying buttresses. The end result is a skeletal system that is anchored at the points of upright buttresses, thereby allowing the wall surface between the buttresses to be replaced by
large expanses of colorful stained glass.

What makes Gothic architecture revolutionary is not that it used
new or different materials. Gothic churches were made of the same
stone, wood, and glass that had been used to build Romanesque
and other pre-Gothic churches; indeed, the Gothic parts of some

27. *The soaring Romanesque transept of Winchester
Cathedral is characterized by solid-looking construction,
rounded arches, plain, thick walls, and dark recesses.*

28. *Winchester Cathedral's Gothic nave features ornate carving and high windows, a dramatic contrast to the Romanesque transept shown in Figure 27.*

cathedrals were built by recycling materials that had been used in Romanesque churches. What was different was the way the Gothic style combined the elements of design to create an entirely new, organically unified whole. Gothic design amounted to a new vision of the way to combine the distinctive advantages of ribbed vaulting and pointed arches with a new system for buttressing high vaults and roofs to create an interior space that was expansive, soaring, and bright (see Figure 30).

The Gothic style, of course, did not materialize all at once in its mature form. According to Frankl, the Gothic style evolved slowly out of the Romanesque, starting from the time when diagonal ribs first were added to groin vaults. The principles inherent in the first

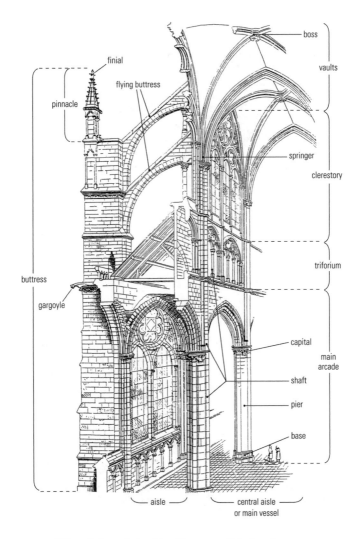

boss

vaults

finial

flying buttress

pinnacle

springer

clerestory

buttress

triforium

gargoyle

capital

shaft

pier

base

main
arcade

aisle

central aisle
or main vessel

29. *This artist's rendering identifies some of the key features of Gothic design.*

30. *The nave of Worcester Cathedral shows how ribbed vaulting, pointed arches, and new systems of buttressing were combined to create a space that is high and bright.*

ribbed vaults, says Frankl, had profound implications for the design of other features, such as windows, shafts, wall arches, plinths, and moldings, eventuating in Gothic style's mature form. The pointed arch eventually came to be combined with the ribbed vault at a later date, and the flying buttress emerged after the pointed arch appeared. But only during the so-called High Gothic period, which Frankl dates from 1194 through 1300, did all the innovations begin to coalesce into a coherent style in cathedrals like Chartres.[8]

Supporting Frankl's thesis is the fact that no name for the style is known to have existed at the time it first appeared. Indeed, it is unlikely that any special name, beyond simply "new work," or *novum opus*, existed for it at the time. The label "Gothic" never appeared until the fifteenth century, when it was used pejoratively to describe things regarded as crude, rustic, coarse, and uncivilized. Frankl tells us that one school of thought, in some unexplained way, associates the style with the Goths who, in A.D. 410, under the leadership of Alaric, destroyed parts of Rome. Another school also associated it with the Germans, but in this case the myth is that it originated in forests. The claim is that the Germans would not cut down trees, so instead they bound the top branches of living trees together, thereby creating the pointed arch. This theory that the Gothic style was born in the forests of Germany persisted with incredible tenacity, and one hears it occasionally even today.[9] Not until the eighteenth century did a more positive view of the Gothic style emerge among art historians. The quest to understand the concepts inherent in this style then began in earnest.

By now it should be clear that the most important part of a Gothic cathedral is its interior space. Here the emphases on geometry and light fuse to create an image of God's house. Of course, the outside appearance of the building mattered, but the primary goal in building these cathedrals was the illumination of interior spaces. Otto von Simson has likened the exterior of the Gothic cathedral to the backstage area in a theater, where props are hung to produce the interior scenery. Others compare it to the "wrong side" of an elaborately designed sweater.[10] From the outside, one sees only the structure that was needed to support the glass and perfect geometric forms inside. At this point one may wonder why geometry and light were so important in designing great churches. Is there a connection to ecclesiastical, theological, and philosophical precepts of the time?

CHAPTER 8

An Image of Heaven

In 1144 a ceremony was held to dedicate the newly completed Gothic choir of the Abbey Church of St. Denis. Otto von Simson writes that, for Abbot Suger, the renovated choir was an embodiment of the "mystical vision of harmony that divine reason has established throughout the cosmos."[1] Suger portrayed the choir as a place where heaven touched earth, a space where the living could glimpse heaven. This description expresses the conception that gave rise to the Gothic style of architecture. The Gothic cathedral was intended as a space where people could get a taste of heaven (see Figure 31).

What does von Simson mean when he says that this medieval bishop conceived of his cathedral as providing an "image of heaven"?[2] To us an image is a visual representation of an object that inherently entails our personal interpretation and perspective. To the medieval theologian, however, the term *image* had a different meaning, closer to the Greek word *mimesis*, which signifies "imitation," or a literal copying of a natural form. It implied the actual embodiment of the thing it stood for, an attempt at a *literal* representation of the thing itself, or—with regard to Suger's remark— at least as literal a depiction of a spiritual ideal as one could achieve in the material world. When Suger said that the new choir provided

31. *The Abbey Church of St. Denis was designed by
Abbot Suger to be a place infused with light.*

an image of divine order, he meant that a literal rendition of heaven was now available to humans here on earth.

But how could a space located on earth and created using ordinary materials become magically transformed into a heavenly enclave? What was it about the stone, wood, glass, lead, and paint used to build Gothic cathedrals that made this transformation possible? The answer lies in the belief of medieval theologians that all visible objects contain within them the potential to reveal the divine— indeed, that through the contemplation of material objects, we can gain a direct experience of God. The medieval philosopher John Scotus Erigena expressed this idea succinctly when he said that we understand a piece of wood or a stone only when we perceive God in it.[3] This property, intrinsic to all physical objects, made them potential "stepping stones to heaven." And the quality that unleashed their intrinsic potential, the thing that enabled a stone or piece of wood to serve as a vehicle for experiencing God, was—*light*. Medieval theologians regarded light as the medium *par excellence* through which physical objects became capable of revealing their divine properties to humans.

In order to construct images of heaven out of ordinary materials, a designer must first picture what heaven is like. So what, we may wonder, did the designers of Gothic cathedrals think heaven looked like? It is here that geometry comes into play. The centrality of geometry in the medieval vision of divine order can be traced to the classical tradition and to the writings of the theologian Augustine of Hippo (A.D. 354–430), who was influenced by this tradition. In his famous essay on aesthetics, *De Musica*, he explained the nature of beauty. True beauty, he declared, is ultimately anchored in divine reality and reflects it. He conceived beauty to be a property that inheres in an object or a sound, an attribute it possesses by virtue of its resemblance to or mimicry of divine reality.[4]

But what exactly is the nature of the divine reality that objects and sounds of true beauty reflect? Augustine found the answer in a famous passage from the Wisdom of Solomon: "Thou hast ordered all things in measure and number and weight." From this statement Augustine inferred that the defining quality of divine order is precise mathematical relationships. Given his belief that true beauty must be rooted in metaphysical reality, Augustine concluded (as others had before him, including the sculptor Polykleitos, eight centuries earlier) that the fundamental quality of true beauty is what he termed "proper modulation." Augustine defined beautiful music, for example, as "the science of good modulation."[5] He believed that beautiful music could be achieved by basing the relationships between musical units on simple arithmetic ratios. Music composed according to these rules would be "ideal," reflecting the true nature of the universe, which, he believed, was constituted of similar ratios.

This conception of beauty seems strange in this modern age. We are accustomed to thinking that beauty is in the eye of the beholder. For Augustine, something could be beautiful only if it exactly mirrored the geometric regularity of divine order, and, if it did, by definition it had to be beautiful. Issues of personal taste and preference were irrelevant to the judgment. In fact, the observer's obligation was to contemplate the object or sound in order to grasp the beauty it held within it.

The connection between the principles of modulation in beautiful music and mathematics are easy to see. But Augustine went on to suggest, as others before him had done, that the principles that hold for sounds also apply to physical objects. He was particularly impressed by the observation that harmonic intervals could be represented as intervals of length along the strings of a musical instrument, inferring that these intervals of length constituted harmonic proportions that would, by virtue of their geometric regularity, be as pleasing to the *eye* as their equivalent in sound was pleasing to the *ear*. This conclusion led Boethius to declare that the ear is affected by sounds in exactly the same way as the eye is by optical impressions, and Augustine to say that one needs to look at a building to understand music![6] From here it was but a short step to assigning cosmic significance to geometry. Through studying the mathematical proportionality of physical objects, by grasping the underlying logic of their geometry, Augustine believed the mind could be guided past the world of appearance to achieve contemplation of divine order. Otto von Simson describes the idea elegantly when he writes, "Music and architecture are sisters. . . . Architecture mirrors eternal harmony [and] . . . music echoes [it]."[7]

Augustine's ideas about geometry were reflected in every aspect of medieval sacred design, probably because they were taught in the twelfth-century cathedral schools whose students became the bishops, abbots, and master builders of the twelfth, thirteenth, and fourteenth centuries. Augustine's philosophy of beauty became part of a powerful intellectual movement in France, especially among the group of eminent Platonists assembled at the Cathedral School of Chartres. The twelfth-century theology and cosmology of scholars at Chartres embraced the sacredness of geometry and the aesthetic consequences of exposure to it. They believed that geometry was a means for linking human beings to God, that mathematics was a vehicle for revealing to humankind the innermost secrets of heaven. They thought the harmony of musical consonance was based on the same ratios as those forming cosmic order, that the cosmos was a work of architecture and God was its architect.

In their view, the primary bodies composing the world were akin to building materials, and these elements, assembled in accordance with perfect ratios, could result in an exact image of cosmic order. This outlook also led them to assume that because the cosmos was stable and enduring, the designer of a great church who planned his sanctuary in accordance with the laws of harmonious proportion would produce a structure that revealed heaven itself. The application of "perfect proportions," as dictated by geometry, thus became a technical necessity as well as an aesthetic postulate if the building was to serve its purpose. Perfect proportions led builders of great churches to conceive of architecture as applied geometry, geometry as applied theology, and the designer of a Gothic cathedral as an imitator of the divine Master.

This approach occasionally led designers to draw disastrous conclusions. Because the builders aspired to model their structures on divine order, they assumed that as long as they did not deviate from a strict geometric proportionality, their buildings would inevitably be structurally stable and sound. They reasoned that because divine order was geometrically proportional and it was manifestly stable and enduring, the same would be true for any similarly designed structure. The reason, they thought, so many structural failures occurred in Gothic cathedrals was that the builders had deviated from strict geometric proportionality. Even worse, some designers assumed that the cure for a work in progress that was showing signs of distress was simply to keep building until geometric regularity was achieved, at which point the entire structure would magically

32. *The builders of Milan Cathedral feared their building would collapse and sought advice from master builders throughout Europe.*

stabilize. The historian Christopher Wilson recounts just such an event in connection with the construction of Milan Cathedral (Figure 32) in the 1390s. Master cathedral builders throughout Europe were summoned to Milan to advise the cathedral builders about how to correct the increasing instability of their structure. One of these consultants, the famous designer of Prague Cathedral, Heinrich Parler, argued vociferously that its height should be *increased* in order to make the section exactly conform to a square (i.e., *ad quadratum*), thereby magically stabilizing it! He apparently believed that the increased stress on structural members would in some mysterious way be offset by the structural soundness ensured by strict adherence to a form that was in harmony with the laws guaranteeing the stability of the divine order. Though Parler's advice was seriously considered, in the end it was ignored in favor of buttresses.[8]

In the last chapter I noted that a devotion to geometry in designing great churches gives them a certain characteristic organic quality. In one sense this association follows directly from Augustine's ideas about geometric proportionality in music. According to Augustine, part of what makes music pleasing to the ear is the pattern that is used for replicating, dividing, contrasting, and timing the octaves, fourths, and fifths that it comprises. In a traditional Western musical composition, the chord that is struck with the left hand on a piano keyboard might have four notes in it, which are sustained while the right hand plays the melody on the keys in the upper register. The notes that make up the melody may be the same as those used in the chord, but several octaves higher in pitch, and these notes are struck with a timing that is regular and divisible into replicated increments. This kind of proportionality leads us to think about how individual segments of a musical composition fit together to form an organic whole. Take, for example, a musical composition with an eight-bar refrain (or another increment of four). Here some element, such as the chords played, the melody line, the harmony, or the timing of the pattern of notes struck, lasts eight bars, then repeats, goes another eight bars, then repeats, and so forth. We can see how the same mode of thought and logic that produces organic unity in musical compositions would, when applied to architecture, result in buildings with organic unity.[9]

The impulse toward achieving organic unity in church design may have been implicit in Augustine's *De Musica*, but it gained its most precise definition and clearest elaboration through Scholasticism. The origins of Scholasticism have been traced to Aristotle, whose works were beginning to be translated in the eleventh and twelfth centuries in the cathedral schools of France. The central figures in this movement were the French philosopher and teacher Peter Abelard (1079–1142) and the Italian theologian Thomas Aquinas (1225–1274), along with his teacher at Cologne, Albertus Magnus (1206–1280).[10]

The art historian Erwin Panofsky, who has brilliantly explicated the connections between Scholasticism and Gothic architecture, terms Scholasticism a "mental habit" espoused by Abelard and his followers. This new mode of thought was instilled in students who attended the great cathedral and abbey schools of France during the twelfth and thirteenth centuries, who applied it to whatever their chosen field happened to be—music, theology, philosophy, art, political propaganda, painting, mythology or architecture. At heart, Scholasticism was an attempt to achieve a unity of truth by combining reason, logic, and faith under a single umbrella, in order to reach what Panofsky describes as "a permanent peace treaty between faith and reason"—"permanent" because the issue had been an unresolved concern of Christianity from the beginning.[11] One version of the story suggests that the scholastics imported the idea from the neo-Platonists of Islamic Spain. Wherever it came from, it reached fruition in Aquinas's writings in the thirteenth century, representing an effort to place reason and logic in the service of faith. The fundamental notion was that, though sacred doctrine could not be *proven* through reason and logic, reason and logic could *disclose* or *reveal* faith. This belief led theologians to apply reason and logic to nearly everything, including reason itself. Many historians think this particular aspect of Scholasticism had the greatest influence on medieval theology and, in the end, on Gothic architecture.[12]

To understand this mental habit and how it worked, it is helpful to begin by explaining the effect it had, not on architecture, but on intellectual and scholarly discourse. Before the advent of Scholasticism, the fame of the towering intellectual figures in religion, philosophy, and other learned disciplines was based not on the originality of their ideas but on their powers of erudition: what they knew, their teaching, their literary artistry. In this tradition classical works of scholarship were simply divided into "books," which contained unrelated ideas that did not follow any particular logical order. These scholars seldom considered, as modern academics typically do, the logical consistency of their positions on different issues. The purpose, instead, was exhaustively to recount everything known and said about a particular topic or writer from classical antiquity.

Scholasticism profoundly transformed the nature of scholarship. Its new goal was to lay bare the logical basis for the arguments being made, to consider all the implications of conclusions drawn about one question for conclusions drawn about other matters. This approach forced a dramatic change in the way scholarly treatises were presented and ultimately produced the characteristic form for organizing discourse that today is taken for granted as the appropriate form for expository writing. Panofsky explains that Scholasticism led to a method for organizing ideas "according to a scheme of division and subdivision, condensable into a table of contents or synopsis, where all parts denoted by numbers or letters of the same class are on the same logical level."[13] Indeed, the rules we follow today for sentence structure and punctuation evolved from this tradition. Scholasticism resulted in a method for presenting discourse that guided the student, point by point, along a logical path of reasoning that clarified the place of each idea within an overarching framework of thought.

Scholasticism, in other words, led theologians to attempt to construct a framework or system of thought within which all positions on a particular issue of theology could be fitted together so that they were logically consistent and reinforced each other. What theologians sought to do with religious treatises, builders then tried to do when they designed Gothic cathedrals. As Panofsky has explained, "Like the High Scholastic *Summa*, the High Gothic cathedral aimed at 'totality' and therefore tended to approximate, by synthesis as well as elimination, one perfect and final solution. In its imagery, the High Gothic cathedral sought to embody the whole of Christian knowledge, theological, moral, natural, and historical, with everything in its place and that which no longer found its place suppressed."[14]

Among the designers of Gothic great churches were some of the greatest scholars of the Middle Ages. Bishops had typically been ed-

*33. The exquisite fan vaulting in the ceiling of Bath Abbey
shows the exuberance of the High Gothic style.*

ucated at the great cathedral schools, and many of them had been
heads of schools before being appointed bishops. The new mode
of thought they acquired and taught had an enormous influence on
the way in which they and their master masons worked to conceive
and execute their designs. Much as theologians elucidated the logical structure of their arguments, builders of Gothic great churches
attempted to elucidate the logical structure for their buildings. The
"mental habit" of Scholasticism led designers to think more explicitly about physical structures as systems that hang together as
coherent wholes. Just as the theologian had been trained to think
through the implications of adopting, say, position A on one issue
for positions taken on all other issues, so the master builder approached his task by thinking through in advance the relationship
of the parts of a building to the whole, contemplating how the decision to configure an arch in a certain way, build a nave to a certain
height or length, or construct a window to a certain width would
affect other parts of the building.

In one sense, this strategy was no different from the way builders of pre-Gothic great churches had proceeded, as no building can be conceived piecemeal, without considering in advance the connections between parts and whole. But Scholasticism forced the designer to articulate this planning clearly, rather than just grasping it intuitively. The intention of Gothic design was for all of the elements to work together to produce the coordinated effect the builders desired; thus, everything had to be designed as a whole and each decision constantly reconsidered in light of decisions made on other elements.

It is easy to see how a Scholastic turn of mind encouraged the production in advance of an organically unified design. The master builders who came out of the tradition of Scholasticism would have planned a system of unitary volumes, working back and forth between the various architectural and sculptural elements until they achieved a logical organization that subordinated all parts to the whole. The organizing principle that emerged was based on repeating spatial modules assembled in additive sequence. The same principles that led to the identification of divisions and subdivisions in a manuscript led to the assignment of component parts of the building to discrete "logical levels" and arrangement "according to a system of homologous parts and parts of parts."[15] As Paul Frankl's careful study of Gothic architecture shows, this approach to great church building was not born whole. He suggests that it began with the appearance of ribbed vaults and gradually led builders to think through the implications of such structures for every other part of the building. In most instances, the approach did not come to fruition until the appearance of the High Gothic form during the period from 1194 to 1300 (see Figure 33).[16]

But what about the most distinctive element of Gothic design—light? In medieval theology God concealed Himself so as to be revealed, and light was the principal and best means by which humans could know Him. A Gothic great church amounted to a neo-

Platonic attempt to materialize and reflect spiritual perfection in the earthly sphere. As the worshippers' eyes rose toward heaven, God's grace, in the form of sunlight, was imagined to stream down in benediction, encouraging exaltation. Sinners could be led to repent and strive for perfection by envisioning the world of spiritual perfection where God resided—a world suggested by the geometric regularity of cathedrals.

As we have seen, Abbot Suger of St. Denis viewed his church as a monument of applied theology. This theology was based on the work of Dionysius the Areopagite, who wrote what is considered one of the most imposing mystical constructs in the history of Christian thought (although Suger erroneously attributed the ideas to his abbey's patron saint, St. Denis).[17] At the heart of the Areopagite's theology was one central idea: God is light. According to this view, every living creature, every material object that is visible, stems from and is connected to this initial, uncreated, creative light. All living creatures and all material things receive and transmit the divine illumination from which they emanate. They do so according to their capacity, that is, their rank in the hierarchical scale of being, the level at which God's intention has situated them within the cosmic scheme of things.

In this view, the universe, born of an irradiance, is tantamount to a descending flood of light that touches everything and unites it, giving order and coherence to the entire world. The Areopagite believed that not only is each material object and each living creature connected to divine order through light, but also that one can move backward, step by step, to the original, ineffable, invisible source of light. God is absolute light, existing more or less veiled within each creature, depending on how refractory that creature was to His illumination, but every creature in its own way unveils God, for anyone open to seeing this can find in each creature its share of light, which holds the promise of leading one back to God. This concept underlaid the new art—an art of light—and every facet of Suger's redesign of his abbey church manifests these ideas. Every partition, everything that interrupted the flow of the divine effulgence, was removed.[18]

The idea behind the importance of light in Gothic architecture is that as the most noble of natural phenomena, the least material, the closest approximation to pure form, light can mediate between what is bodiless and what is corporeal. It became essential in Gothic architecture because it was capable of revealing the divine reality that Gothic churches were meant to disclose. To serve their intended purpose, sanctuaries demanded that light penetrate every corner of the interior space. The quest to achieve greater openings to admit more light necessitated piercing the walls, which led to a concern with points of support, and this led builders to perfect the coordinated interplay between ribbed vaults, pointed arches, and flying buttresses that distinguished the Gothic style. In essence, new structures and forms were invented to solve problems created by theological purposes. At the same time, these new expanses of glass could be used for another purpose, namely, to adorn the interior of the newly created Heavenly Jerusalem.

CHAPTER 9

A Pragmatic View
of Cathedral-Building

The explanation for the elements of the Gothic style given in the preceding chapter has much to commend it. However, this approach is highly deductive, starting with basic theological principles and deriving from them the fundamentals of Gothic design. It underplays the fact that cathedral-building is very much a hands-on, empirical activity. If, instead, we approach cathedral-building inductively, we might ask how the basic conditions under which cathedral-building projects were carried out affected their design. Three features of Gothic cathedral-building projects strike me as particularly significant: (1) their complexity, (2) the inordinately long period of time it took to complete them, and (3) the fact that the building process was repeatedly interrupted.

Gothic cathedrals were probably the most complex building projects undertaken during the medieval period in western Europe. Their organic unity, the extraordinary ornateness required of their exterior and interior spaces (see Figure 34), the daring heights the builders sought to achieve, and the resulting need for elaborate systems of buttressing, the great towers the style demanded, and the massiveness of the great west fronts were unrivaled by any other building projects during the period.

34. *Salisbury's interior is one of the plainest of all Gothic
cathedrals, but even here the stonework is elaborately detailed.*

The master mason assigned to design and build a typical Gothic great church had no way of knowing how long it would take to complete the project. He would almost certainly not expect it to be finished during his own lifetime. In rare instances, a Gothic great church could be built relatively quickly, say in a decade or two, and certain components of Gothic structures, such as the choir and crypt of St. Denis, were built from start to finish in less than four years. But, as indicated in Chapter 2, the typical structure took two or more centuries to complete. This meant that at the outset the designer had to conceive of ways to encode the fundamental features of the design in a way that could be transmitted to successive generations of builders who were unfamiliar with the project's beginnings. The plan had to be in a form that would be intelligible to future builders and that would help them to construct a building resembling what the original designer had in mind. Given what we know about medieval rates of literacy and numeracy, the absence of usable numeric systems, the lack of paper on which to make detailed drawings, and so on, the impact of time on the building project was no small matter.

Complicating the problem of time was the inevitability of frequent and maddening interruptions to the construction work. Builders faced both interruptions whose timing they could anticipate and whose duration they could predict, and disruptions they might know were apt to occur but whose timing and extent they had no way of anticipating. Among the predictable interruptions were those due to the annual building cycles and the daily rhythm of work described in Chapter 3. A second source of disruption was the liturgical calendar adopted for a particular year, including holy days, saints' days, feast days, and so on. On high holy days or days commemorating particular saints, all work ceased; no work was permitted on the Sabbath; and these work stoppages involved not only the specific days in question, but most or all of the afternoon of the days preceding them. Using Richard Jones's estimates for the number of hours of daylight during the building season for the year 1253, when Westminster Abbey was under construction, I have tried to measure the impact of liturgy and Sabbath celebrations on the total amount of time worked. During the period from April 1 to September 30, there would have been approximately 2,140 hours of daylight when work could have been done. Taking into account the number of days lost because of Sabbaths, holy days, and feast days, and the number of hours lost to scheduled breaks that were taken during the workday, 715 daylight hours were lost, shrinking the total hours available for productive labor to 1,425 per building season—a loss of 33 percent of the total available time.[1]

When sources of interruption were known, presumably the master mason could take them into account in developing his long-term work plan. But other disruptions could not be planned for in the same way. The most common problem was unpredictable cash flow. If a cathedral chapter failed to meet a weekly payroll, the skilled workers might simply leave to search for employment elsewhere.[2] The mechanisms for funding cathedral-building projects that were available to cathedral chapters were whimsical. Such funds came from a multitude of sources, including tithes, absolutions, indulgences, donations from pilgrims, and loans. Every one of these sources was ultimately traceable to agriculture, and medieval agricultural yields were notoriously unpredictable. The bishop or canons of a cathedral chapter might pledge a portion of their prebendary income—the income from the lands that went with the position of bishop or canon—but no one could know for sure how much money such a pledge might amount to. Agricultural yield was at the mercy of the elements and could be diminished by droughts, floods, and unseasonably cold or wet weather. Moreover, prebendary income depended on the canon's ability to collect duties and taxes from the peasants who farmed his land, and collection often proved difficult and was subject to a good deal of caprice. Therefore, a cathedral chapter might know that each of its canons was prepared to contribute a tenth or a quarter of his prebendary income, but the treasurer would have no way to know how much total income would come in during any given period, because no one could accurately predict the figure on which the tithe would be based.

Moreover, no system of banking existed that would allow chapters to borrow as protection against uneven cash flows. Unless a cathedral chapter or monastic order was exceedingly wealthy and had managed to build up huge reserves of liquid capital, the unevenness in the flow of money contributed greatly to the unevenness of the pace of work. This problem is illustrated in Stephen Murray's study of the construction of Troyes Cathedral, which spanned the 312-year period from 1220 to 1532.[3] Funding problems forced the builders to alter their implementation of the original design. Periodically, they had to stop work entirely or take shortcuts, which included using inferior materials and building walls so thin that some of them collapsed.

Certain building projects, such as those at Lincoln, Westminster, Winchester, and Exeter, relied on moneylenders for help in getting through periods of financial shortage, but because usury was considered a sin, officially at least, the church discouraged money lending by Christians. To get around this problem, bishops worked with monarchs to enact ordinances forbidding Jews to engage in any form of trade or commerce *except* money lending. This guaranteed a source of money that would allow bishops to meet their payrolls, while "off-loading" the sin of usury onto non-Christians. Bishops sometimes became so heavily indebted to Jewish moneylenders that they could not meet their loan obligations. When this occurred, a bishop would solve his problem by offering the sitting monarch— the designated "protector of Jews"—substantial indulgences in exchange for canceling his debt to the moneylenders.[4]

Disruptions caused by a lack of funds were extremely serious. They almost always meant that work had to stop, even if it were in mid-project, such as a tower partially built or a roof or a vault half-finished. When work began again, many of these half-completed projects had to be undone and restarted. But far more serious was the fact that when funds were exhausted, the teams of skilled workers might disband and find work elsewhere, along with the laborers who aided them. Even when new sources of funds were found, there was no guarantee that the same crews could be reassembled. In most cases skilled artisans had migrated elsewhere, and newly hired workers were often unfamiliar with the project or the site.

Another unpredictable source of disruption was the need to allow lime mortar time to set. As noted previously, the rate at which mortar hardened dictated the pace at which masonry could be laid. A high wall could not go up quickly, because the resulting load might squeeze mortar out of the lower courses before it had time to cure properly. At the point of every arch and the curve of each vault, where the thrust was not downward but oblique, workers had to allow the mortar to cure before removing the supports, and further construction might have to stop until the mortar had hardened. Because the rate of hardening depended on atmospheric conditions, the time required was not always predictable. If there were no other projects to work on, nothing else could be done until the mortar had cured, regardless of the funding situation.

Weather, too, was a serious and unpredictable source of disruption. For example, evidence from tree ring studies indicates that during the forty-six years when the main part of Salisbury Cathedral was being built (1220–1266), twenty-two years were exceptionally wet and cool. Not only did wet weather make building difficult or impossible on some days, it would have required much of the workforce to abandon the construction project to respond to the needs of their farms.

Indeed, it was agriculture that posed the greatest challenge to planning for the master mason. As noted in Chapter 2, nearly 98 percent of all people living in England during medieval times relied directly or indirectly on farming for their wealth and livelihood, including those whose money helped to pay for cathedrals and, just as important, the unskilled workers whose labor supported the skilled artisans. Depending on the style of a cathedral project, two-thirds or even more of the total workforce consisted of unskilled laborers. Much of this labor was almost certainly local and drawn from the peasant population. The few scraps of information from account books that have survived indicate that the wage rates paid to unskilled laborers were low, certainly no more than 2 or 2.5 pennies per day, and often less. Common laborers who had to migrate from their homes to distant work sites would have had to pay for room and board. At building sites such as Vale Royal Abbey, the fee charged to workers to live on the site was 1.5 pennies a day for room and 1 penny a day for board.[5] Only the skilled artisans could afford to live away from home for long periods of time. For this reason, most people who joined the "grunt labor force" at cathedral sites were probably locals who "commuted," if not daily, then certainly weekly.

The workforce data presented in Chapter 2 show that the number of workers on site at Westminster Abbey and at Vale Royal fluctuated widely from week to week. Together, the low rates of pay and the variation in the amount of work available from one week to the next suggest that much of the unskilled labor pool came from local peasant families whose primary livelihood was farming. As explained in Chapter 2, I believe that they lived off the land and supplemented their earnings at large building sites in the vicinity. This is why the organization of agriculture during the Middle Ages, especially the obligations of ordinary peasants to the lord of the manor, were significant factors affecting cathedral-building projects of the time.

To build a cathedral under these conditions was an awesome task. The extreme complexity of the project, the lengthy period of time required for construction, and the repeated interruption of the building process made cathedral-building unlike anything in modern engineering and architecture. Formidable though the challenge was, the master builder did have complete control over one extremely important resource: the way in which he organized himself and his workers to carry out the project. No cathedral builder could predict weather, famine, drought, plague, or war, or if sufficient funds would be available to keep the building project on course. But he could control how the construction work was organized. So how might a cathedral builder have gone about planning in order to enhance the likelihood that the building process could carry on? What might he have done at the outset to guarantee that the building would eventually be finished and, when it was, that it would bear a reasonable resemblance to the originally intended design?

That Gothic cathedrals are complex organic wholes suggested to me an approach to the puzzle that the medieval master mason had to solve. Can complex organic unities be organized in just any way, I wondered, or do certain forms of organization enhance the likelihood of a favorable outcome? If so, what are these forms? An intriguing answer comes from systems theorist Herbert Simon. In an essay on complexity, he describes common properties among diverse types of complex organic systems—systems in which the constitutive parts are mutually dependent or intrinsically related, as is true of Gothic cathedrals. Simon presents a parable involving two watchmakers who adopt different approaches to assembling watches, his metaphor for organically complicated phenomena. One watchmaker employs modularity, subdividing the work into discrete, self-contained units that, once assembled, can be left as complete until it is time to put them all together. The other uses a continuous process of assembling the entire watch piece after piece, involving no modular components; this approach obviously would be inefficient. The point of his example and the assumptions he invokes is to show why modularity is an essential principal in creating any object characterized by organic unity. His analysis suggests that without modularity, organic complexity is not attainable.[6]

One implication of Simon's essay for understanding Gothic cathedral-building seems to be that the probability of a successful outcome for this complex task, which is subject to recurrent interruptions, is much higher if the work is organized in modules. Indeed, with a continuous form of organization, the chances are that the builder will never complete the cathedral at all. To erect a cathedral over a long period of time, with the risk of frequent and often unpredictable interruptions, a modular approach to organization appears to be essential.

Recall Panofsky's description of "the principle of progressive divisibility" in Gothic design. He talks of "the arrangement according to a system of homologous parts [i.e., having a similarity attributable to common origins] and parts of parts . . . graphically expressed in the uniform division and subdivision of the whole structure." He notes how this principle of progressive divisibility "increasingly affected the entire edifice down to the smallest detail," how "the very principle of homology that controls the whole process implies and accounts for the relative uniformity which distinguishes the Gothic from the Romanesque," and how "the whole is composed of [the] smallest units which are homologous [and that] as a result of this homology, we perceive [a] hierarchy of logical levels."[7]

I am suggesting that the *conditions* under which designers and builders of Gothic great churches had to work forced them to organize the work in a particular way, using a modular system of design and construction. Simon's parable is a simple, elegant way of describing the fundamental principles of Gothic design: a recurrent series of identical modules, each of which derives from a master geometric code and, with the use of templates, can be assembled as a subunit of the larger whole. But how do we reconcile this explanation with the idea that Gothic great churches adopted the precise mathematical proportions believed to underlie cosmic unity and that their organic unity is a product of Scholasticism?

On the one hand, we might argue that the proponents of Scholasticism such as Abelard, Aquinas, and their students were astonishingly lucky. Not only did their system of thought reflect a theological vision, but it was by pure chance ideally suited to the practical purposes at hand. In this view, Scholasticism gave them the Gothic image, which required a plan of action and form of organization that was exactly suited to building a structure according to the philosophical dictates of Scholasticism. On the other hand, we might say that the reverse was true, that the inspiration for a Gothic cathedral led to a planning process that, it soon became clear, had to have certain features if it were to proceed. Once this became apparent, Scholasticism was applied to the emergent design in an effort to render it theologically coherent, not to say theologically determined.

For various reasons, I don't find either of these arguments compelling. The first strikes me as improbable, and the second leaves the origin of the particular inspiration unexplained. I propose a third alternative—that in a complicated, dialectic process thinkers and builders went back and forth between an abstract ideal and the real conditions under which builders work. In this view, the core ideas that are implicit in Scholasticism preceded and gave rise to the Gothic ideal, but the ideal had to be greatly elaborated in response to the exigencies of the building process, resulting in a form that had to have the properties it exhibits in order ever to have been completed.

THE RELIGIOUS EXPERIENCE

Sacred Force and Sacred Space

The Concept of the Sacred

My colleague William Mahrt, a professor of music at Stanford University, specializes in medieval church music and liturgy. I once asked him what a cathedral is for. A cathedral, he replied, exists for the performance of liturgy. He then explained that liturgy refers to the language, gestures, and actions that members of a religious body use to commune with and venerate God. The *Oxford English Dictionary* defines *liturgy* similarly, as the authorized forms of rites, observances, and procedures prescribed by the church for public worship. Communication with God is engaged in as an end in itself and also in the hope that God will adopt and retain a benevolent attitude toward those who worship Him and toward the groups on whose behalf they pray.

Most people probably imagine God as a force that is omnipresent. At the same time, people also believe that God is uniquely present and available to them in certain places for veneration and worship, and that the divine is uniquely concentrated in certain objects. Such places are sacred spaces, and such objects, sacred objects. Gothic cathedrals, of course, are prime examples of sacred spaces, and the relics, statuary, altars, and other material objects they contain are examples of sacred objects.

Understanding how people conceive of a place, say a cathedral, where the sacred spirit is uniquely present requires an understanding of what people imagine the essential nature of the divine to be. Where exactly does its sacred force come from? What is its form in its natural state? How does it come to inhabit particular spaces and objects on earth but not others? Once there, what keeps it from leaving, and how should a person behave in its presence? Answers to these questions yield valuable insights into cathedrals as socially constructed spaces: how they are designed, what existential project the space is created to accomplish, how the space is arrayed, who is permitted to enter it, what takes place within it, and more.

To understand cathedrals, then, we must understand the idea of the sacred. The *Oxford English Dictionary*'s definition of the word *sacred* includes such terms as "made in awe," "revered," "considered deserving of veneration," and "consecrated." Terms such as "holy" and "hallowed" are employed in elaboration. A conception of a force that evokes such emotions and feelings in people seems to be universal. Though the specific content of ideas about the sacred varies across different peoples and historical eras, most students of religion agree that societies everywhere have such a concept.[1]

Libraries abound with scholarly works on the nature and role of the sacred in human society. Those most relevant to my interests disclose the common core of ideas that humans hold about the sacred and the key dilemmas they face in their efforts to venerate and communicate with it. For me, one of the most instructive works on the topic is Émile Durkheim's classic *The Elementary Forms of Religious Life*. Although I first read this book long ago in graduate school, only now—in my search for an understanding of the sacred—did I truly appreciate its brilliant insights.

Durkheim's approach to the study of religion and society is analogous to that of the cell biologist who attempts to understand complex life forms by studying single-cell organisms. He examines the religious practices of small tribal societies (mainly in Australia) in an attempt to expose the fundamental anatomy of ideas and practices associated with the sacred that he believes are common to human groups everywhere. Of Durkheim's many observations about the sacred, the following points gleaned from my reading of his book are particularly germane to interpreting cathedrals as socially constructed spaces.

The divine, from which the quality of sacredness emanates, is typically conceived to be without shape or form. It has no persona. It is basically shapeless, anonymous, impersonal, and enduring. It is imagined to have existed long before those experiencing it were born and to persist long after they have died. Generations will come and go, the places where humans worship it will crumble and decay, but the force itself endures.

Even though it is imagined as being incorporeal, people do not experience it in this way. Through their words and actions, they clearly seem to regard the sacred force as being as tangible, as concrete, as the wood, stone, and metal of the temples or the statues and other objects they believe the sacred has come to occupy.

However, people's belief that the divine is both omnipresent and also localized in certain spaces and objects means that the force is external to places where it alights. That is, it does not inhere in the places and objects to which it attaches; rather, it enters them from without and above.

This impression in turn suggests that originally the raw materials used to create sacred spaces and objects or employed in the enactment of holy rites were indistinguishable from other, ordinary materials of their type. At a certain moment, however, they became infused with a divine presence, transforming them from something ordinary into something sacred. For example, the high altar of a cathedral is considered the most sacred location in the building and the great cross sitting atop it, its most sacred object (see Figure 35). Neither exists in nature; both had to be manufactured by ordinary craftspeople working with common metals and woods. The sacred force thought to occupy them was not there in the raw materials from the start. It entered only at a certain moment.

35. *The high altar of Winchester Cathedral is rendered more dramatic by the magnificent stone reredos behind it.*

Rituals are required to effect the transition from ordinary materials to sacred objects. Human notions about the sacred and the nature of this transition from ordinary to special occur in all religions and are powerfully illustrated by a passage from David Freedberg's book *The Power of Images*, which presents a prototypical example of such a ritual. He explains that Ceylonese (now Sri Lankan) Buddhists believe that the spirit of Buddha enters his statue only when the eyes are painted on it. Until this happens, it is regarded as just ordinary material. Once the eyes are added, "bringing an image to life," it is considered to be sacred, the equivalent of a god. As Freedberg describes,

> The ceremony is regarded by its performers as very dangerous and is surrounded with taboos. It is performed by the craftsman who made the statues, after several hours of ceremonies to ensure that no evil will come to him. This evil . . . is imprecisely conceptualized, but results

from making mistakes in ritual, violating taboos, or otherwise arousing the malevolent attention of a supernatural being, who usually conveys the evil by a gaze (bälma). The craftsman paints in the eyes at an auspicious moment and is left alone in the closed temple with only his colleagues, while everyone else stands clear even of the outer door. Moreover, the craftsman does not dare to look the statue in the face, but keeps his back to it and paints sideways or over his shoulder while looking into a mirror, which catches the gaze of the image he is bringing to life. As soon as the painting is done the craftsman himself has a dangerous gaze. He is then led out blindfolded and the covering is only removed from his eyes when they will first fall upon something which he then symbolically destroys with a sword stroke.[2]

Once the divine force has been localized in a now sacred space or object, however, it is not bound to remain there. It is imagined to have the capacity to go elsewhere or, for that matter, to disappear entirely. As a result, even while venerating and worshipping the divine force, humans worry that it might, at any moment, leave. (In ancient Greece, once a statue was invested with life, it was sometimes chained down in order to stop the god who occupied it from escaping!)

In addition, a sacred force is also thought to have a radiating quality; that is, its power is believed to diffuse and radiate out, in the process occupying objects and spaces adjacent to it. The power is believed to diminish with distance, so that the farther one is from the source, the weaker its effects. As we will see in Chapter 12 when we discuss the medieval cult of saints (see "The 'Special Dead'"), this idea permeates beliefs about saints' relics. Such objects were thought to have a quality similar to radioactivity that affected anything they touched. The belief was that the farther one stood from the object, the weaker was the effect. Thus, a person who hoped for a miracle cure needed to have direct or near-direct physical contact with the relic.[3] Because of this tendency to radiate, if a sacred object is left unconfined and exposed, its powers will dissipate, like oil being carried along the surface of a running body of water. For this reason, care must be taken to construct a container to house it that is made of materials appropriate to the task of holding and containing the sacred force.

These last observations hint at the magnitude of the existential project entailed in designing and building a space for the sacred to occupy. The design and appearance must attract the sacred and induce it to settle and to stay. At the same time, the space must be substantial enough not only to contain and confine the sacred, but also to ensure that it will remain strong, vibrant, and alive—keeping its powers from dissipating. Accomplishing all this entails a delicate balancing act; indeed, it is difficult to imagine a more daunting human enterprise.

Embracing the concept of the sacred and believing that it is uniquely present in a particular place automatically sets up another, opposing type of place and realm of existence—one that is not sacred. Just as "up" implies "down," the sacred implies the profane, or secular. In most religions, this distinction between the sacred and the profane is absolute and antagonistic, in the sense that things may belong to one realm or the other but not to both. Sacred things must then be set apart in special places to protect them from becoming polluted or tainted through physical contact with things that are profane, and clear boundaries must mark where one realm ends and the other begins. Finally, rituals are needed to cleanse, purify, and prepare those coming from the realm of the secular before they enter the realm of the sacred.

Durkheim shows us that practices designed to commune with and venerate the divine are almost always *communal* activities. Even in the early monastic communities, where worship was sometimes performed in solitude, the form, content, and process of worship were often communal. Thus it is accurate to say that most religious practices take place in group settings, assemblies arranged in an attempt to evoke, maintain, and recreate particular states of mind about and experiences of the sacred among group members. Religious worship is therefore *constitutive of the collective*. To use Durkheim's apt phrase, such ceremonies "make the collective happen" by setting collectivity in motion.[4] People experience the sacred most intensely when they are in the company of other people, united around the same ideas, with the same focus of concern and the same forms of action. When acts of collective worship end, members go their separate ways, returning once again to the secular world. As they do, their sense of the collective begins to fade and lose its vibrancy and sharpness. The periodic gatherings that religious practice provides for and requires enliven it again. Through group experience, the experience of the sacred is renewed, largely because groups serve as the vector that arouses these sentiments in the first place. In this respect, Durkheim reminds us, the true function of religion is not to make us think, but to make us strong and to help us to live by strengthening our experience of belonging, thereby enabling us to better endure the inevitable trials of existence and to overcome them.[5]

Creating Sacred Space

We have seen how, in the minds of those who designed and built them, Gothic cathedrals were intended to mirror heaven as medieval theologians imagined it to be. The cathedral was supposed to be a setting in which humans could glimpse heaven, thereby experiencing a foretaste of the hereafter. It served to draw people toward heaven. Durkheim's ideas about the sacred, however, suggest a different, almost opposite view of the cathedral's purpose—in which the cathedral is a place designed to draw the divine down among people.[6] We might say this is done by creating a congenial *habitat* for the divine. Working within the limits imposed by ordinary materials, builders aim to erect a setting reminiscent of the place from which the divine emanates. People then enact rituals in this space that they believe will please God, encouraging the divine spirit to enter the building and occupy it. In this sense, the Gothic cathedral is akin to a great lens created to gather the diffuse ambient light of the divine spirit and focus it to a particular geographical location, where it becomes available for human worship and supplication.

These two views may seem antagonistic, but I do not believe they are. Each appears plausible yet incomplete. A fuller understanding of the Gothic cathedral requires us to view it both as a place where humans were meant to cast their eyes toward heaven and as a setting in which humans endeavored to lure the divine into their midst. The second endeavor is actually reflected in the building's design and layout, as well as in what transpired within it.

To people in the Middle Ages, it was obvious that sacred spaces had to be *created* and that the act of creating them demanded the highest forms of *artistic expression* of which human beings were capable. The medieval worldview did not lend itself to the idea, present in other cultures, that natural places—caves, tree hollows, or forest glens—might be suitable settings for attracting the divine into the human midst. On the contrary, they believed that fashioning a sacred space in a setting of God's very own creation might be viewed by Him as demeaning or a slight. It was taken for granted that sacred spaces had to be *built*. Moreover, such spaces had to be constructed of materials that could be seen as suitable to the purposes at hand. In theory, all that is required to create a sacred space is a place apart and separate from the secular world; the boundary lines between secular and sacred realms could be marked by mud, twigs, or mounds of dirt, and processional ways designated with chalk or pebbles. But in the mind of the medieval cathedral builder sacred spaces demanded substantiality. *Stone*, whenever available, seemed required, and, in its absence, wood or brick. Of all natural materials available during the Middle Ages, stone was preferred because it alone had the requisite qualities of durability, heft, timelessness, and permanence that a house meant for the sacred demanded.

The philosopher John Sallis captures the nub of this sentiment in his fascinating book *Stone*. "Stone," he explains, "is ancient, not only in the sense that it withstands the wear of time better than other natural things, but also in the sense that antiquity is of the order of the always. . . . Stone comes from a past that has never been present, a past inassimilable to the order of time in which things were and go in the human world."[7] Its appearance of invulnerability to the whims of history, human foibles, or the winds of change, its marked capacity for providing safe shelter and protection, ideally suited it to the task of creating a sacred space.

In the medieval world, a sacred space demanded art—not just any art, but the most beautiful, exquisite, and refined expressions of human artistic endeavor available. Abbot Suger voiced this idea when he said of his plans to renovate the Abbey Church of St. Denis that "everything that is most precious should be used above all to celebrate the Holy Mass."[8] The German philosopher Hegel helps us to understand why. Art, he suggests, originates when humans produce through their own resources a new object, one capable of presenting a spiritual content that does not appear in natural things. It reflects the deep human need to make something special.[9]

The very existence of art made it imperative to use it in decorating sacred spaces. People feared that a failure to use the best of human creativity might be interpreted by the divine as a slight, an indication of something less than full devotion. Therefore, medieval people felt compelled to draw on all of their artistic, engineering, and craft-based creative impulses to create the finest space of which they were capable. Doing so allowed them to make manifest a highly personal expression of their piety and devotion, one that belonged to their community alone. When Abbot Suger announced his plans to build a new choir for his abbey church, his longtime friend and fellow abbot, Bernard of Clairvaux, criticized him for wanting excessive opulence. Bernard asked,

> What is the good of displaying all this gold in the church? . . . You display the statue of a saint . . . and you think that the more overloaded with colors it is, the holier it is. And people throng to kiss it—and are urged to leave an offering; they pay homage to the beauty of the object more than to its holiness. . . . Oh vanity! vanity! and folly even

greater than the vanity! The church sparkles and gleams on all sides, while its poor huddle in need; its stones are gilded, while its children go unclad; in it the art lovers find enough to satisfy their curiosity, while the poor find nothing there to relieve their misery.[10]

Here is Suger's reply:

We maintain that the sacred vessels should be enhanced by outward adornment, and nowhere more than in serving the Holy Sacrifice, where inwardly all should be pure and outwardly all should be noble.... If, according to the word of God and the prophet's command, the gold vessels, the gold phials, and the small gold mortars were used to collect the blood of goats, the calves, and a red heifer, then how much more zealously shall we hold our gold vases, precious stones, and all that we value most highly in creation, in order to collect the blood of Jesus Christ.[11]

Everything about the medieval cathedral—from its physical design, including its special use of light, through its decorations, to its daily rituals of prayer, including the texts used, as well as the music, vestments, processions, and incense—reflects this effort to use art to help make the space worthy of and welcoming to the divine. Soaring heights, delicate arches, magnificent stained glass, and fine stone and wood carvings are there for all to see (Figure 36). But there were also subtler, less obvious ways in which the intended perfection of the building was expressed. I know a young woman named Jenny Jacobs, a stone mason who specializes in restoration work. She has worked on many recent projects, including the restoration of the tower, spire, and west front of Salisbury Cathedral; the west front of Bath Abbey; and the interior of St. Paul's Cathedral. She once told me that she finds the finest expressions of spirituality in these buildings not in spaces that can be seen up close, but high in ceilings and on towers. She also describes exquisite works of carpentry and masonry out of sight in the attic areas beneath roofs and above vaults or behind the massive stones forming west fronts. There are also stained-glass windows high up in the clerestory, not

36. *This doorway at Burgos Cathedral is a stunning example of the stone carver's art in the service of the divine.*

visible from the floor level. She especially admires the west front statues that are "back-carved"—carved in the round, including the areas that do not show. Occasionally, she has even uncovered bits of wonderfully carved statuary concealed in places where no one may have seen them for hundreds of years. Why are they there, and what purpose do they serve?

Her interpretation, which I accept, is that works of fine craftsmanship done to exacting standards are found in concealed places for good reason—they allowed the craftsmen who built the cathedrals to declare emphatically that the building was intended as a monument to God, created by humans solely for His benefit. Few humans may ever see these examples of artistic expression, but God, as witness to all things, can. (Of course, to make this point, it is necessary to reveal the existence of these works. They are the worst-kept secret about Gothic cathedrals I know!).

Before all these delightful treasures could be appreciated, medieval designers had to attract the divine to the cathedral. To do so, they aimed to demarcate the realms of the sacred and the secular, and show that the sacred would be protected from adulteration. The physical layout of the building clearly reflects this intent, beginning with massive walls that form the boundary separating the sacred from the profane. Entrance into the walled-off enclosure of sacred space is gained through the great doors of the enormous west front, often referred to as the "Gates of Heaven."[12]

On entering a Gothic cathedral, however, a person does not confront the full essence of the sacred immediately. Instead, the cathedral's interior space is divided into zones of successively more concentrated sacredness from the westernmost to the easternmost end of the building. The transition from one zone to the next is always marked in some way, most commonly by one or more steps, which signal an increase in the degree of hallowedness. The part of the nave where one enters at the western end of the cathedral is customarily the lowest level of the main interior space. (For ease of reference see Figure 3, on page 18, which displays the floor plan of Salisbury Cathedral.) Typically, at the eastern end of the nave, up one or more steps, a massive stone screen separates the nave from the eastern arm of the building (see Figure 37). Called a "choir screen," it marks the western perimeter of the building's sacred core, which was enclosed by walls on the other three sides as well. The choir screen denotes a new zone of sacredness, denser in concentration, so to speak, than that found in the nave, and in medieval times it underscored the distinction between the clergy and the laity. Entry into the space east of the great choir screen was generally restricted to those who were officially designated as spiritual mediators, that is, members of clergy, such as canons and monks, who used it as a special setting for performing their daily round of prayers. Within this area, called the "presbytery," is another set of steps marking off the high altar. The high altar is the most sacred of all spaces within a great church's inner sanctum, the place where the

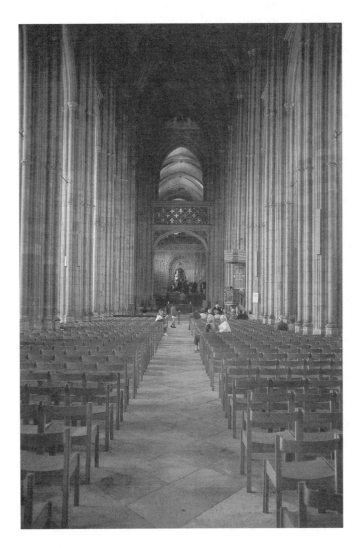

37. *By walking the length of the Canterbury Cathedral nave, from the entrance at the west end to the central crossing, and then up the stairs through the door in the choir screen, one can make the journey from the secular world outside the cathedral walls into its most sacred spaces.*

38. *The choir screen of Canterbury Cathedral was designed to hide the inner sanctum from the eyes of the common people.*

power and concentration of the sacred force are said to be most intense. For this reason, it is reserved for the holiest of sacred objects, such as the image of Christ affixed to the cross.

The choir and presbytery are often surrounded by ambulatories separating them from the building's outer walls. These were used for processions and, in cathedrals and abbeys that housed the shrine of a saint or a special chapel devoted to Mary, they served as pathways to guide pilgrims as they made their way from the great west front to the eastern end of the building, where shrines and lady chapels were typically placed.

Of the English cathedrals I have visited, Canterbury provides the most impressive example of this axial pattern of sacred architecture.

One enters the building through a side door on the westernmost end of the south wall (as is the custom elsewhere, the great west doors are used only for special ceremonial occasions). At the far end of the nave (Figure 37), at the point of the crossing formed by the east-west axis of the building and its principal transept, one encounters a magnificent staircase consisting of first three steps, then four more, then ten more leading up to the base of an immense stone choir screen (Figure 38). The central door to the choir screen, itself two steps above the top of the staircase, provides entry into the choir area, nineteen steps above the floor of the nave. Continuing eastward, at the far end of the choir is another set of eight steps leading to the high altar (Figure 39). Beyond that are eleven more steps leading to the throne of the first Archbishop of Canterbury, the seventh-century St. Augustine of Canterbury, and the site of the shrine of Thomas Becket. In all, from the floor of the nave to the site of Becket's shrine, there are thirty-eight steps, resulting in a difference of perhaps twenty-five feet of elevation from the one to the other.

William Mahrt explains that the configuration of sacred space within a Gothic cathedral is both axial and concentric in design.[13] It is axial in the sense of a movement, as just described, through zones of increasing degrees of sacredness from the westernmost to the easternmost end. It is concentric in the sense that the fortress-like exterior walls separate the outside world from the inner world, where the sacred may be found, and the nearer to the heart of the interior space one gets, the more sacred the space is considered to be. Thus the choir and presbytery area amount to a walled-in inner sanctum surrounded by ambulatories, which are themselves encased by exterior walls, and these in turn, at least in English cathedrals, are enclosed within the walled domain of the cathedral close. In most cathedrals this sense of encapsulation is heightened further by roof vaults, which seal the inner vessel from the exposed timbers of the roofs.

Within this space of increasingly concentrated degrees of

39. *Canterbury's mysterious and majestic choir is rendered
even more breathtaking by the fact that it cannot
be seen until one passes through the screen.*

sacredness, various techniques were used not only to create a space to accommodate a divine presence, but to heighten the impression that the divine was indeed there. The aim was to evoke astonishment, disbelief, and awe. Heavy pieces of stone were made to appear light, delicate, even ephemeral, to float and soar in ways that seem impossible. The rich tones of the primary colors used in stained glass, the sound of music written to resonate with the inner chords of the soul, and the manner in which the building drew the visitor into it—all combined to make a Gothic cathedral one of the most astonishing settings ever built.

A particularly interesting way of enhancing the impression of a divine presence in medieval times was the use of exclusion. Laypeople were generally barred from the cathedral's inner sanctum, where the clergy performed in honor of the divinity. The laity could hear the service from the nave, where they were permitted to stand, but the service was recited in Latin, a language they could neither speak nor understand. The arrangement seemed calculated to evoke an even deeper sense of the mystery of the divine, thereby enlivening and enriching people's experience of it. As theater—complete with stage sets, scripts, costumes, dramas, and musical works—great cathedrals evoke what they are meant to evoke perhaps more successfully than any other forms of architecture. An additional confirmation of the sacred force's presence came through the occurrence of miracles (see "The 'Special Dead'" in Chapter 12). That cathedrals, which often housed the remains of saints and other holy figures, were the site of ongoing miracles served as proof of the divine's presence and that the efforts to ensure its benevolence had been effective.

As I mentioned earlier, the fear persisted that the sacred force might abandon the spaces humans had created for it. The power of this fear is evident in accounts of the fire of 1194 at Chartres, which destroyed the entire city along with its treasured cathedral. Chronicles of the event tell that the people fell into a state of general despair because they believed that the fire indicated the Virgin's extreme displeasure with the citizens of Chartres, whose immoral and heretical conduct had caused her to destroy the basilica she had previously considered to be her earthly home. She had even allowed the destruction of their most sacred relic, the tunic she wore at the time of Christ's birth, as an indication that she had decided to abandon the city and migrate elsewhere. The tunic was subsequently discovered unburned—taken as miraculous proof that she intended to remain but preferred a grander edifice.[14]

Another expression of this fear appears in Patrick Geary's fascinating book about relic thefts, *Furta Sacra*. He recounts the history of the robust, profitable, and widespread trade in stolen relics during the medieval period. Part of what fueled this trade was the fact that every cathedral, abbey church, and monastery required some sort of sacred relic as a magnet for pilgrims, a need that developed at the very moment when the Church of Rome was endeavoring to regulate what had fast become an unwieldy collection of saints (see Chapter 12). The tension between these two developments fostered a flourishing market in stolen relics, which were believed to be more valuable than ones that had been gained legitimately. The reason was that the monks at the relics' new home could claim that the saint had deliberately, though clandestinely, arranged for the theft in order to be moved to a preferred site. This site was, of course, the setting preferred by the purchaser of the stolen relics.[15]

These examples suggest that medieval people accepted the idea that a sacred force could leave a structure to which it had been drawn. This danger called for actions to ensure that it would not leave. The clergy, who were charged with mediating the relationships of ordinary individuals to the divine, needed to devise ritual practices meant to communicate to the sacred spirit at a particular site that it remained admired, esteemed, and continuously welcome. Above all, everyone was to avoid giving it any reason to leave. This brings us to the principal activity that engaged almost all of the time and energy of members of a monastic order or cathedral chapter: the performance of liturgy.

Protecting Sacred Space

Liturgy comprised daily, weekly, seasonal, and annual cycles of worship engaged in by the canons of a cathedral community. Enactment of liturgy took place each day of the year and demanded the energies of chapter members during most of their waking hours and even into the night. Each day was organized into a sequence of eight prayer services termed the Divine Office; the core of each service was a recitation from the Book of Psalms, and all 150 psalms were sung in their entirety over the course of a week. Alongside the Divine Office was the Mass, which each appointed member of the cathedral community was obliged to celebrate every day. Overlying this principal cycle of daily prayer were supplementary liturgical observances, including special psalms, a daily office of the dead, and a daily little office of the Virgin, not to mention the annual cycle of liturgical seasons and feast days.[16]

All of these activities resulted in an extremely complicated, tightly ordered calendar of prayer services that lent structure to the entire year. In one widely adopted form of the liturgy, the *Sarum Use* (named for the cathedral church at Sarum, i.e., Salisbury), one of thirty-five different possible calendars was selected as a guide for each particular year.[17] According to this densely packed calendar, most of the day and significant parts of the night were spent in prayer. Each service had its own set of rules. These were contained in two sets of books: the *Ordinal* and the *Customary*.[18] Each ran to fifteen volumes and regulated in detail the behavior, demeanor, stance, expression, intonation, posture, and dress of each participant, as well as the text, music, and actions of each service. Together, these books stipulated the where, what, and how of a foundation's entire round of worship for each day of the year. The cathedral, as a setting to which the sacred force presumably had been drawn, provided the ideal space for carrying out this complex project.

Devotion to such a program of worship, day in and day out, over the course of an entire year sent a clear message that in this place the divine was valued above all else. In this regard, an interesting feature of the daily performance of liturgy warrants special mention. Of the eight main services of the daily office, the longest, most demanding, most difficult one to perform is Matins—the service performed in the dead of night. Among the many possible reasons for performing it at this hour, I would suggest that, in an effort to demonstrate their total devotion to the sacred, monks and canons chose to disrupt their sleep and engage in the most complex, demanding, and difficult service of the daily office at the least convenient time.

Special celebrations used the sacred space of the cathedral in elaborate ways. At certain times, in connection with particular liturgical ceremonies, the entire monastic order or cathedral chapter engaged in processions that took them all around the interior spaces of the church. These parades were occasions for displaying the social order of the community, with each class of members identifiable for all the others to see, and a place for each within an overarching framework. At the same time, they were acts of renewal in which the force of sacredness that inhabits, let us say, the objects housed in the innermost sanctum of the building such as the cross, the relics of a saint, or relics of the Passion of Christ, were marched about the church to reconsecrate and renew the sacredness of the places and objects within the building that are located at a distance from the inner sanctum.

One such procession took place at Salisbury Cathedral on Palm Sunday, one of the most important days of the year. (Figure 40 depicts a fictional medieval liturgical procession; Figure 41 diagrams the Palm Sunday processional route in Salisbury.) The procession began in the choir area with a recitation of prayers by the assembled canons, presided over by the bishop. The bishop then led the entourage out of the choir into the central crossing, and the procession turned left into the southeast transept. At that point it *exited* the cathedral and proceeded around three sides of the cloister (see Figure 42). From here it left the cathedral building completely

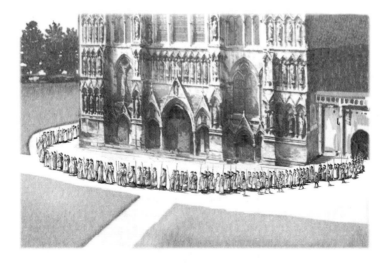

40. *An artist's rendering shows how a medieval procession at Salisbury might have looked.*

and proceeded along the exterior of the west front, turning right toward the great north porch.[19]

Up to this point the only object the procession included would have been a plain wooden cross. However, when it reached the north porch, the main procession was met by a separate, smaller procession of canons carrying the Corpus Christi, which had been removed from its place of special honor at the high altar. It was brought to the door of the north porch, where it was handed over to the bishop. At this point a mass would be said as the cross bearing Corpus Christi was exchanged for the smaller wooden cross, which was taken back inside. The cross bearing Corpus Christi then headed the procession along the remainder of its route.

The procession then continued along the exterior aspect of the entire north side of the cathedral, across the east end, along the south side and the exterior cloister and back again to the west front, stopping from time to time to pray. When the procession finally reached the west front, the great doors would be opened, and the assembly

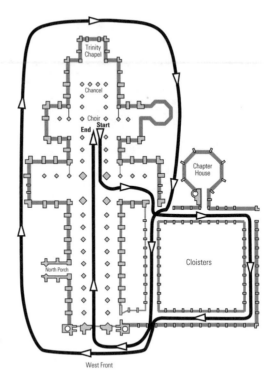

41. *The medieval Palm Sunday procession at Salisbury Cathedral used the entire building, inside and out. The route was dictated by the Sarum Use, the official liturgy of the cathedral.*

would enter the church, commemorating Christ's triumphal entry into Jerusalem. They would proceed up the center aisle of the nave and back into the choir, where the Corpus Christi was returned to its place of highest honor.

The ritual actually poses a puzzle. The round of daily, weekly, and seasonal prayers in which the cathedral canons had engaged for an entire year was carried out in a fashion designed to ensure that the cathedral's powers of sacrality remained contained, concentrated, and in place. Why, then, would they risk dissipating the force of the most sacred object they possessed by removing it from its container and taking it outside? The procession took several hours to complete, and for much of this time the Corpus Christi remained open and exposed. It is almost as if the purpose of the procession was to deliberately disperse its sacral properties, to empty it, as it

42. *Salisbury's cloister is a space built especially for processions.*

were, of its accumulated sacredness. Why should a community of worshippers want to do this?

My reading of Émile Durkheim's pioneering work in the sociology of religion suggests several possible answers. One pertains to where in the annual liturgical calendar this particular processional occurred, namely, on Palm Sunday, in the period leading up to Christ's crucifixion and resurrection. Perhaps depleting the store of sacrality that had presumably accumulated in the Corpus Christi during the course of the year would make way for a new infusion of sacredness that is symbolized by the Easter celebration. Another explanation could lie in the communal nature of the procession. By taking its most sacred object out of the setting built to house it and exposing it to the secular world, the community expressed symbolically the idea that it, too, was in extreme danger. In this ceremony, it reenacted Christ's danger as its own. Finally, when carried around the perimeter of the building, the most sacred of all objects served as a resource for redrawing, renewing, and strengthening the line between the sacred and the profane, which is marked by the walls of the cathedral and is one of the primary reasons for the cathedral's very existence.[20]

CHAPTER 11

Imagining the Cathedral

We have seen how the physical form of the Gothic cathedral, its geometric regularity and emphasis on light, related to medieval theological ideas. So it may be astonishing to learn that some of the first cathedral spaces humans conceived were never meant to be built. Only later were these visualizations translated into actual spaces. Here I am not talking about tangible "plans" for cathedrals. Rather, I am referring to a way of thinking about the divine. To explain this, I need to describe a technique for remembering known in ancient times as "the art of memory."

The art of memory was a technique that enabled a person to recall large amounts of information. This method for retaining information dates at least to the ancient Greeks, who devised it as an adjunct to oratory. A trained memory enabled a speaker to deliver lengthy orations without ever having to refer to written notes. Greek masters taught the art in conjunction with their instruction in rhetoric.

People who mastered the art of memory were capable of prodigious feats of recall. The Greek poet Simonides was renowned for his ability to remember events and accurately reconstruct them from memory. A story is told of a banquet he attended at the home of a famous nobleman. At a certain moment Simonides was summoned outside, and just as he left, a devastating earthquake completely destroyed the house. The collapsed roof and walls crushed those inside, and so badly mangled were the bodies that even relatives were unable to identify them. Because Simonides had committed to memory the names of the scores of people in attendance and where they were sitting, he was able to identify the dead according to where in the collapsed building their bodies were found.[1]

Another master of the art of memory, Seneca, amazed his audiences by repeating the names of two thousand people in the exact order in which they had been given to him, and further astounded students in his class of two hundred by asking each to recite a single line of poetry one after the other. When the last student had finished, Seneca reportedly recited all two hundred lines of poetry back to the class—in reverse order! In a similar vein, Julius Caesar was said to be able to dictate four letters simultaneously to four different secretaries, each letter on a different topic, and each composed a few sentences at a time, all the while writing a fifth letter in his own hand. Augustine of Hippo once told of a man he had met who had committed the entire works of Virgil to memory, which he recited to Augustine backward![2]

Thomas Aquinas, like Caesar before him, regularly dictated materials to several secretaries at once, each dictation dealing with a different topic, each letter or chapter spoken a few sentences or paragraphs at a time. It was also claimed that Aquinas would compose an entire book in his head and then summon a team of secretaries and dictate it to them, whole chapters at a time. So complete was his command of his material that he could begin reciting the text for any given chapter at any point and proceed forward or backward at will. As if this weren't enough, his talent included providing completely accurate, often lengthy, quotations from the works of other authors to whom he wished to refer in his own writing.[3] How did Simonides, Seneca, Augustine, Aquinas, and others achieve these prodigious feats of recall? Of what did the art of memory training consist? How did they learn it and how were students tutored in its use?

Mnemonics

The ancient Greeks called the art of memory *mnemonics*. This complex and intricate system for creating and storing images in memory entailed a sequence of steps. First, one had to create in one's imagination a place where the materials to be remembered could be stored. Such imagined places were ordinarily based on architectural metaphors (the first hint of the connection between the art of memory and cathedrals)—what one student of the subject, Mary Carruthers, terms "the architectural mnemonic."[4] Augustine of Hippo describes the inner memory buildings he imagined and used as "vast courts and boundless chambers."[5] Another master, Quintilian, taught his students to imagine a vast building. He instructed them to make it spacious and varied in its parts, to define it in great detail and to remember its constituent elements, for example, forecourts, living rooms, parlors, dens, kitchens, bathrooms, and pantries. Once the imaginary edifice was "built," Quintilian showed students how to use it to store the things they wished to remember.[6]

The rules Quintilian established for building these imaginary structures are fascinating. He recommended that they be set apart in the imagination, in a place that could be envisioned as solitary and free from crowds. He advised that they be distinctively different from other structures one is accustomed to seeing in daily life. They should be composed with great precision, by which he meant that the spatial dimensions of the various parts should be precisely known, so that the relationships of the parts to one another could be grasped intuitively by the imaginer. Such a building was to have an overall shape that would enable the student to grasp it in its entirety and to navigate with ease from place to place within it as circumstance and need dictated. (Similar techniques are used today by computer gamers to create virtual reality in cyberspace.)

Next Quintilian taught his students to develop in the imagination *icons* (also known as *simulacra*) for the things that were to be remembered. The technique entailed linking the contents of what was to be remembered with the icons that stood for them. These icons were then placed in a particular room or spot within the place the student had built in his or her imagination, where they were kept until needed. To retrieve them, the student simply imagined going to the place where the icon had been stored and "pulling it up," so to speak—then, the detailed information for which it stood would magically appear. Once built, these imagined places could be used over and over again for storing different kinds of information as circumstance demanded. Reuse was made possible by simply deleting the information stored behind an icon and replacing it with new material, much as one does with the computer today. This did not, of course, preclude the invention of new icons.

Much attention was given to learning the rules for creating icons. To practice the art of memory, two kinds of icons were required: icons for forms and icons for words. Icons for forms were needed to remind one of "things." Examples might be a particular line of argument, a specific event or sequence of events, or a particular concept. Icons for words stood for specific words. According to this scheme, icons for things denoted subject matter; icons for words denoted the language in which this subject matter was cloaked. But what kinds of icons were to be used? Quintilian taught his students that ordinary, banal icons would be of little use for remembering. Instead, he counseled, the more remote a simile was from the subject to which it was applied, the greater would be the impression of novelty and surprise it produced (see Figure 43). To serve their function, then, images had to be extraordinary. For this reason, Quintilian taught his students to use icons that were unusual, beautiful, grand, striking, ridiculous, unbelievable, ugly, grotesque, ludicrous, breathtaking, ethereal, or extreme. The interior spaces of the imaginary memory buildings came to be filled with icons of every sort—hideous, comical, obscene, beautiful, ugly, and grotesque icons—all placed there to aid remembering.

43. *This modern-day "grotesque" at Salisbury Cathedral is in the tradition of memory icons used in medieval times.*

These ancient techniques for training memory remained in use for a long time, well into the Middle Ages. Very little had occurred to diminish the importance of memory as a rhetorical device, and the need to remember texts, arguments, and lessons had become, if anything, more urgent. It is estimated that only about 5 percent of the entire European population could read and no more than 2 percent could write. For those who could write, paper was scarce and difficult to obtain, and vellum, the other main substance on which people wrote, was extremely expensive, difficult, and time-consuming to make. The printing press would not appear until about 1450.

The Middle Ages was a time of great evangelism. Clergy were responsible for preaching to common people about the Christian virtues, warning them of the dangers of vice, instructing them about the path to eternal damnation, and explaining the way to eternal salvation. The craft of teaching the articles of faith drew on the principles of mnemonics in at least two ways: one to aid the listener and the other to aid the sermon-giver. Clergy were instructed in using mnemonic devices for rhetorical purposes just as the Greeks had been. Teaching the lessons of Christian virtue required them to recite biblical texts on command, a skill made possible by creating great imaginary warehouses. At the same time, they created icons in their sermons to help ordinary people remember the lessons they were meant to learn. Aquinas instructed the priests he trained with these words: "To make people remember things, preach to them in 'unusual' similitudes, for these will stick better in memory than the spiritual intentions will do, unless clothed in such similitudes." The craft of preaching, then, required clergy to use stark, extreme, grotesque, and beautiful images—what Aquinas termed "corporeal similitudes."[7]

But there is a deeper connection between the art of memory and religious experience, a connection that contributed directly and significantly to the emergence of the cathedral as an architectural form. It pertains to the monastic movement and to the role that memory played in its most basic aims. Christian monasticism originated during the third century and remained a vital force within Christianity for the next twelve hundred years. One of its purposes was to achieve a state of grace, permitting its practitioner to achieve communion with and experience the divine. In pursuit of this quest, the art of memory was crucial.

The monks used a method similar to the one the Greeks had devised. It called for creating an imagined interior mental space in which sacred texts could be stored so that they would be readily available during meditation and study. The technique used tropes and figures as icons for the things to be remembered, and the rules for creating icons were similar to those the Greeks had employed. For example, monks were taught that ornamentation was vital to creating memory icons, because ornateness had the potential to capture and orient the worshipper's attention. In this respect they followed Quintilian's admonition that we remember best what is unusual and what most attracts our attention. Like the Greeks, monks favored the use of an architectural metaphor for organizing items to be remembered, and the icons were stored in an orderly fashion.[8]

Their purposes, however, were different. For early monastics, the purpose of cultivating and mastering the art of memory was not, as it had been for the Greeks, to enable the speaker to repeat an entire text exactly from memory or to have full and ready access to all that he had learned. Rather, memory was a tool for attaining enlightenment. The monks believed that a state of grace was possible only if the mind was prepared, that preparation required oral recitation of sacred texts and elaborate rituals, and that the art of memory provided the most effective tool for proper engagement in these activities.

For members of monastic orders, using memory was a creative act that facilitated their ability to think about, meditate on, and ultimately gather their thoughts about God. In the words of Carruthers, memory served as a matrix "for reminiscing, cogitating, shuffling and collating 'things' that had been stored in a random-access memory scheme, a memory architecture, a library of information, texts, experiences and so on that had been built up over a lifetime for the express purpose of using it inventively to find one's way to God."[9] To the monks, meditation was the craft of making thoughts about God, and memory was the tool that made this craft possible.

In the hands of monks, memory was a highly creative skill. Because its goal was not rote recitation but creative eloquence, it was employed to facilitate invention, to make invention possible. In this context the term *invention* has two meanings: creating something new and creating an inventory. The second sense facilitated invention in the first sense by allowing the monk who was meditating to attend to interruptions and asides without becoming distracted or lost. An inventory was a device to prevent monks from losing their way.

I have said that the monastic schemes for remembering provided a place for everything and assigned everything to its place, and that the metaphors employed were architectural. Because the materials to be remembered (i.e., the sacred texts) were used for meditation, the practice of the art of memory required imaginary movements through the imaginary spaces. It was almost as if the monks "processed" (in the sense of moving in a processional fashion) from icon to icon, back and forth, around and about, along an imagined path made possible by the carefully inventoried way in which memory about sacred texts had been stored. Carruthers captures this dynamic, moving quality of meditation that the memory technique made possible:

> In the minds of monastic writers, every verse of the Bible . . . became a gathering place for other texts, into which the most remote . . . and unlikely matters were collected. . . . A student is to use the mental building he has laid out as the foundation of his . . . knowledge of the Bible . . . as a structure in which to gather all the bits of his subsequent learning. . . . Such [memory] superstructures are useful . . . as collecting and re-collecting mechanisms with which to compose the design of one's own learning. . . . The shape or foundation of a composition must be thought of as a place-where-one-invents. Everything is fitted onto it . . . so the edifice of one's life (so to speak), although created from stories available to all citizens, is also a fully personal creation, an expression (and creation) of one's character. . . . Thus, because it builds entirely through the associations made in some individual's mind, memory work has an irreducibly personal and private or "secret" dimension to it.[10]

Visualize, then, an imaginary inner space filled with ornate icons behind which are stored sacred texts, the icons laid out in a precise and orderly manner relative to one another so that they become readily available to recall. In such a scheme, meditation amounts to movement through this space, an imaginary form of pilgrimage in which the monk transports himself at will in his imagination from one place in the structure to the next. In this sense, memory structures required imaginary pilgrimages and gave special meaning to the notion of following a "way," or path, among places. This patterned order of processional movement the monks termed *ductus*.

Meditation as a Communal Activity

So far I have emphasized the internal practice of the art of memory, describing the thought processes of individual monks who, through meditation, sought to find their way to a state of grace. But monastic existence was communal, and the very being of the individual was experienced in a communal context. The memory system that monastics used was not the idiosyncratic creation of distinct individuals but the product of the collective enterprise. The system was shared by members of the community, was intended to be used communally, and was employed in communal settings. The texts the monks committed to memory, the icons they used to help them, the spaces in which the memories were stored, and the imaginary actions in which individual monks engaged as they moved from place to place in the inner, imaginary warehouses were, in effect, communally constructed and communally used. In sermons, and on occasions of collective meditation, monks were invited to conjure up the image of a common building in which they processed together as a community in an imaginary way.

As Carruthers explains, "In monastic teaching . . . the ordinary practice was to construct a wholly fictional building, rather than to use an actual one. When invoking a building plan as the device for a compositional structure, monastic writers did not customarily use the monastic buildings that they lived in daily, but rather laid out a typical exemplary construction." She cites examples of how this practice worked. One involves a monk, Peter of Cellar, who imagined an entire monastery and invited his audience to enter and use it together with him. Another is Hugh of St. Victor, whom she describes as

careful to show exactly how each piece [of his imaginary building] is articulated in the scheme of the entire structure, and how the story and rooms are divided in them to 'place' information in the form of images within these divisions, used as mnemonic loci. . . . Hugh saw this building in his mind as he composed: he "walked" through it and . . . he used it himself as he advised others to, as a universal cognitive machine.[11]

A third example was Augustine of Hippo, who in his sermons painted a literary picture of a tabernacle and then invited his fellow monks to look around and walk about it with him.

Perhaps the most intriguing example I have found of this practice is the Plan of St. Gall, an elaborate architectural plan for a monastery that provided the ideal space for engaging in liturgical processions and meditation in pursuit of the path to enlightenment (see Figure 44). Significantly, the monastery was never actually built, but it was nevertheless used in imagination by the monks of St. Gall as a space in which to meditate individually and as a community. This was done by presiders at moments of communal worship, who summoned the image of the plan and invited monks to join in imaginary processions through it.[12]

There is much more to be said about the art of memory as practiced in early Christian monastic communities. Yet we can see how some great churches may have first existed in the shared imagination of the monks who used them for communal acts of worship that actually took place in the far more humble and austere settings of their early monasteries. The imaginary buildings were understood as cognitive devices to be conjured up for the purposes of meditation and prayer. Only eventually did cathedrals become material expressions of these imagined structures. As Carruthers explains, cathedrals and monastic churches were "compelling expressions of monastic rhetoric," and it could be said they were "previsualized in the manner of rhetorical invention and of meditation, of which the actual stone is the 'imitation.'" In this sense the building itself is no more than a "'recollection' of the mental composition, itself composed or 'gathered' from the inventory of the artist's memory."[13]

On what were these imaginary tabernacles modeled? The obvi-

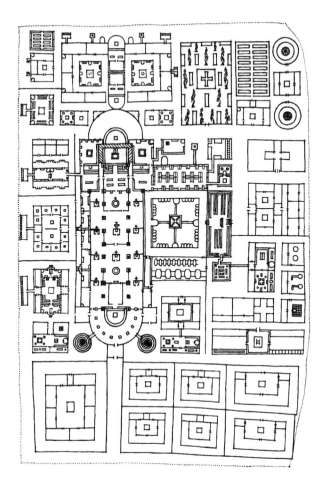

44. *The Plan of St. Gall, an elaborate and detailed blueprint of a monastery, was used by monks as a tool for meditation.*

ous answer is that the model was the shared image of the Heavenly City to which the monks aspired to ascend. Consistent with the understanding of divine order, these imaginary spaces were orderly, precisely geometric in design, filled with light, soaring in dimensions and appearance—in other words, imaginary cathedrals. It is no accident that students of the art of memory commonly refer to these imagined spaces as "inner memory cathedrals."

Although imagination is hardly the whole story behind the origins of Europe's cathedrals, I believe it is an important part that is commonly overlooked. It is good to remind ourselves of this point for at least two reasons. First, the great ecclesiastical buildings of Europe are structures of such audacity, grandeur, and breathtaking beauty that it is easy to underemphasize the fact that human beings conceived, designed, and built them. One source of their inspiration was spiritual, but the form itself arose out of the human imagination. Second, the context in which the form arose was not one of isolation; it was the quintessence of community. The imaginary materials out of which the first such buildings were constructed were shared, the rhetorical and literary materials contained within them were collective representations, and the uses made of them were first and foremost communal (for more on this, see Chapter 15).

CHAPTER 12

Honoring the Dead

Of all of the different groups involved in building Gothic cathedrals—from prelates, monarchs, and pious laypeople, through master builders, craftsmen, and vendors, to ordinary wage laborers and peasants—the group most often overlooked is the dead.[1] The dead were at least as important as the living in making cathedral building possible. For one thing, the dead proved to be effective fund-raisers. Their departure from this world became the basis for an entire industry involving endowed masses celebrated on their behalf by clergy, who often performed them in special chapels, built with gifts from the deceased. In addition, shrines dedicated to what the medievalist Peter Brown aptly calls "the Very Special Dead"—those elected to the society of saints—helped ensure a steady stream of visitors to cathedrals.[2] As an act of veneration, pilgrims were told, they should bring gifts of coins, food, wine, cloth, precious metals, and other items of value, most of which made their way into the cathedral's treasury.

The Ordinary Dead

During medieval times, when people died they did not cease to be members of society. Rather, they retained a vital, palpable presence within the world of the living. Beliefs about their continuing presence and importance in this life were framed within a larger context of assumptions about the universe. Its existence was believed to date to no more than a few thousand years before the birth of Christ, and prior to A.D. 1000, people generally assumed that Judgment Day would arrive on or shortly after the millennium. With the advent of the year 1001, this view obviously had to be modified, but the idea that Judgment Day was vaguely at hand persisted. Within this framework, the abode of the dead was imagined to be nearby—somewhere beyond the moon.[3] From their realm, the dead were thought capable of influencing the world of the living. In this sense, the dead and the living together formed a single universe of being. (So deeply held were these beliefs that the living imagined that the dead returned at times to share meals with them, so that on special occasions places were set aside for them at the table.)[4]

The same rules of reciprocity that applied to the living applied to the dead. They were accorded certain rights and in exchange were expected to fulfill certain responsibilities toward the living. The dead had an obligation to aid those they had left behind. The living depended on them to warn of potential sources of harm and impending dangers. They were expected to protect the living against violence and the forces of nature. They were also expected to provide the living with vital information about the hereafter, and those who had become saints were viewed as capable of interceding with God to promote miracles.

In addition to aiding the living, the dead were deemed capable of harming them. They could call down misfortunes on people, particularly those who had hurt loved ones of the dead. Moreover, the dead might take action against loved ones if they failed to honor their obligations to remember their dead. According to the historian Patrick Geary, the living were supposed to preserve the names of the dead in a variety of ways—by giving them to newborn family members, by placing them on property deeds, by listing them on documents written to preserve family memories, and, most important, by citing them in liturgical remembrances, such as special prayers and masses for the dead in the weeks, months, and years after they had died.[5]

People believed that fulfilling their obligations to the dead was vital to the deceased person's fate in the afterlife, limiting the amount of time spent in purgatory and reducing any punishment. For this reason, neglecting to pray for the dead or failing to remember them in appropriate ways invited harmful intervention by the dead in the lives of the living. Such "revenge" was greatly feared, for the dead, it was believed, had the power to torture and punish the living, and could even invoke the full wrath of God.

In the early Middle Ages, obligations of "memoria," or remembrance, were assigned to family members generally, but especially to widows, who were responsible for praying for the souls of their dead fathers and husbands. This obligation fell to widows rather than children of the marriage because the children would incur obligations of their own through matrimony. On average, if women survived childbearing, they outlived their husbands by approximately two decades.[6] By assigning their wives the role of remembering, men hoped their names would not be forgotten for years after their death. Over time, however, religious orders gradually appropriated this function by signing contracts with men guaranteeing that monks or canons would pray for their souls after death and, in particular, commemorate the occasion of their passing. Beginning in about the eleventh century, and continuing for the next two hundred years, members of religious orders contested the role of women as rememberers of the dead. They portrayed women and children as fickle—pointing out, for example, that widows might remarry and as a result feel less obligation to pray for their previous husbands, and that children would incur conflicting obligations later in life. In contrast, members of religious orders could assure complete fidelity in this regard. Moreover, religious orders could assure that obligations of memoria would continue long after the widow herself died, because the responsibility would rest with an entire institution, not an individual, and it could be recorded in writing and catalogued in the library.[7] Obviously, in this dispute, women were significantly disadvantaged, so in the end the clergy prevailed. Of course, the valuable services they performed on behalf of the souls of men came at a price. Contracts between monastic and secular orders and those who wished to be remembered had to be sealed, and this was often done by exchanging property. In this way, religious orders were able to gather capital to support their own operations and building projects.

The great power that beliefs about the dead held over the living is illustrated by how these beliefs were used to devise a kind of crude "civil defense system," protecting against violent attacks. Patrick Geary presents a fascinating analysis of the ways in which members of monastic communities played on beliefs about the dead and obligations of reciprocity in order to protect themselves and their property and to work their will within the larger community.[8] I described earlier how, under feudalism, monks took responsibility for praying not only on behalf of the entire community but also for the salvation of particular individuals to ensure their spiritual well-being after death. In addition to prayers, clerics undertook daily rituals—celebrations of the mass, performances of the Divine Office, and veneration of saints' relics—to keep heaven benevolently disposed toward the people under their care. These acts of veneration fulfilled the community's obligations in the reciprocal relationship between a community and its protector saint. Monastics, who lacked military or police forces of their own, came to parlay this mediating role between the living and the dead into a way of protecting their orders from human attack. They staged what today we would call "job actions," "work stoppages," or "strikes."

As Geary explains, if an individual offended a monastic order, the affected monks might try to sanction him by publicly substituting curses for prayers on behalf of the offender or his or her dead relatives. The monks would pray for eternal damnation of the malefactor, effectively devising their own version of excommunication.

If the grievance was against an entire community or its political leaders, the monks adopted a different strategy. They performed liturgical rituals called the *clamor*, in which the monks cried loudly to the Lord for divine intervention, and the *humiliation*, in which they demonstrated dramatically the harm that was being done to the saint by the continuing conflict. Geary presents an example of how these rituals might be enacted. Depending upon the seriousness of the offense committed by the malefactor, the clamor could be performed alone or include a protracted humiliation, lasting for days, weeks, or even months.[9] The clamor was made during the celebration of the mass by interjecting a prayer that explicitly called attention to the abuses committed against the monks and their monastery which prevented them from engaging in regular rituals of prayer and veneration. While such prayers were being recited, members of the monastic order would prostrate themselves before the Eucharist to display their humiliation in a highly public way.[10]

In extreme form, these prayers were accompanied by the humiliation of relics or images of the saint, and perhaps other sacred objects as well. In such cases, the monks would bring the church's most important relics and images from their places of honor and set them on the ground before the high altar on a coarse cloth such as a hair shirt, covering them with thorns. In this way the monks meant to demonstrate to the community that its saint had joined the prostrate monks in their gesture of humiliation. If the offense was comparatively minor, the relics would be returned to their rightful places following the prayer of the clamor, but if the offense were especially serious, more severe acts of humiliation would be performed. In such cases the relics remained in a state of degradation after their public abuse until the monks got their way.[11]

All sorts of other devices were used to drive home the point. For example, in certain versions of the clamor, verses and prayers were not sung in the customary way, holding the final syllable for as long as the breath would last. Instead, the singers defiantly cut off the final notes, as if in anger. Another technique was to explain in their prayers to the saint that the enemies of the monastery, acting out of pride, were harming it. Since pride was considered a cardinal vice, the monks were in effect stating that the offense was not being committed against them personally but against the house of the lord.[12]

Geary recounts one story of a tenth-century figure, the Count of Anjou, who committed certain serious offenses against a local monastery. Several times he had entered monastic grounds with armed soldiers, damaged the houses of canons, and stole from the treasury. The canons held that, as a monastic order, they were immune from the count's jurisdiction and viewed his attacks as an atrocity. Having no soldiers of their own, nor court in which to plead their case (the count controlled all the courts), the monks chose instead to humiliate the relics of their saint as well as the crucifix—and in this case they did even more. They locked the doors to their church against the count and members of his family, barring anyone related to the count and his men from entering to worship. Those who were admitted, including local pilgrims, could see that their saint was being humiliated. Members of the community could see that the saint could not be expected to continue providing protection to the community at large.

In addition, the monks' action prevented the count and his family from entering the place where their own ancestors were buried, preventing them from engaging in rituals of memoria, prayers of remembrance on behalf of their own relatives. This meant that the count's dead relatives would be at risk of further suffering in purgatory, for which they would presumably reap suitable revenge against their living relatives.

How effective were their actions? Geary writes, "The count, regretting his actions . . . and seeking forgiveness, by his own free will entered the cloister and went to the house [of] the master of the students. From there, barefoot, he humbly entered the church with some of his followers [where] he promised God and [the saint] never to do such a thing again. Then he made satisfactions."[13]

Humiliations and clamors worked by mobilizing public opinion against an offender. Though directed at specific evildoers, the rituals effectively mobilized support, sympathy, and concern among third parties who in turn pressed the offender to negotiate. In effect, the monks were declaring a strike by refusing to perform their primary tasks, which were to venerate Christ and his saints on behalf of the community. This left the community feeling powerless against the malevolent forces of nature and society, from which the saints in question were believed to offer protection. In essence, the clamor and the humiliation were the monastic equivalents of the papal interdict, which is a ban on holding religious celebrations and services. By mistreating sacred objects, degrading them, or sequestering them, the monks created a public impression of disrupting the proper relationship between the world of the living and the world of the dead, a disruption that threatened dire consequences for the community. Along with the curse, the clamor and the humiliation thus became important parts of the spiritual arsenal that religious communities used to protect themselves and to gain the upper hand in any disputes.[14]

The *"Special"* Dead

Among the dead, saints had perhaps the greatest impact on cathedral building. Venerating a saint by visiting and praying before his or her tomb or relics was one of the most meaningful expressions of piety during the Middle Ages.[15] Since most important shrines to saints were located in cathedrals, fulfilling this obligation brought tens of thousands of ordinary people to cathedral doorsteps (see Figure 45).

Saints attracted money because pilgrims were expected to leave gifts to honor the saint and ownership of such goods could be claimed by the cathedral chapter. The largest crowds gathered on feast days in honor of the saints. Crowds drew merchants, merchants joined fairs, and, for cathedral chapters, fairs meant income—from sales of licenses to vendors and from taxes on their profits. Also, saints brought prestige. The cathedral that successfully claimed to

45. *Pilgrims kneel and pray at the "pilgrims' pillar" before entering the Cathedral of Santiago de Compostela.*

be the earthly home of an important saint (or, in the case of Chartres, the earthly home of the Virgin Mary) was immediately elevated to the top ranks of sacred places in Christendom.

Though few complete accounts survive regarding the contributions of pilgrims to cathedral "fabric" (i.e., building) funds, the information we have suggests that the many gifts to saints were important in carrying on building campaigns. Surviving accounts list coins, bread, wine, jewelry, fowl, grains, fruits and vegetables, livestock, cloth, precious metals, clothing, household goods, and other items of value. Wax was frequently contributed in the form of candles, which, according to the custom of the day, had to be the same size as the donor's body or, in the case of appeals for healing, the same weight and length as the afflicted body part. The great medieval historian André Vauchez describes the contents found at the tomb of one of England's most famous medieval saints, Thomas Cantilupe, located at Hereford Cathedral. According to Vauchez, the list included "170 silver ships, 41 wax ships, 129 silver images of a person or of human limbs, 1,424 wax images of a person or of human limbs, 77 animal figures, 108 crutches, 3 wooden vehicles."[16] W. H. Vroom's study of the financing of cathedral-building campaigns indicates how important these gifts were. A typical Gothic cathedral-building campaign was usually financed in several stages. In order to get the project under way, bishops and chapters contributed substantial sums of their own money. But, following the initial infusion of capital, this source of contributions dried up, as did contributions made by secular authorities and municipalities. In the long run, Vroom found that the offerings of the faithful, together with sales of indulgences, occasional loans from moneylenders, profits from fairs held in connection with feast days of saints, and periodic gifts from monarchs, were what made it possible to complete a project.[17]

At St. Denis the contributions of pilgrims, together with profits, license fees, and other revenues associated with Lendit (the royally authorized annual fair), made up *three-quarters* of the total cost of Suger's renovation of his abbey church, and Thomas Becket's memorial at Canterbury has been described as "one of the greatest concentrations of portable wealth in England."[18] During the first half of the thirteenth century, the annual take from gifts left by Canterbury pilgrims was on the order of one thousand pounds, a fortune in that day. In fact, in the year 1220, gifts from pilgrims made up almost two-thirds of the total income of the monastery. In the year 1275 cathedral accounts show that Becket's shrine was the hub of Canterbury's fiscal activities, with the shrine's keeper routinely making loans and gifts to other departments of the cathedral.[19]

The medievalist Jonathan Sumption also emphasizes the importance of pilgrims' contributions to the treasuries of major shrines.

He refers to an entry by an eleventh-century chronicler at the shrine of St.-Trond near Liège, where rumors of miracles brought thousands of pilgrims bearing gifts of every kind. The chronicler writes, "herds of animals. . . . Palfreys, cows and bulls, pigs, lambs, and sheep. Linen, wax, bread, and cheese arrived; and above all purses full of money." So much money was given that several men were needed to collect it in the evening and put it in a safe place, and a number of monks worked full-time as guardians of the shrine. According to the chronicler, these offerings exceeded all of the other revenues of the abbey combined.[20]

What drew pilgrims to the shrines of saints, and why did they shower them with gifts? What did they expect and hope to gain? And how did they judge whether their contributions were worthwhile?

THE QUEST FOR MIRACLES   One reason people visited cathedrals was to express their piety by venerating the saint whose relics were placed there. But at least as important was the quest for miracles, fueled by the belief that the saint might be willing to intercede with God on the worshipper's behalf, rewarding his or her piety with miracles. Some people actually felt that saints *owed* rewards to those who worshipped them.[21]

The miracles people sought took many forms, including cures for illnesses, protection from or revenge on enemies, protection against catastrophes like drought and plague, and protection of villages, towns, or nations from invasion.[22] These hopes are not difficult to understand in light of the dire conditions of existence during medieval times and the insatiable appetite for miracles that these conditions produced (see Chapter 13). Patrick Geary summarized the situation well when he observed that belief in the possibility of gaining access to supernatural powers "provided the only recourse against the myriad ills, physical, material and psychic, of a population defenseless before an incomprehensible and terrifying universe."[23]

Appeals to the divine at sacred shrines came from individuals on their own behalf or on behalf of collectivities—villages, towns, monasteries, or entire nations. In either case, the vast majority of appeals fell into two categories: appeals for "acts of mercy" and appeals for "acts of power."[24] Acts of mercy included relief from disease and suffering, a logical request, given the prevailing view that physical disease had spiritual causes.[25] Acts of power involved miracles aimed at gaining advantage over adversaries. One could pray for divine protection for oneself, one's family, or one's community against threatened attack by an enemy. Sometimes saints were even petitioned to bestow diseases on enemies, showing no "mercy."[26] There is little doubt that most people believed deeply in the protection of saints and feared that harm would befall those who offended anyone who was protected by a saint. Von Simson recounts the uses made by the city of Chartres of its cathedral's most sacred relic, the tunic worn by Mary at the birth of Christ. Twice it was displayed in an effort to rescue the city from siege. The first time was in 911 when the Norman invader Rollo laid siege to Chartres. On that occasion the Bishop of Chartres displayed the sacred tunic atop the city gate, allegedly causing the invader and his force to flee in panic. The second time was in 1119 during a war between King Louis VI and Bishop Thibault of Chartres. When the tunic was paraded before the king in solemn procession, he was persuaded to spare the city.[27]

Medieval people certainly had compelling reasons to believe in miracles and to convince others that they could access divine powers. But how were these impressions fostered, how were they conveyed, and what sustained them? To answer these questions, we must turn to the system of beliefs that surrounded saints and to the rituals engaged in by people who came to saints' shrines.

It was considered unseemly and inappropriate for ordinary mortals to appeal directly to God for miracles. People believed that God would perform a miracle only for a saint, out of admiration for the saint's own virtues, rather than the virtues of the suppliant. As André Vauchez explains, "It was as if the servants of God had acquired, through the sufferings they had endured during their lifetime, a means of putting pressure on God, in a sense obliging him to intervene on behalf of whoever had put themselves under their protection."[28] Therefore, to be heard, a request for a miracle had to be addressed to an intermediary whom God admired and on whom He looked with special favor.

In the Christian tradition, saints were persons of great virtue to whom God had granted a special force, termed *virtus*, which was not only present during their lifetime, but endured and gained even greater power after their death. This force was manifested in various ways, including the supposed incorruptibility of the saint's flesh. Bodies of dead saints were believed not to decompose and were said to emit a unique odor, termed "the odor of sanctity." *Virtus* persevered and even gained in power in the saint's corporeal remains and in objects he or she had possessed. Medieval people believed that the force infused anything that had direct physical contact with the saint, including portions of his or her body, clothing, the tomb, and the soil that abutted the tomb. Indeed, it is recorded that liquids that sometimes oozed from beneath the tombs were highly prized, because the saints' powers of healing were thought to be concentrated in them.[29]

Jonathan Sumption explains the literal sense in which *virtus* was understood. He cites an account by Gregory of Tours, who offers the following advice to those who visit the tomb of St. Peter: "Should he wish to bring back a relic from the tomb, he carefully weighs a piece of cloth which he then hangs inside the tomb. Then he prays ardently and, if his faith is sufficient, the cloth, once removed from the tomb, will be found to be so full of divine grace that it will be much heavier than before."[30]

Relics and reliquary sites became inseparable, and people came to think that relics could lose their special powers if removed from the sites where they were housed. Relics were therefore only rarely brought to people wishing for miracles; people in search of miracles had to travel to the relics, which gave added impetus to the age-old practice of pilgrimage.

Because the relics of saints were believed to sanctify the physical spaces they occupied, abbeys, monasteries, and cathedrals were anxious to obtain them as a way of discouraging attacks from predators and enemies, who would fear incurring divine wrath. As explained earlier, relics that could be represented as stolen were especially valued—so much so that according to one authority, abbeys and monasteries that had come by relics legitimately often went to great lengths to claim that they actually had been stolen.[31] The reason was that the act of stealing a relic could be represented as a sign that the saint was displeased with the previous site of his or her earthly remains and preferred them to be relocated to the site to which they had been moved. Stealing relics thus had the effect of enhancing their protective powers by signaling to the community at large that the new site to which they had been transferred was now under the saint's extra-special protection.

Relics were regarded as being surrounded by force fields of spirituality, which could be transmitted to those who touched them. They were thought to emit what historian Ronald Finucane colorfully describes as "a kind of holy radioactivity which bombarded everything in the area, [in such a way] . . . that objects placed next to them would absorb . . . their power."[32] The sine qua non of venerating a saint in hope of receiving a miracle became close physical proximity to his or her relics, and a fundamental tenet of popular religion in early medieval times was the belief that saints would respond only to prayers uttered in the vicinity of their remains. For this reason, medieval pilgrimages to shrines were made not to see but to touch the relics. A surviving example is the base of St. Osmond's tomb at Salisbury (Figure 46), which had holes through which a pilgrim could insert his or her head and hands to get closer to the saint himself.

Saints were numerous, so how did people decide which saint or saints to venerate? To venerate saints indiscriminately would seem

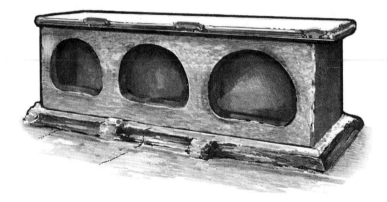

*46. The base of the tomb of St. Osmond in Salisbury
Cathedral allowed the pilgrim to place his hands and
head inside, to be closer to the relics of the saint.*

fickle, just as celebrating the feast in the saint's honor on the wrong
day was considered heretical.[33] One obvious basis for such choices
was related to the nature of the miracle desired. By the thirteenth
century, an entire society of saints had developed within Christianity, specializing in miracles of every kind. Various saints gained
renown for curing afflictions such as blindness, rickets, arthritis,
or madness. Certain saints became famous for their ability to avert
or end drought, prevent violence, or protect people against the
ravages of fire. St. Roch and St. Sebastian were famous for curing
plague, St. Job for curing the pox, St. Margaret for protecting mid-
wives, St. Cosmus and St. Damian for curing botches and biles, St.
Clair for correcting eye disorders, St. Appolin for curing toothache,
St. Agatha for healing sore breasts, St. Oswald and St. Faith for healing sick animals, St. Osyth for protecting against fire, and so on.[34]

Cutting across these notions of specialization, a supplicant also
had to consider where in the celestial hierarchy a saint stood. In
thirteenth-century Christianity, beings that dwelled in heaven were
imagined to form a pyramid-shaped hierarchy. Christ, of course,
stood at the apex, and immediately beneath Him dwelled the Vir-

gin Mary. Then came the twelve apostles, as well as John the Baptist and a few of the most renowned saints, such as St. Francis of Assisi, St. Anthony of Padua, and St. Isidore of Seville. At the bottom of the pyramid were the humblest, least famous saints, simple people of virtue who were known locally to members of a particular village or perhaps even only to a single family. Between the apex and the base dwelled hundreds of others, figures revered greatly for their good deeds, including martyrs, abbots, bishops, popes, prelates of every rank, church fathers, patriarchs, prophets, and seers.[35]

The significance of this imagined celestial hierarchy for seeking divine intercession presumably lay in the idea that the more distant the venerated saint stood from the apex of the hierarchy, the more levels a plea would have to cross to reach God. Certain saints were considered to occupy particularly strategic places in heaven, and those of a lesser stripe, such as local saints, could invite God's influence only through the intercession of these more influential beings. People tried to access the celestial hierarchy as close to the top as possible, not only because saints there were believed to have greater influence with God, but also presumably because the more levels through which an appeal had to ascend, the greater the risk of distorting or misrepresenting the intended message.

How was it decided in the first place that someone was a saint? Incorruptibility of flesh, the odor of sanctity, a luminous appearance, and the appearance of stigmata were some of the criteria used by the Church to make judgments about canonization. In certain cases determining sainthood was little more than a matter of biography, as, for example, would have been true for people closely associated with Christ during His lifetime or, for those born later, made famous by extraordinary acts of virtue, sacrifice, or heroism, especially martyrdom. But in the end, the most compelling criterion, particularly among the general population, was the report of a miracle. Miracles attributed to those who had died were considered proof that they were divinely blessed and had been assigned a place of honor in heaven. Indeed, in the eyes of the laity the sine qua non of saintliness was the ability to perform miracles, and the more miracles that could be attributed to a dead soul, the more exalted his or her place in heaven was thought to be.[36]

DEFINING A MIRACLE   Reports of miracles abound during the medieval period. Robert Finucane has documented approximately three thousand reports of miraculous events during the period 1066 to 1300 at nine prominent medieval shrines—seven in England and two in France.[37] The largest recorded collection of miracle cures is associated with the shrine of Thomas Becket at Canterbury. According to one source, Becket's shrine was the site of seven hundred miracles in the fifteen-year period following his murder in 1170—an average of one miracle every seven or eight days![38] At the Holy Rood of Bromholm in Norfolk, during an undisclosed time period, thirty-nine people were reportedly raised from the dead and twelve others were cured of blindness.[39] There are similar reports of miracles at other such shrines throughout Europe (see Figure 47).

Given the hope and promise that miracles offered and all that was at stake for individuals, families, communities, clergy, monarchs, and societies at large, widespread reports of miraculous occurrences and general acceptance of them should come as no surprise. Claims that the blind were made to see, the lame to walk, the dead to return to life, and the sick to become well were based on reports by people desperate to believe them, told to audiences eagerly seeking evidence of saints' efficacy, and verified by a clergy whose social power could only be enhanced by confirming the claims. Perceptually, then, every individual and every group in society was "primed" to find evidence of miracles, even in the most mundane events.

Careful investigation of the miracles that were reported and groups who visited medieval shrines has led historians to conclude that the overwhelming majority of the claims should be regarded as exaggerations. For our purposes, however, the truthfulness of miracle reports is largely beside the point. Claims about miracles

47. *Miracles were associated with medieval reliquaries,*
like this one, housing the remains of an important saint.

were widely believed at the time, and therefore they were consequential. The claims of miracles associated with medieval shrines—
the great shrines as well as local ones—are best understood as social constructions possessing what social scientists call "facticity,"
products of an emergent consensus. In this case, they were made
possible by individuals with particular needs who sought to satisfy
them in contexts that were special and unusual.

The question of how particular events came to be regarded as miracles is extremely difficult to untangle. The evidence that remains
is fragmentary, but we know enough to make a few general observations. First, when we consider the numerous reports of miracles
that occurred at medieval shrines, we must recall that, for people
living during the Middle Ages, a miracle was *anything* that hinted
at the earthly presence of God.[40] This definition granted a tremendous degree of interpretive latitude, not to say license, to the witness of events. If we recall the widely shared assumption that *all*
things known and seen were possessed of God and therefore held

the potential to reveal Him, we can see why many apparently unremarkable events could be interpreted by medieval people as miracles. As Sumption explains, "Even the most normal incidents of daily life were interpreted as signs of divine favour or disfavour. Simple men were terrified of the dark.... Thunder storms brought panic.... A flash of lightning created havoc.... Terrible cries were heard during an eclipse of the moon.... All such phenomena sprang not from natural causes but from the direct action of God."[41]

This way of thinking applied especially to miracles involving disease and illness. People understood and interpreted bodily sensations as evidence of a divine presence inside them; thus, any change in the way someone felt could be explained as evidence of a miracle. The disappearance of a feeling of weariness following rest, or of indigestion following a fast, the breaking of a fever, recovery from dizziness or nausea, or relief from ordinary aches and pains were all understood as due to acts of God, and therefore they counted as miracles.

These interpretations were powerfully reinforced by the general ignorance about human physiology. The state of a person's health or sickness was little more than a matter of social consensus or collective agreement. A particularly interesting illustration of this point was the persistent debate over how to determine whether or not someone had died. Different people used different criteria. Some believed that death was to be judged only by temperature, others by skin color, others by respiration or muscular rigidity. Only a few believed that it could be decided by the absence of a pulse. Finucane cites cases in which doctors declared patients dead because they had lost their sight or hearing or because they could not speak. He recounts an event in Ely in the first half of the twelfth century, when an argument arose about whether to bury a man who several said had died. In the end the parties to the debate agreed to permit his body to lie in state for three days before they buried it, by which time the man regained consciousness, leading them to declare his awakening a miracle.[42]

At the shrine of Thomas Becket, there was so much uncertainty about whether a person had died that the monks who managed the shrine always met for extensive consultation before deciding. Finucane tells us that William of Canterbury, one of Becket's shrine-guardians, "claimed that revival of the dead after a period of a few days was quite common," and when it happened a miracle was recorded. This inability to distinguish definitively the dead from the living probably accounts for many miraculous "revivals from death," which constituted one-tenth of all official reports of miracles in the fourteenth century.[43]

If there was so little agreement about whether someone had died, we can imagine how much room for interpretation there was regarding cases of ordinary illness. Studies of medieval miracles indicate that cures for human afflictions were the overwhelming majority of miracles that were recorded.[44] Given our current use of the term *miracle*—an event that seems to transcend or contradict known natural or scientific laws—we might imagine that these were dramatic cures. But historical research indicates that at medieval shrines such cases were rare exceptions. As Finucane explains, "Most medieval miracles were not sudden, and if we expected to find as a daily occurrence cripples flinging away their crutches or mute pilgrims breaking out in a *Te Deum*, we would be disappointed. Certainly a few cases were sudden, taking place as soon as the supplicant approached the holy dead, but they were not typical."[45] The great majority of miracles recorded at medieval shrines involved partial recoveries and reports of temporary improvement in health. No particular limit was placed on how much time could elapse between a visit to a shrine and a cure, and even people who began to feel better a year or more after their visit were regarded as cured by miracle. The degree of change was disregarded, and relapse was common, with reports of persons said to have been cured at one shrine appearing on the register of other shrines later on.

Some reported miracles may actually have resulted from changes in diet due to the act of traveling on pilgrimage. One student of the subject, historian Sister Benedicta Ward, recounts a twelfth-century outbreak of ergotism, an illness caused by a rye fungus that thrived during wet summers. Sufferers from this disease who went to shrines located in drier areas recovered spontaneously because they were eating bread made from unaffected grain. Because the cause of the disease was not known, these cures were counted as miracles and credited to the work of the Virgin.[46] Other events that were recorded as miracle cures involved illnesses that medicine today would regard as instances of "self-limiting" diseases, that is, disorders that disappear naturally with time. But, to reiterate, when we consider the combination of ignorance about death and disease, an abiding conviction of divine omnipresence, and the hardships of life in a hostile world, it is not surprising that people were ready to see miracles everywhere and to believe deeply in the miraculous healing powers of saints.

This powerful system of belief adds an important ingredient to the story of miracles. A considerable body of scientific evidence—especially in the field of psychoneuroimmunology—has now revealed the roles of belief and suggestion in alleviating symptoms of physical illness, not just "psychogenic" illnesses or illnesses involving conversion reactions. Studies of placebo effects have demonstrated that inert substances administered as if they were real drugs can sometimes be remarkably effective under certain conditions, especially when both doctors and patients believe they will work. Such studies also show that the placebo effect is greatly heightened if the administration of the inert substance is accompanied by a high degree of ritual performance.[47]

Studies of medieval miracle cures repeatedly state that elaborate rituals and dramatic ceremonies were performed around sacred shrines. Such practices established a context in which the miraculous powers of the saint whose relics were housed there were unquestioned. A powerful sense of suggestibility was carefully cultivated in the minds of pilgrims, and ritual and liturgy were carefully orchestrated to induce miracles to occur. According to historian Keith Thomas, these features worked together "to create an environment ideally suited for curing cases of self-limiting and psychogenic illness." His analysis of ritual drama and the system of beliefs that characterized the environment of the medieval shrine leads Thomas to conclude that "the greatest asset of the sacred shrine was the pilgrim's imagination. . . . In view of what is known about the potentialities of any cure in which both doctor and patient have complete faith, its power cannot be disregarded."[48]

REGULATING THE MIRACLE MARKET   Belief in miracles was not without its problems for the medieval Church, however. The claim that it was possible to access divine powers for the benefit of humankind created at least two difficulties. First, it inadvertently legitimized belief in magic, and created the problem of explaining to lay people the often mystifying distinction between magic and miracles. Second, it created the potential for what amounted to an unregulated market in saints and their miracles.

Relic cults and the miracles associated with them had a long history that predated Christianity. Indeed, reports of miracle cures at pagan shrines were common. Perhaps this was why, in the earliest years of Christianity, miracles played a comparatively insignificant role in the story of Christ. The four evangelists did mention miraculous powers attributed to Christ, but they neither exploited nor extolled them, nor did their immediate successors. It is not that pagans would necessarily doubt Christ's miracle-making powers; rather, such powers would in no way distinguish him from a great number of itinerant magicians and healers who made similar claims.[49]

Following the acceptance of Christianity by monarchs, however, missionaries set out to convert barbarian populations throughout Europe. During this effort, they found miracles valuable, but their persuasiveness had a high price. Many accepted Christ because they believed his followers held greater sway with the divine than did the pagan priests. Subtleties of doctrine and the true messages of Christianity escaped them. As a result, Ronald Finucane explains, "Miracles and saints' relics attained a significance far beyond what the missionaries may have intended. The beliefs promoted by missionaries in the heat of conversion were often an embarrassment to later generations of churchmen in a peaceful Christianized Europe when the battle to evangelize had been won; but by then the damage had been done."[50]

The making of saints became similarly problematic. In the early years when Christians were being persecuted, the only saints recognized by the Church other than the apostles, John the Baptist, and the Virgin Mary, were martyrs—disciples who had remained true to Christ without faltering under threat of death or actual execution. Once Christianity became a tolerated religion, by Constantine's declaration in the year 313, the Church expanded the basis upon which sainthood was granted. Now, in addition to martyrs, confessors might also be elevated to sainthood. (Confessors were the faithful who deserved veneration because of the pain they had suffered or inflicted upon themselves for the love of Christ.) The Church named as saints people it felt exemplified Christian ideals, but the populace at large bestowed the title on people of lesser stature and often of lesser moral standing, who were candidates for sainthood only because miracles of one kind or another had been attributed to them.[51]

The populist sentiment about sainthood proliferated, producing an explosion in the number of people worshipped as saints by local villagers. Every region and every village, indeed even individual families, claimed the protection of one saint or another. Who the saint was and how he or she became so designated was a judgment made entirely by members of the local populace and the local priests who served them. Perhaps the most unusual was St. Guinefort, associated with the small French village of Villars-les-Dombes. St. Guinefort was a dog who had suffered an unjust death. The story is that the dog had been left alone by its master with a child and had killed a snake that had crawled into the child's crib and threatened its life. When the master returned, he found the child soaked in blood. Thinking the dog had attacked the child, he killed it. The truth soon emerged, and a devotion to the animal developed that included reports of miracles, resulting in its elevation by the villagers to the status of a local saint.[52]

This state of anarchy was bound to cause problems for the Church and inevitably invited some form of episcopal intervention and control. The more miracles there were, the less significant any single miracle became. Too many miracles claimed by what we might call "wildcatters" threatened to weaken the value of all miracles. Jonathan Sumption tells us, for example that "so many miracles were performed by St. Swithin of Winchester . . . that the monks began to find them wearisome."[53]

Since anyone could establish a sacred shrine by claiming and advertising a miracle, the power of the clergy as sole mediators between human beings and the divine was threatened. Moreover, the marketing of miracles and the fantastic wealth it could produce attracted unscrupulous opportunists who threatened to undermine the doctrine and belief system upon which shrines depended. The need to control the proliferation of saints at the local level eventually gave rise to the officially sanctioned process of canonization that was developed, implemented, and controlled by the Church.[54]

Initially, local bishops and abbots tried to control the market in sainthood. Papal involvement in canonization did not begin until the tenth century, when bishops sought to enhance the legitimacy of their own candidates for sainthood by requesting the stamp of approval from the pope. Inexorably, over the next two centuries the papacy demanded more and better evidence of virtue and proof of miracles, and the role of the Church of Rome loomed larger and larger in the process. This "mission creep" culminated in the proclamation of 1215 by Pope Innocent III that no one should "presume to announce newly-found relics unless they should have first been approved by authority of the Roman Pontiff."[55]

In authorizing canonization, the Church of Rome had two basic concerns: evidence of sanctity and proof of authenticity of miracles. Investigative procedures became increasingly elaborate and cumbersome. Papal courts required detailed written accounts of miracles and the exact circumstances of their occurrence. These petitions had to include details about the people to whom the miracles had happened—their lives and their illnesses and afflictions that were said to have been cured—as well as names and details of witnesses to these events, with letters attesting to *their* character.[56]

Most canonization processes began at the local level, initiated perhaps by a village priest or members of a local parish church. If their petitions were to proceed at all, they typically required the support of local authorities and influential people in the region.[57] Indeed, by the thirteenth century, petitions for sainthood were unlikely to go forward unless they were enthusiastically endorsed by the leading bishops and the monarch of the originating country, and even then a petition frequently had to be resubmitted numerous times before the papacy granted permission to proceed.

Once this was given, an inquiry was convened consisting of three commissioners, one of whom had to be a bishop. They investigated the life of the proposed saint, gathering evidence of sanctity and virtue, and information about miracles that were claimed to be associated with his or her relics. Their report was submitted to the pope for his consideration. According to André Vauchez, early investigations proceeded with reasonable speed, but from the thirteenth century onward, they took longer and longer. The investigation of Yves of Trequier in 1330, for example, lasted forty-three days and received the sworn testimony of 7 to 8 witnesses per day, and during the investigation held in connection with the canonization of Pope Urban V during 1374–76, some 659 witnesses were questioned. An investigation required an army of official recorders, notaries, interpreters, translators, and administrative clerks of every kind. A medieval version of the modern survey questionnaire was produced and had to be filled out with great care.[58]

The report of a commission, once submitted to the papal court, was turned over to members of the College of Cardinals for further study. This step entailed another lengthy and detailed investigation, which could take several years to complete, culminating in a document arguing the merits and demerits of the case. Only then would the matter be put before the pope for final action.[59]

The costs of shepherding the canonization process along were tremendous and had to be borne by those who began it. They had to provide funds for maintaining the commissioners and their retinues throughout their visits to the sites where the saint had lived or miracles had occurred, and pay the expenses of witnesses and the fees for notaries and interpreters. Once a petition had reached the papal court, they were expected not only to pay all the administrative costs, but also to give monetary favors to important persons to insure that the application did not bog down in the bureaucracy.[60]

Not surprisingly, the cumbersome and expensive process led to a marked decline in petitions for sainthood. As the Church tightened its control over the process of canonization, the number of saints canonized dropped dramatically, and the composition of membership in the cult of saints changed as well. Vauchez's study shows that between 1198 and 1431, the rate of canonization dropped from one new saint every 3.1 years, on average, to one every 13.5 years. Because the effort and sums involved were beyond the means of ordinary people, the society of saints became increasingly populated by members of ecclesiastical and other elites. In addition, there is considerable evidence of nepotism and favoritism operating in the process.[61]

Even though the Church had monopolized control over the canonization process, the phenomenon of populist saints did not die out. If anything, it flourished. Most people seemed to prefer venerating individuals who were closer to them in space and time than the saints recognized by the Church of Rome, and the number of local saints continued to increase. Ultimately, a compromise was reached in which the Church continued to monopolize the formal canonization process while turning a blind eye to local parishes that preferred to venerate lesser known figures reputed to have performed miracles. Vauchez describes "a gradual development of two sectors in the sphere of the cult of saints: on the one hand, a tiny

band of the privileged, who had been lucky enough to emerge un-
scathed from the pitfalls of the canonization processes; on the other
hand, a throng of the obscure and the failed, who continued nevertheless to be venerated."[62] The former were referred to by the
Church of Rome as the sanctified *(sancti)*, the latter as the beatified
(beati). The beatified were almost always local people whose fame
had not spread beyond the local village or region where they had
lived. Many of them, including St. Guinefort the dog, would never
have been canonized by the Church of Rome for all the money in
the world.

One interesting phenomenon is that, although people were commonly skeptical of the miracles attributed to local saints, their skepticism, as Durkheim would have predicted, was reserved for claims
from *other* parishes and regions. As Vauchez notes, "The truth is
that they really only believed in 'their' miracles, that is, those performed by members of the religious order or local community to
which they belonged or by persons in whom they recognized
themselves."[63]

To explain the role of the dead in the world of the living, we have
had to roam far afield from the subject with which we began, Gothic
great churches. But saints and other members of the world of the
dead stand at the very center of our story about cathedrals and great
monastic churches. Cathedrals stood at the very center of the world
of the dead, because they housed many of the shrines that pilgrims
came to visit. This gave pilgrims glimpses of the world the saints
inhabited and provided the settings in which the strength and force
of the world of the hereafter could be implored to serve a human
purpose. In exchange, the world of the dead provided cathedral
builders with the financial means for seeing their grand projects
through to completion.

PART V

THE GOTHIC COMMUNITY

CHAPTER 13

Medieval Living Conditions

In a book originally published in 1922, the sociologist Max Weber wrote, "The most elementary forms of behavior motivated by religious . . . factors are oriented to this world," and as an example he quoted the prayer at Deuteronomy 4:40, "that it may go well with thee . . . and that thou mayest prolong thy days upon the earth."[1] To understand religious practice in any society, including the building of magnificent sacred spaces, we need to know something about people's everyday lives, their "days upon the earth."

Citizens of modern, developed countries can never fully understand and appreciate just how precarious life was for those who lived during medieval times. Inevitably, our attempts to understand their lives are filtered through the interpretative lens of our own experience, and the resulting picture is not completely accurate. Nevertheless, we can gain some understanding from historians who have studied the basic conditions of human existence in the Middle Ages. Details are sketchy, but the data that have survived show clearly that for most people life was difficult, precarious, and at times downright terrifying.[2] Daily life was lived out against a backdrop of fear— fear of violence, bloodshed, and brutality, fear of starvation, fear of dying, and fear about one's fate in the hereafter. For the true believer, perhaps the greatest fear of all was the fear that Judgment Day was at hand.[3]

Numerous accounts tell us that sickness and death abounded. According to some estimates, almost one-third of all infants born alive during the medieval period died before the age of five, and even the nobility, whose standard of living and diet were far better than those of ordinary people, had an average life span of no more than thirty years. (The comparable figure today exceeds seventy.) Members of the gentry who survived to age twenty could not expect to live much past fifty, and people of the poorer classes died even sooner. Indeed, the accepted definition of *senectus*, the age of reaching seniority, was forty-five to fifty.[4] These statistics did not improve for centuries. One study by the seventeenth-century English demographer John Graunt of the birth and death records from London for the year 1662 shows that of every one hundred live births, *sixty* children died before the age of sixteen—thirty-six of these during the first six years of life and twenty-four more in the next ten years.[5]

For those who did manage to survive, malnutrition, disease, and illness were common, mostly because the food supply depended so heavily on the weather. More than 90 percent of all people living during the Middle Ages depended on agriculture, and most of them lived hand to mouth. Good weather meant enough food for everyone, with perhaps a small surplus to store or to sell at market.[6] Poor weather meant a meager harvest, resulting in less food on each plate and nothing to sell. Truly bad weather, which occurred on average every six years, forced many peasants to starve their livestock so that they and their families could eat the animals' fodder.

A dramatic description of the impact that weather could have on agriculture and the resulting havoc appears in William Chester Jordan's *The Great Famine*. Jordan documents in impressive detail the seven years of catastrophic subsistence crisis from 1315 to 1322. This famine encompassed the whole of Germany, the Baltic region to the borders of Poland, the southern portion of Scandinavia, the whole of northern France and, except for northern Scotland, all of the British Isles. In all, Jordan estimates that the famine affected a population of thirty million people living in an area of four hundred thousand square miles. The "Great Famine" was caused by a combination of seven consecutive years of incessant rains from spring to fall, combined with bitterly cold winters. This came in the midst of a twenty-year period that was one of the two worst for winter weather during the entire Middle Ages. Twice the Baltic Sea and the North Sea froze.

Jordan's account of the conditions created by the Great Famine is at once riveting and chilling. He describes how seedbeds were soaked by the unceasing rains and explains that the few grains that managed to ripen had to be left to rot. Pastures flooded, fish traps were destroyed, and dikes were washed away by floods. Meadows became too wet to mow, turf too soggy to cut, and quarries too flooded to work. Vast expanses of fertile topsoil were washed away, leaving acres of gravel on which nothing could grow. Animal herds were devastated by epidemics of often fatal diseases that flourished under wet conditions. The flooding also made salt harvesting impossible, which deprived people of one of the few methods they had for preserving food to get them through the winter. The severe food shortages brought about by this extreme weather pattern were compounded by a crisis of food distribution caused by the endemic war and civil unrest of these decades, much of it in the regions most adversely affected by weather.[7] The cumulative effects over seven years took a horrible toll on the population.

Even without a famine, life was precarious and difficult. Peasants were always at the mercy of weather, and even the very wealthy were never free of its tyranny because most of their wealth derived from agriculture. A poor harvest diminished the wealth of landowners, drove up the price of food on the open market, deprived wealthy consumers of disposable income for the purchase of manufactured items, and halted the purchase of nonessential goods. A succession of crop failures sent economic shock waves throughout a region or country.

Even when food was abundant, the diet of ordinary peasants was extremely poor. For the most part, they lacked a dependable source of protein, as well as such essential vitamins as A and D, iron, and other vital minerals. The typical diet left people weak and vulnerable to illness and disease, including incipient night blindness caused by the shortage of vitamin A. Crop failures, of course, further diminished people's already compromised ability to fight infections, so such common illnesses as colds, influenza, and fever could quickly turn lethal. Moreover, during droughts and floods, food supplies were rapidly consumed, and many people had only rotten meat and mildewed grain to eat, thus adding food poisoning to their list of woes.[8]

Housing for the typical citizen was extremely primitive. In her account of the everyday life of peasant families in late medieval England, *The Ties That Bound,* Barbara Hanawalt describes a typical medieval dwelling as a squat, poorly lighted, badly ventilated one-story hovel. It had wooden framing with turf, cob, or wattle-and-daub used to fill the interior wall spaces, which were crude, colorless, and undecorated. The sole sources of external light were tiny windows, usually unglazed but shuttered to protect against inclement weather. To compensate for a lack of glass, some peasants used sheep or cattle gut stretched across the window frame, so only a dim, gray-tinted light entered. The only interior source of light was from the hearth fire or an occasional candle. Furnishings were few and crude, and the earthen floors were covered with straw. Animals freely entered the interior rooms. Most houses had an open hearth for heating and cooking, but water sources and latrines were usually located in the closes around which peasant huts were built.[9]

In most villages and towns, the drinking water was polluted, and sanitation systems were unknown. Outbreaks of typhoid, cholera, and dysentery were common, as were epidemics of contagious diseases such as measles, smallpox, diphtheria, and scarlet fever. In addition, poor indoor heating led to severe and debilitating bouts of pneumonia and tuberculosis, particularly during the long, cold, dark winter months. To these trials was added a significant rate of disability and death from accidents in the home and the workplace. Taken together, these various conditions exacted a frightening toll of death and suffering, especially among the young.[10]

Then there were the devastating effects of recurrent epidemics of plague. The Black Death swept across Europe in the mid-fourteenth century, killing between one-third and one-half of the major urban populations. It was preceded and then followed by lesser epidemics spaced a few years apart. For instance, during the 110-year period from 1369 to 1479, England experienced successive waves of plague every 5 to 12 years. From 1515 until the second great epidemic in 1665, there were only 12 years when London was entirely free of plague. In the Netherlands plague appeared every 2–3 years between 1360 and 1494; in Paris it appeared eight times between 1414 and 1439; and on the Iberian Peninsula plague occurred fourteen times between 1391 and 1457. On average, about 5 percent of the population died during each of these epidemics.[11]

Starvation, malnutrition, illness, and disease, then, were daily concerns, but these were not the only significant problems confronting medieval people. Another source of fear and havoc was fire, especially in towns. The densely concentrated houses and other structures were mostly built of wood and were heated by open hearths ventilated by wooden chimneys mounted atop thatch roofs. Floors were covered in straw. This combination of design and materials provided tinder that erupted in flames with even a single spark. Once a fire broke out, little could be done to stop it. People seldom had a dependable water supply nearby for dousing the flames, and in any case they had no way to project dense streams of water to the roof level. Mostly, there were only leather buckets, wooden ladders, and hooks for pulling burning thatch to the ground. This meant that once a fire had ignited, there was little to do but let it burn itself out.[12]

Yet another pervasive source of risk to life and limb was violence, which contributed greatly to the general sense of insecurity. Acts of violence occurred almost daily and affected people at every level of the society. Neighboring settlements fought with each other over the farming and gleaning rights to contiguous lands. Nobles regularly resorted to violence to defend their domains, and they launched predatory forays to expand their holdings and amass new wealth. Holders of the crown fought with pretenders for control of the monarchy, and nations fought with one another over issues large and small. Defenses in villages and towns were usually weak and often absent, so most ordinary citizens were exposed, defenseless, and extremely vulnerable to attack.

Even everyday activities could be hazardous. Venturing into the forests that surrounded human settlements, for example, was extremely dangerous. Wild animals abounded in the woods, including boars, whose foraging for food extended to human beings. Just in traveling from one village to the next through dense forest, it was easy to get lost and disoriented, and once night fell, one was completely exposed to the elements. The zone between human settlements also provided a habitat for society's outcasts, who lived by attacking and stealing from travelers. Writing about life during the fourteenth to eighteenth centuries, historians William Naphy and Penny Roberts state, "Fear was all pervasive and omnipresent within society, and . . . the population of Europe at this time experienced unprecedented levels of anxiety and pessimism."[13]

What defenses did people have against such harsh living conditions? Especially when social institutions were weak, people sought help in religion. One of the bedrock convictions of medieval civilization was that God could protect people from harm or bring down upon their heads His terrible wrath. An absolute premium was therefore placed on developing and retaining benevolent relationships with God and with the saints who dwelled with Him in heaven. As we have seen, a saint could intercede with God to heal afflictions; ward off disease; relieve pain and suffering; guarantee a bountiful harvest; protect against violence, plague, or drought; and grant advantage over adversaries, or, better still, bring ruin to them. André

Vauchez writes, "The belief in the omnipresence of the supernatural and in the constant intervention of the inhabitants of the hereafter in the world of the living was a basic feature of the medieval mentality. In medieval eyes, the miracles of the saints constituted one of the principal ways in which this close relationship between heaven and earth took concrete form."[14] Without this conviction, people would have had no sense of protection and security.

An equally powerful conviction was that humans owed God His due, that unless they venerated Him properly, appropriately, and continuously, divine punishment would ensue. When misfortune struck, whether in the form of fire, plague, drought, flood, or war, the most common explanation was that the victims had failed to venerate and worship God as He required. In his study of the Great Famine of 1315 to 1322, William Chester Jordan shows that people at the time saw it as a sign of God's anger at them. "For them," he explains, "it was God who was unquestionably bringing famine in order to mete out the legitimate recompense for sin. . . . Sin, hatred of the visible church, empty faith, and lack of loyalty offended God and explained why he permitted the foul weather to linger for such a period of time."[15]

The concerns I have sketched here, of course, are scarcely unique to the Middle Ages. The harsh conditions of life, along with faith in divine protection against them, lasted at least until the eighteenth century in western Europe, and are still the norm in much of the world today. Our interest here is not so much in people's impulse to seek divine protection as in understanding the forms of its expression, at both the personal and the institutional levels, in the period when Gothic cathedral-building was at its prime.

During medieval times, the project of devising ways to engage the divine led to the emergence of a specialized institution, the Church, and a special class of professionals, the clergy, to whom authority was ceded to manage and mediate relationships between the secular and sacred domains. The Church served the vital function of ensuring that God adopted and retained a benevolent disposition toward the entire social collective and its individual members. It had the solemn responsibility of drawing the Holy Spirit into society's midst and keeping it available for the protection, succor, and support of the community. This role automatically placed the clergy in a privileged category and set them apart from ordinary people; therefore, responsibility for managing religious practices was bound to become the foundation of power and authority in the secular world.

CHAPTER 14

The Spiritual Brokers— Priests and Monarchs

In any society where people thirst for the protection of religion from the harshness of life, anyone who can claim special access to the sacred and special relationships to sacred places has an important basis for political and cultural power. In the medieval world, two elements of society—prelates and monarchs— made these claims, at times competing for primacy, each claiming the ability to secure for the community God's benevolent and protective powers. Because cathedrals and great abbey churches were considered to be the best settings for engaging the sacred, this competition naturally focused attention on them.

Like other important matters during medieval times, issues of political and cultural power were embedded in a dense thicket of beliefs about universal order. People assumed that when God created the earth, He established a strict coherence between heaven and earth. They were seen as two facets of a single, homogeneous universe, built to the same strictly hierarchical plan and reciprocally related to each other (see Figure 48).

In heaven God stood at the top, with Christ at His right hand, the Virgin nearby, and apostles, saints, and other exemplary Christians arrayed beneath. This vision is depicted in the arrangement of statuary on the west fronts of cathedrals, on altarpieces, and in stained-

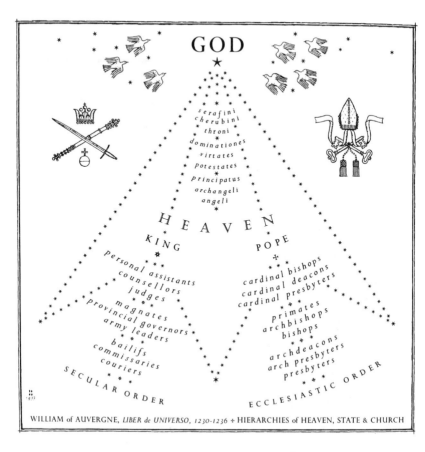

GOD
★

serafini
cherubini
throni
dominationes
virtates
Potestates
Principatus
archangeli
angeli

HEAVEN

KING
✿

POPE
✣

Personal assistants
counsellors
judges
magnates
Provincial governors
army leaders
bailifs
commissaries
couriers

cardinal bishops
cardinal deacons
cardinal presbyters
primates
archbishops
bishops
archdeacons
arch presbyters
presbyters

SECULAR ORDER

ECCLESIASTIC ORDER

WILLIAM of AUVERGNE, *LIBER de UNIVERSO*, *1230-1236* ÷ HIERARCHIES of HEAVEN, STATE & CHURCH

48. *Hierarchies of heaven, state, and church, reproduced from the Plan of St. Gall.*

glass windows. Heaven was superior to earth and was meant to serve as a model for it. In particular, its superiority was expressed by its ideal order, a system that it was humankind's duty to emulate on earth. Order in the earthly realm was reflected in strict, God-given divisions among different classes of people, divisions that reflected God's mission for members of the two highest-ranking classes of society: priests and monarchs. Both were concerned with providing leadership in the world of the living. Priests were meant to turn their faces toward heaven, praying to God on behalf of the community and of its prominent members. They were entrusted with the responsibility for engaging the divine, communicating with it on behalf of fellow human beings, and handing down God's rules of conduct for all people. Kings and princes were meant to turn their attention to earth. Their responsibility was to enact God's rules of conduct and enforce strict adherence to them. The roles of both classes were dictated by these responsibilities and in carrying them out, great churches—cathedrals and great abbey churches—played a crucial role.[1]

Priests

Priests proclaimed themselves masters of the spiritual. Their assertion was deeply rooted in official Church doctrine, which held that the relationship of ordinary humans to God required mediation and that clergy were the only members of society who could be trusted with this audacious function. At the head of the Church hierarchy stood the pope, the embodiment of Christ on earth, who had been anointed by the Lord's anointed. The pope's direct representatives, the bishops, were God's special representatives within a given territory, the diocese. In his diocese the bishop was the preeminent pastor, entrusted with the ultimate responsibility for the care of souls in his flock and for dispensing the sacred. The bishop, in turn, delegated his sacral duties to those he anointed and ordained. Those he ordained shared his special powers, so the act of ordination extended a hierarchical chain linking God to the pope, the pope to his bishops, and the bishop to his clergy. In principle at least, no act of religious worship, communal or private, could be conducted or engaged in without the direct or indirect instigation of the bishop, through the priests he appointed.

The anointing of bishops conferred not only exclusive authority for stipulating the time, place, and form of worship for individuals and the community, but also exclusive access to truth. The words of bishops, based as they were on their command of the scriptures, were considered as coming from God and therefore taken as final, the authoritative interpretation of God's own word in the domains over which the bishops ruled. In this scheme, to anoint a priest as a bishop was to situate him at the very point where earth and heaven joined. He was believed able to communicate with either realm, bringing words of truth handed down from heaven to humans, and bringing pleas from humans for divine intervention in their lives to heaven.[2]

Within this system of belief, we can see why the heresy of the Albigensians, described in Chapter 4, was treated so harshly. Their most scandalous heresy consisted not so much in criticizing the clergy for their excesses or denouncing their peccadilloes, but in arguing that people did not even need the services of priests, that every human had sole and unmediated control over his or her relationship to God. Georges Duby expressed this heresy issue succinctly when he asked, "Why should certain men, setting themselves apart from the rest, claim custody of the extraordinary privilege of administering the sacred? How was one to justify the exercise of such a monopoly by a small group which thereby gained the power to bend the rest of society under its yoke?"[3]

Proclaiming dominion over spiritual brokering is one matter; legitimating it in the minds of other members of society is quite another. How did the priestly class persuade others that they actually were masters of the sacred and that only they could perform the functions they claimed for themselves? A principal means of establishing legitimacy, of course, was through church teachings. From the very beginning, priests instructed members of the laity in the requisite orthodoxy and bound them by oath to accept it. Another method was through performance of liturgy—the hourly, daily, weekly, and yearly worship engaged in by priests on behalf of the communities they represented. Different systems of liturgy were regarded as more than just alternative ways of praying to and venerating God. They were treated as secretly held master codes by which humans were able to communicate with God—secret because the liturgy was said in Latin and performed behind great stone choir screens, out of sight of the general public. Indeed, a succession of popes, bishops, and monarchs tried to have only *their* versions of liturgy adopted, with competing versions forbidden and stamped out.[4]

As we have seen, the legitimacy of the clergy was also expressed in the grandeur of the cathedral that served as the bishop's seat. In Chapter 6 I explained that bishops regarded cathedrals as reflecting their standing in society and, by implication, in the overall cosmic scheme of things. To fulfill its function, a bishop's building had to be bold and intimidating. It had to embody a sense of commanding authority, of total dominion by the social institution that created it and the class of professionals who occupied it. In this respect, cathedrals expressed in material form the symbolic function served by their occupants (see Figure 49).

In addition to the cathedral's grandeur and size, its decorations, the ceremonies that took place within it, and the grand style in which rituals were enacted further strengthened the bishop's legitimacy. I have said that during this period all art was considered sacred. Its purpose was sacrificial—works of art were offerings to God to win His favor and appease His wrath. Spaces that were built to underscore the legitimacy of the clerics' claims to power thus had to be repositories of fine art.

In these magnificent settings, rituals performed in connection with public liturgical services were enacted with a fine eye to achieving maximal dramatic effect. Two aspects of these services stand out.

49. *The moral and temporal authority of Wells Cathedral is depicted on its imposing west front.*

The first is that both the buildings themselves and the liturgy imposed a strict sense of ordering. The performance of liturgy by medieval clergy created an atmosphere in which time and place were strictly ordered in accordance with a grander cosmic scheme. Enacting the liturgy imparted to observers and participants alike a clear, firm sense of cosmic regularity, coherence, and structure that was lacking in much of ordinary life. This order was imposed not for a day, or week, or month, but for the entire year, and its regulation extended all the way down to the individual moment. Cathedrals thus stood apart from and in stark contrast to the turmoil, chaos, and violence of ordinary daily life. To enter a cathedral was to cross an important threshold between the secular and the sacred, and their occupation of the sacred space implied that the clergy were connected to the sacred realm in a way that ordinary people simply were not.

This aspect of liturgy was especially highlighted in certain kinds of ceremonies in which worshippers were made to glimpse the chaos and perdition of hell that regular performances of liturgy were designed to hold in check. In cathedrals they took the form of special services during which darkness gave way to light. The Anglican Church today celebrates an Advent service that is a modern version of this age-old ritual. In one version of the service, all sources of light are extinguished so that the interior is totally dark. The organ then booms out cacophonous noise, as painful and terrifying as possible, which mimics the chaos of hell. (In medieval times, this noise would have been produced by the priests with shrieks, screams, clanging metal objects, and wailing.) After a prolonged period devoted to this imitation of hell, candles are lighted, and the cathedral's interior gradually becomes filled with the blaze of a thousand lights. As the gloom diminishes, cacophony is supplanted by the measured tones of sacred music. Light and divine order replace darkness and chaos. Dramatic portrayals along these lines in medieval times would, one imagines, have done much to heighten the impact of liturgy in the minds and hearts of the faithful and strengthen the legitimacy of the priests' claims as spiritual mediators.

This practice of contrasting order with chaos extended to architectural features of cathedrals as well. The art historian Michael Camille, in his fascinating book *Images on the Edge: The Margins of Medieval Art*, discusses this facet of cathedral architecture. Camille points out that the grandeur, geometric orderliness, and awesomeness of Gothic cathedrals sometimes blind us to the presence in these buildings of numerous grotesques, creatures that portend a different, chaotic, terrifying, or base existence. Cindy Davis's drawings of such figures appear throughout this book (see also Figure 50). Gargoyles, serpents, lascivious men and women, baboons, monkeys, pagan Green Men,[5] and fabulous figures that are half animal and half human mysteriously emerge from the foliage of carved capitals. They adorn the corbels of vaulted ceilings and jut out from the

50. *An artist's rendering of some of the grotesque images found high atop pillars and hidden under choir seats in cathedrals throughout Europe.*

arms of choir stalls. They are carved on the undersides of choir seats (misericords) and poke out from behind massive columns. Camille asks, "What do they all mean, those lascivious apes, autophagic dragons, pot-bellied heads, harp-playing asses, arse-kissing priests and somersaulting jongleurs that protrude at the ends of medieval buildings, sculptures and illuminated manuscripts?" His answer is that the incoherence of marginal art is there to stand against and highlight the Word of God. "The centre," he argues, is "dependent upon the margins for its continued existence."[6] It is as if such marginalia act, metaphorically, as a counterthrust to hold up the system of strict ordering that the liturgy embodies, just as flying buttresses hold up a building's roofs and vaults.

To return to the special liturgical ceremonies, it seems clear that they were written and performed so as to first arouse and then allay anxieties and fears. In this regard, they belong to a category of human activity that anthropologists term "ritual performance." Such performances enable people to simplify their world by orienting them to a very small number of salient concerns and actions. They reduce many varied relations to fewer, more orderly, concentrated, and schematic ones. The notion is that in order to comprehend and control the world, to live in it free of fear and paralyzing anxiety, we must reduce complexity and increase our sense of order.[7] The elaborate rituals of medieval liturgy (and similar cultural rituals) seem ideally suited to allaying dread by focusing attention on detail, thereby imparting a sense of security, protection, and wellbeing. To the extent that the rituals succeeded, those who engaged in or observed them experienced a reassuring sense of calm. This feeling, when interpreted for participants as evidence of God's presence, presumably significantly enhanced the perceived efficacy of the ritual and further legitimated the power of the Church.

Another resource on which priests drew to substantiate their claim as spiritual mediators was the occurrence of miracles. From the earliest days of Christianity, when missionaries set out to convert barbarian hordes to the Christian faith, the clergy knew the value of coupling sermons based on sacred texts with displays of miracles as a means of persuading skeptical lay folk that Christian clergy were more effective than pagan priests in summoning the powers of the sacred into the human midst and putting them to use for secular purposes. In *Religion and the Decline of Magic*, historian Keith Thomas tells us how this reliance on displays of miracles came about. He points out that in all primitive religions priestly classes offered their followers access to supernatural powers while representing themselves as mediums through which this access became possible. Beginning in the fourth century, conversion of nonbelievers and skeptics to Christianity was simplified and facilitated by convincing skeptics that the new religion offered not only hope for salvation in the life to come, but cures for illnesses and other afflictions in this life. As a result, the staging of miracles became a standard technique of conversion.

Performing miracles soon led to performing acts of exorcism, conjuring the devil out of some object by pronouncing prayers over it and invoking God's name. Thomas tells us that by the early Middle Ages special ecclesiastical benedictions were associated with almost every object or event. Medieval books of liturgy included rituals "to bless houses, cattle, crops, ships, tools, armor, wells and kilns. There were formulae for blessing men who were preparing to set off on a journey, to fight a duel, to engage in battle or to move into a new house. There were procedures for blessing the sick and for dealing with sterile animals, for driving away thunder and for making the marriage bed fruitful."[8] The medieval Church became a nearly bottomless reservoir of supernatural power, which, in exchange for gifts, it dispensed to the faithful to help them cope with every imaginable type of problem and situation.

Monarchs and Nobles

In its attempt to monopolize mediation between the sacred and the secular realms, the Church sometimes faced competition from monarchs. A succession of kings wrapped the monarchy in images of sacredness to strengthen and extend control over their domains. Monarchs represented themselves as soldiers of God.

As we have seen, European society in the eleventh century was conceived according to an image of the City of God, a kingdom based on order, hierarchy, and strict adherence to the sacred text. Initially, under Charlemagne, the king stood at the apex of the earthly city; the weaker monarchs of the ninth and tenth centuries, however, became uneasy co-chairmen with the popes. As I mentioned earlier, much of the conflict that developed between the Church and the state centered on the investiture of bishops. The question of who had the right to appoint men whose role was the care of souls raised the issue of who among living beings—

pope or king—was to be considered first in the eyes of God. This issue was central to events surrounding the building of the first Gothic basilica at the Abbey Church of St. Denis (see Chapter 5). It figured as well in the intense interest shown by a succession of monarchs in sponsoring major ecclesiastical building projects, including grand monastic churches and ornate chapels, as well as cathedrals. According to art historian Suzanne Lewis, Henry III's sole patronage of the east end of Westminster Abbey was motivated by a desire to create a great church that would rival the episcopal power of St. Paul's Cathedral, a structure that dominated the skyline of London. It was also intended to rival the splendor of Ste.-Chapelle, the grand chapel built under the patronage of Henry's rival, Louis IX of France. Lewis argues that the project was motivated by a wish to promote "an image of sacred rulership . . . creating an ideological base from which Henry III could claim the right to exert royal power over the bishops." She concludes: "The project provided a perfect vehicle through which Henry's public piety and love of ceremony could promote his expansion of royal authority into the jurisdictional affairs of the Church."[9] Historian Christopher Wilson discusses this issue as well, describing Henry's motives in this way: "Westminster Abbey embodied Henry's elevated view of the place of kingship within the divinely established order. To his English subjects it was intended to proclaim the king's role as God's anointed vicar and lord of all men in the kingdom, clergy as well as laity."[10]

Even though people thought that God had set the monarch apart to serve as secular leader, maintaining control over the secular domain was a source of constant concern to every medieval monarch. As detailed in Chapter 3, various challenges, such as poor systems of transportation, the precarious nature of an agricultural economy, and the feudal lords' independent power, conspired to make ruling any kingdom extremely difficult and uncertain. To meet these challenges, every monarch tried to draw on the power of the sacred, linking his position to a higher force that legitimated it. The monarch who successfully represented himself as an earthly embodiment of God might then use God's reflected powers to establish his claims to legitimacy and thus coerce subjects into obedience through fear of offending the Almighty.

Medieval kings therefore displayed a deep interest in religion and religious practices and sought ways to manipulate religious symbolism for political purposes. Kings were as interested in sacred spaces as the prelates who occupied and ran them, and they customarily made generous gifts to cathedral chapters. Charles IV, for example, conceived of Prague Cathedral as the centerpiece of the newly emerging Bohemia. Wilson reports that in 1341, when Charles was co-regent, a tenth of the very large royal revenues from his Bohemian silver mines was granted to the cathedral chapter specifically to meet the costs of building. In 1344 the king personally negotiated with the pope to separate the archdiocese of Prague from that of Mainz, and in 1355 he acquired relics of the cathedral's patron, St. Vitus. By 1358 he had remade the shrine for the relics of St. Wenceslas, "a canonized representative of the previous indigenous dynasty."[11]

Since art was considered sacred, as were kings, the monarchy became a principal source of support for artistic enterprise. Kings and great churches of every kind were thus intricately linked; in a sense the great church expressed the idea of God's and the king's sovereignty in equal parts. As Georges Duby explains, "The churches were in a sense royal buildings par excellence, for God revealed himself to mankind as sovereign of the world, crowned and seated on a throne, there to judge the living and the dead."[12] The Christianization of the king's powers made him the focal point of all Church ceremony, and anointing the king with holy oils, in a sense, made art an inherently royal affair. One meaning of the word *sovereign,* the person anointed by God to govern man, is "he-who-gives." Kings and princes were meant to give to God and also to humans, and it was appropriate that the ruler should be identified with beautiful works of art and that they should flow to him and from him into the hands of his subjects.

Throughout much of the medieval period, then, the king was regarded as a sacred figure anointed by God to rule mankind. According to the doctrine of the three orders of society, the king, as sovereign, was to protect and guide the populace—nobles and peasants alike. His goodness, mercy, and justice determined the health and moral standing of the entire realm. If he was virtuous, so was his realm, and if he became corrupt, so did his entire kingdom. Because the king was considered to be a sacred or at least a quasi-sacred figure, claims were made for him that were similar to the claims priests made for themselves. One of the most interesting was the claim that kings could perform miracles. It was quite common for medieval monarchs to claim the power to heal. An intriguing analysis of this phenomenon appears in Marc Bloch's book *The Royal Touch*. Kings were thought able to cure scrofula, a form of tuberculosis of the lymph glands, by touching the patient—the power was popularly known as "the touch for scrofula."

Though accounts of miraculous powers possessed by European monarchs date from at least the tenth century, by the twelfth century they seem to have become more pronounced. The French monarch Louis VI (1108–1137) was reportedly able to cure scrofula and other disorders by touch, and similar cures were commonly reported in England during the reigns of Edward the Confessor (1042–1066) and several of his successors, most notably Henry I (1100–1135), Henry II (1154–1189), and Henry III (1216–1272). The practice appears to have peaked at the very time when European kings were most aggressively engaged in monarchy-building, in Capetian France and Norman England, and did not subside until the close of the Middle Ages.

The number of persons suffering from scrofula (or other disorders mistakenly diagnosed as scrofula) who sought cures from kings was not trivial, though it was never as great as the number seeking cures at important pilgrimage shrines (see Chapter 12). During the 106-year period covering the reigns of Edwards I, II, and III in England (1272–1377), large numbers of people were granted royal audiences in hopes of a cure. For example, Edward I received 983 such persons during a single year of his reign, and more than 1,200 in another. Crowds were no doubt attracted by an additional custom connected with receiving the Royal Touch: a gift by the king of one penny per person touched.[13] Kings of England also distributed "cramp rings," said to hold other miraculous powers to cure. These rings were made from coins offered at a Good Friday service; the king first presented them as gifts at the high altar and then retrieved them for eventual distribution to his subjects.

Reports of miracle cures achieved through the touch of a monarch reinforced the impression that monarchs were close to God and imbued with special powers to make the miraculous forces of heaven accessible to ordinary humans. Through being anointed by miraculous oils, performing miracles, and other means, kings sought to elevate themselves above ordinary mortals, even the clergy, to the status of half-sacred, half-human figures. To the extent that they succeeded, their claims to power were, of course, strongly bolstered.

Medieval society, then, comprised three groups—priests, kings and nobles, and commoners. The three were bound in a vision of organic unity emanating from heaven, and cathedrals, abbey churches, and other exemplars of sacred space were important settings for expressing this unified order and its link to heaven. At the same time, as we have seen, cathedrals powerfully legitimated the powers claimed by the Church and the monarchy alike.

CHAPTER 15

Cathedrals and Community

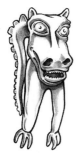Cathedral-building by medieval bishops often threatened the power, economic resources, and social standing of local nobility, fostering conflict, violence, and even murder, as we saw in Chapter 6. But it seems to me that a more powerful and enduring effect of cathedral-building was to bring people together. Durkheim portrays religion as constitutive of community—participating in religious rituals, he claims, makes the social happen. This insight could be extended not only to the religious ceremonies in which worshippers participate directly, but to the act of building a cathedral itself.

Initiating and bringing to completion a project of such scope and magnitude as the building of a Gothic cathedral obviously could not have occurred without having an enormous impact on the community that built it. Inevitably, a grand cathedral became a focus for communal identity on the part of the cathedral chapter responsible for building it. In addition, the process of creating such a building almost certainly generated a renewed and enlarged form (and in certain cases, an entirely new form) of *communitas* among ordinary citizens living in the shadow of the building. A cathedral-building project provided a potentially defining focus, a master narrative, for collective identity among members of the community in which it was built, not unlike the sense of collective pride in achievement that so many Americans felt after the United States placed a man on the moon. Such accomplishments help foster a profound sense of communal efficacy. Building a cathedral entailed an ongoing, difficult, yet energizing form of collective enterprise in which people could take enormous pride and around which they could rally a community.

Salisbury Cathedral affords an example of what I have in mind. Prior to 1220, the official seat of the Bishop of Sarum was situated at the hundred-year-old Norman cathedral inside the hill fortress now called Old Sarum. The cathedral site was too small to expand the building, and access to the cathedral was controlled by the soldiers who guarded the fortress within which it lay. On at least one occasion castle guards barred the bishop and canons of the cathedral chapter from reentering their own cathedral after returning from a religious celebration at nearby Wilton. Such problems eventually led the Bishop of Sarum to petition the king and pope for permission to build a new cathedral on a virgin site on the bishop's own land. The petition was ultimately granted, and work began in 1220. What is interesting here is that the petition made to the king entailed more than just permission to build a new cathedral. Permission was also sought to establish an entirely new municipality, the present-day city of Salisbury, and for a license to hold a weekly market there. In this instance, the new cathedral led to the creation of an entirely new form of *communitas* that quite literally did not exist previously. The entire community was under the exclusive control of the Bishop of Sarum for several hundred years.

The Salisbury story was unique in its details, but it was part of a trend. In the Gothic enterprise that began in 1134, part of the motivation was the interest on the part of bishops throughout Europe to use cathedral-building projects to strengthen the areas they controlled, to challenge kings and feudal lords for dominion over the territories they occupied, and to make the cathedral the centerpiece around which local forms of collective identity became organized. To fulfill this purpose, each building required a style that gave it its own special character. Each diocese required its own unique cathedral building. For this reason, though all cathedrals share certain commonalities in their basic floor plans and component parts, they can vary enormously. Each has its own distinctive personality, what the Dean Emeritus of Salisbury cathedral, Hugh Dickinson, terms its *daimon*, or spirit.

The Gothic cathedral, then, was an instrument for creating, strengthening, and extending forms of *communitas*. Given its vitally important role in this respect, it is interesting to speculate about the consequences of two aspects of cathedral-building projects. One is their sheer audacity, and the other is the great length of time required to complete them. To some extent, the strength and depth of the collective identity that grew during the process of building a Gothic cathedral arose because what was being attempted defied belief. The more impossibly grand the project appeared to be, the more challenging its execution, the more powerful and profound was the resulting sense of collective identity and communal efficacy. Building a Gothic great church was undoubtedly an enormous accomplishment, but in the end they *were* built—the task was not beyond the reach of human possibility. Building a great church mostly took persistence, hard work, and dogged determination over a long period of time. Yet their design suggests that it was important to make the task *seem* more difficult than it actually was, to create the illusion that the building itself defied the laws of nature and had come about through an act of magic. One of the defining qualities of the Gothic style is that it made the doable seem impossible.

Consequently, the communities that built such monuments were themselves strengthened in corresponding measure. One imagines that those who built Gothic cathedrals or monastic abbeys would be pleased to know that future generations who gaze upon them do so with wonder, asking how human beings could possibly have accomplished what they had done. It was this, perhaps, that led to the incessant quest for greater and greater height, for more and more grandeur, for more effective ways of evoking the sense of a divine presence. When people could stand back and proclaim proudly, "We did this. We built this great building," they simultaneously experienced a renewed and heightened sense of the power of their own society. It made them feel strong because they were strong, not least because building such a monument to the divine almost certainly meant that God would be on their side.

We might also imagine that the long time required to build Gothic cathedrals added to the depth of the collective identity they engendered. It almost seemed to serve their purpose that they should not be completed too quickly. It takes time for a collective identity to form, develop, and harden. The knowledge that Canterbury Cathedral, for example, was 365 years in the making is a very important part of the collective identity that has developed around it.

We are accustomed to asking how communities of people managed to build cathedrals, but we can turn the question around and ask how cathedrals built communities. The sheer scale of the undertaking, which engaged generations of people as workers, witnesses and monitors, proponents, and skeptics, for periods of time measured not in decades but in centuries, strengthened existing forms of *communitas* and collective identity, and gave rise to new ones.

Learning from Stonehenge

Our story began with the great cathedral church in Salisbury, England. Eight miles away, at the north end of the Woodford Valley, stands another grand monument, the famous Neolithic stone circle of Stonehenge. When Julia and I lead tours to Salisbury and neighboring cathedrals, we often include a visit to Stonehenge. The more I have learned about Stonehenge, the more I have been struck by the similarities between it and cathedral-building projects.[1]

A good deal of the scholarship about cathedrals on which I have drawn is suffused with discussions of the religious dogmas of the people who built them. The scholarly accounts are rooted in the same tenets of Catholic theology that bishops, kings, abbots, and master masons used to formulate for themselves and explain to others what they were doing. Religious doctrine is clearly important in accounting for the Gothic enterprise, but we may lose a valuable insight if we look only at Christian explanations. Some of the same forms and impulses that lay behind cathedral-building projects are present in Neolithic monuments, which were built thousands of years before Catholic theology existed. Appreciating the similarities, I believe, adds an important comparative dimension to our understanding of Gothic cathedrals.

The Stonehenge monument we see today is a magnificent ruin, a hodgepodge of the remains of three separate building projects. It is customary to refer to these as Stonehenge I, dating to circa 3100 B.C.;

Stonehenge II, dating to circa 2150 B.C.; and Stonehenge III, dating to circa 2100 B.C. Stonehenge III includes three stages (usually designated Stonehenge IIIa, IIIb, and IIIc), which together spanned the 600-year period from 2100 B.C. to 1500 B.C. Today's ruin is therefore an amalgam of building activities that spanned a period of about 1,600 years and ended about 1,500 years before the birth of Christ.

There is also a nearby landmark that some refer to as Stonehenge 0. It was first discovered in 1966 during construction of the present parking lot, which is located about 275 yards from the center of the stone circle. Excavation work uncovered three sockets, each approximately three feet in diameter, containing pine posts (unimaginatively dubbed Posts A, B, and C) and wedges apparently used to keep the posts upright. Radiocarbon dating of the wood in Post A dated it to 8000 B.C. and in Post B to 7000 B.C.! This dating places Stonehenge 0 well back into the Mesolithic period, when an ice cap still covered most of present-day Norway, when the glaciers covering Scotland were just beginning to shrink, and when the Salisbury Plain was covered with coniferous forests. Though little is known about the peoples who populated Salisbury Plain during this period, they probably lived a seminomadic life, roaming the river valleys and forests of the area and living in temporary camps along the banks of the two main rivers, the Avon and the Till.

In addition to Stonehenge 0, the wider environment is densely populated with monumental earthen and stone landmarks—henges, earthen circles, monuments of wood and stone, offering pits, long barrows, round barrows, and processional avenues. Some of these monuments have features that are strikingly analogous to those of Gothic cathedrals: the careful separation of sacred from secular space, the orientation on an east-west axis, processional paths, and the careful use of light.

The separation of sacred from secular space is especially striking. All the monuments in the greater Stonehenge area are configured so as to clearly mark the sacred spaces inside them. Stonehenge III, for example, included a series of stone circles and a

51. *An artist's rendering of Stonehenge III, built c. 2100–*
1500 B.C. The huge sarsen stones with their lintels were
surrounded by rings of bluestones and sarsen stones,
within a circular ditch.

600-foot, embanked entry avenue. One approached and entered the
monument via the avenue at the eastern end of the site. The monument itself was enclosed by a great ring of sarsen stones linked by
connecting lintels (see Figure 51).[2] Within the ring formed by the
outer sarsen stones was an inner ring of bluestones (remnants of
Stonehenge II), and within it, near the center of the monument was
a horseshoe comprising five great, linteled trilithons, four of them
twenty feet high (including lintels), and a main structure, the so-
called Great Trilithon, which extended two feet above the other four.
In front of it stood the Altar Stone, a gigantic slab measuring sixteen feet in length and more than three feet in width. The lintels had
obviously been designed to be exactly horizontal and to rise in tiers
to the monument's focus, the area marked by the Altar Stone and
the Great Trilithon. In addition, the outer and inner rings of stones
appear to mark zones of increasing sacredness as one moves from

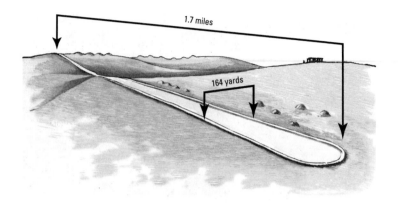

52. *An artist's rendering of the Great Cursus one mile
from Stonehenge, a monumental processional
way built c. 3500–3200 B.C.*

the threshold of the outside world, marked by the extreme eastern
end of the long avenue, down the embanked avenue, into the monument and thence to the Altar Stone.

It is believed that the long avenue was intended as a processional
way, but Stonehenge Avenue was not the only such landmark in
the area. Among the numerous earthen monuments nearby is the
so-called Great Cursus, an excavated space approximately one mile
north of Stonehenge and running on a true east-west axis. Evidence
suggests that it was dug out over the course of a three-hundred-
year period beginning in 3500 B.C., or an estimated three hundred
years before work began on Stonehenge I. This monument has been
called a *cursus,* meaning "movement" or "course," because it is believed that the Great Stonehenge Cursus was created as a long processional way. It was enormous (see Figure 52). Its causeway was
1.7 miles long and 164 yards wide. It was marked by a boundary
ditch on each side that was 10 feet wide and 40 inches deep, and it
had an inner bank on each side that was 40 inches high. (There is
another, smaller processional pathway, the so-called Lesser Cursus, a short distance away. The largest cursus known in the south-

53. *Stonehenge I, c. 3100 B.C., was a simple but massive
circle of earth and chalk designed to reflect moonlight. The
stones for Stonehenge II and III were placed inside the ditch.*

west of England is in the neighboring county of Dorset: it was 6
miles long.)[3]

In design, this Neolithic processional space is strikingly similar
to the great processional spaces of Romanesque and Gothic cathedrals, except, of course, that the latter were roofed. The interiors
of Winchester Cathedral (554 feet long), of Canterbury Cathedral
(540 feet), and of Old St. Paul's in London (600 feet) come to mind
as roofed processional ways reminiscent of the Great Cursus at
Stonehenge. But the cathedrals are only one-fifteenth the length of
the Great Cursus!

Consider also how light was employed at Stonehenge. Stonehenge I, begun in about 3100 B.C., was a henge monument, marked
off from the immediate area by a surrounding ditch (see Figure 53).
Stonehenge I was 377 feet in diameter—so large that Hereford

Cathedral could have fit inside the ditch.[4] Stonehenge I was laid out at the same time that the famous Avebury stone circle was being built about twelve miles to the north. (Avebury was the preeminent ceremonial building project of the day in that area. It was four times larger in diameter than Stonehenge I and created of enormous stones placed within its massive ditches and banks.)

In creating Stonehenge I, the first step was to erect a central post, extend a rope or vine sixty yards in length from it, and walk the rope around a 360-degree arc to mark out a circle (excavations have located some of the estimated fifty or sixty post holes that were dug to establish the circle). The rope was then extended roughly another sixteen feet, and the process was repeated, marking out a perimeter ring with an inner and outer boundary. The turf between the two rings was scraped off and neatly stacked to form an embankment outside the outer perimeter. The builders then dug out the topsoil underneath the sod and piled it on the sod to create a low outer bank, estimated to be twenty inches high. All of this work was done with antler picks by men and women who at the same time had to engage in agriculture, home building, hunting, fishing, and other tasks essential to daily survival.

The Salisbury Plain is a great bed of chalk covered with a thin layer of turf and topsoil. Once the Stonehenge people had dug down to the chalk, which lies no more than six to eight inches below the surface, they began to pile it on the inside of the circle. They continued to dig until they had created a ditch twenty feet across and several feet deep. The chalk they had dug out was used to form an inner bank of pure chalk five feet high. This construction indicates an intention to create a monument formed by a higher inner bank of pure white chalk, surrounded by a wide ditch that would also have been white, enclosed by a smaller bank of darker turf and topsoil. Given the location of Stonehenge on the Salisbury Plain, it would have stood out brilliantly on the horizon when seen from a distance, and acted as a reflector and intensifier of light from the moon and the sun, which shone directly into the monument's center.

Light was clearly important in later versions of Stonehenge as well. For example, the inner surfaces of the sarsen stones that formed the outer ring of Stonehenge III, as well as the surfaces of the great trilithons that marked the inner sanctum, were treated with gypsum to make them glow. Clearly, in addition to its presumed astronomical function, the monument was always designed to draw light to it and amplify it, an intention that later was central to the design of Gothic great churches.

Careful thought also went into achieving the directional orientation of all three Stonehenge monuments. This is illustrated by the positioning of Stonehenge I, which is astonishingly precise. Its main entrance was at the northeast, where there was a wide gap in the ditch and circle. Studies of the monument's position indicate that it was painstakingly oriented to the moon. A series of post holes have been found at the entrance, dug before the excavation work I have just described was ever begun. These post holes exactly correspond to the position of the rising moon on the horizon as seen from the center of the circle. The rising moon follows an arc along the horizon, progressing from the extreme southeast to the extreme northeast and back again, in a cycle that takes 18.6 years. Rows of post holes mark the northernmost rising of the moon on the horizon for each year of the cycle, and there is not one row of postholes, but six. This suggests that Stonehenge people had been tracking the moonrise for 112 years—five or six generations—before work on digging the monument ever began! Even today it is difficult to imagine such a precise and sophisticated level of planning.[5]

Then there is the sheer effort required. Rodney Castleden provides a useful metric for comprehending its magnitude. Using data from modern studies of the productivity of workers using Neolithic tools—antler picks and shoulderblade shovels—he estimates the volume of soil and chalk a single worker could dig and carry in an hour. He then translates this measurement into an estimate of productivity per eight-hour shift, posits a workforce of twenty people, and calculates how much work would be required to build a given earthen monument if a hypothetical crew of twenty people worked eight hours a day, seven days a week, all year. Obviously, such a

54. *Stonehenge II, c. 2150 B.C., seems to have been planned as a ring of bluestones. Before it could be completed, the stones were moved away to bring in the sarsen stones that became Stonehenge III.*

concentrated effort would not have been possible, but Castleden's estimate gives us a way of comparing the amount of physical effort that would have been required to build these large monuments. Applying this hypothetical metric to the Great Cursus at Stonehenge, Castleden estimates that it would have taken his typical work crew 21.4 years of continuous, uninterrupted work to dig it. The archaeological evidence suggests that the work was actually spread out over three hundred years, from circa 3500 B.C. to 3200 B.C.[6]

The magnitude of the effort involved in building Stonehenge and the degree of forethought required are further illustrated by considering the problem of transporting the stones used to create Stonehenge II, begun circa 2150 B.C. (see Figure 54). If Stonehenge II had been built according to its original design (fifty years into the

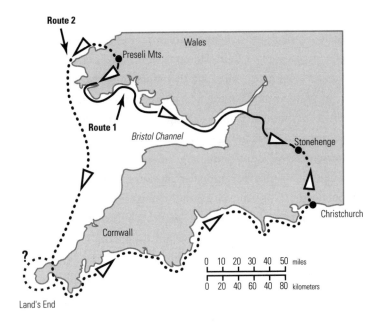

Map 2. *Possible routes for transporting the four-ton bluestones from Wales to Stonehenge, c. 2150 B.C*

project it was disassembled to change the design to Stonehenge III), it would have required a total of 125 large bluestones—82 upright, 42 lintels, and 1 immense Altar Stone. In all, 85 bluestones were actually brought to the site, weighing an average of 8,750 pounds. The mystery about these stones is that they came from the Preseli Mountains of western Wales, some 135 miles as the crow flies from Stonehenge (see Map 2). No one knows how the Stonehenge people even knew they were there, much less how they organized the vast effort involved in transporting them. To get them from Wales to Wiltshire, they must have used a combination of land portage and water transport.

Castleden hypothesizes that one of two routes was probably followed. The first one has the stones portaged off the Preseli Mountains, where large pieces of bluestone lay on the surface of the mountains, to the nearest river, then floated on lashed-together canoes along the Bristol Channel and up a series of rivers to a point near the present city of Bath. Here the stones were again portaged over land for about 5.5 miles and then floated up two more rivers to the present town of Amesbury, where they were unloaded and carted across the final 2 miles of downs to the monument site. A second route has them going by water from near the Preseli Mountains around Land's End and along the south coast of England to Christchurch, up the river Avon to Amesbury, and thence overland to Stonehenge. This route is 400 miles longer than the first and includes floating the stones in small craft through some of the most treacherous waters on the south coast of England.[7]

Experts continue to argue over which route was the likely one. I have traced out both routes on survey maps, and I can only say that either one boggles the mind. A recent demonstration project, organized by adventurers who tried to follow the first route, got a short distance out into the Bristol Channel when a strong wind blew up. They attempted to turn back but capsized, and the stone they had lifted off the top of the Preseli Mountains sank to the bottom of the channel, where it now rests.

The planning and effort involved in creating Stonehenge are also evident when we consider the sarsen stones that were used to build the trilithons of Stonehenge III. These came from the Overton Downs, an open-field quarry adjacent to Avebury, some eighteen miles north of Stonehenge. In all, there were forty such stones (not including lintels). The thirty smaller stones that formed the outer ring stood fourteen feet high. Eight larger stones, with lintels attached, towered twenty feet above ground and formed the three sides of the horseshoe-shaped inner sanctum. The Great Trilithon, twenty-two feet tall, rose eight feet above the tops of the lintels of the outer ring. The largest of these stones was thirty feet long and weighed almost twenty-nine tons.

No one knows for certain how the Stonehenge people transported these behemoths to the monument site. No river or sea route con-

nects Avebury to Stonehenge, so the route must have been overland, using sledges. (Wheels could not have been used, because
without iron or bronze bearings they would have broken apart under the extreme weight. It is also unlikely that wooden rollers could
have been used, because of the uneven terrain.) Three routes have
been postulated, and each one would have required hauling the
stones up hills and maneuvering them through narrow passes. Rodney Castleden favors a route that involves hauling the stones up one
very steep hill. He estimates that it would take the combined strength
of a hundred oxen to manage the climb, but he leaves unexplained
how teams of this size could have been assembled and harnessed
together to pull in a single coordinated manner.[8]

Other aspects of the construction also entailed feats of human
engineering that are beyond our comprehension. You may have
heard the most common questions: How were the stones lifted into
upright position and placed so precisely? How were the lintels,
which weighed several tons, lifted twenty feet off the ground and
set in place? By comparison, building Salisbury Cathedral seems
simple.

Stonehenge and Salisbury Cathedral provoke our wonder. Why,
we may ask, were these great monuments built? How can we explain
the affinity that the builders of both had for light and for processional
ways? What compelled peoples whose lives were separated by five
thousand years to undertake the extraordinary feats of planning,
resource mobilization, and engineering that both projects involved?
What is it about harsh and unforgiving conditions that leads people
who, to an outsider, seem least able to undertake such efforts not only
to launch them but to see them through? Answers to these questions
continue to elude us, but in concluding I would like to offer one or
two insights into where the answers might lie. Both reflect themes
to which we have returned repeatedly.

Archeological studies of Stonehenge indicate that the first earthen
monuments began to appear in the area during the fourth millennium B.C. Their appearance coincides with changes that were tak-

ing place in the basic way of life of the peoples inhabiting the Salisbury Plain. Beginning in about 4500 B.C., evidence suggests that Stonehenge peoples, previously seminomadic, began to clear the land for pasturing cattle and swine. Herding would have required a more settled and organized existence, including cultivating crops for fodder and human food. One hypothesis is that cultivating crops forced a heightened awareness of the annual rhythms of the agricultural cycle: planting, tending, and harvesting grains and vegetables; dormancy; and then another cycle of planting.

Clearing the forests for agriculture probably had an immediate and devastating consequence. In his study of Stonehenge, Castleden cites findings from a recent Danish experiment in forest clearing that was conducted in an attempt to imitate the conditions and practices of the Neolithic period. The researchers found that once forests had been cleared and crops of native wheat planted, the crop yield fell so rapidly that by the third year, planting was no longer worthwhile. The combination of soil exhaustion from successive planting cycles and soil erosion caused by tree clearing laid waste the landscape.[9]

I suggest that the landmark monuments that are scattered around the Stonehenge area, many of which were built to track the movement of the sun and the moon, came into existence in connection with this devastation. It is almost as if the impulse to build them were born of a desperate attempt to appease the forces of nature emanating from the sun and the moon, drawing them, as people during the medieval period tried to do, down into the tribal midst where they could be worshipped and transformed into friendly allies. Castleden makes this point when he writes, "The first farmers would not have understood what was happening in ecological terms and understandably resorted to religion to help them out. . . . Each successive monument in the Stonehenge landscape can be seen as a new cry for help."[10]

My second point is related to the first. When we consider human existence during the Neolithic period, we are struck by a feature of it that sets it apart from life as we know it today. In modern Western culture, individuals are embedded in a dense network of social institutions that protect and buffer us in ways that are often so effective that we scarcely notice them. Institutions of health care can prevent and cure illnesses, relieve pain and suffering, and restore and maintain health. Legal institutions provide us with some recourse to justice. Civic institutions such as the police, firefighters, public health workers, sanitation workers, and agencies responsible for protecting the quality of our drinking water, our food supply, and our air, all help to maintain a relatively problem-free existence. In the modern world, we are largely protected from harm, and we can dial 911 when we need to be rescued.

The Neolithic and medieval periods of history we have been discussing had no 911 number to dial. The core institutions of those societies were, by modern standards, underdeveloped, nonexistent, or powerless to protect their members. About all that stood between people and chaos was their culture. The culture embodied and celebrated beliefs that imparted to everyday life a sense of order, safety, and certainty that it otherwise lacked, and this culture also transmitted the knowledge necessary to manage and survive day by day from one generation to the next.

Because culture made human existence possible and tolerable, because a people's sole source of protection and security was shared beliefs, it became important to make this system appear larger than life itself. Making *communitas* appear powerful and efficacious was a way of reassuring people that they did not stand alone against the terrifying forces of nature and the difficult conditions of human life. Planning and executing incredible feats of construction is a tangible way of empowering the culture that protects us. Mundane activities can never compete, because they are too easily taken for granted or dismissed as unexceptional or ordinary. A Stonehenge, a pyramid of Giza, or a magnificent Gothic cathedral cannot be disregarded in the same way. All three evoke in us the same sense of amazement and awe that ordinary people using ordinary materials could have built them.

In the end, the question with which we began—How ever did

they do that?—expresses one of the most important reasons for building a Gothic cathedral in the first place. It is there to make a profound statement about the power of the community and the constituent institutions out of which it grew. Happily for us, though the buildings may deteriorate and crumble, these feelings remain as alive today as they were then. They link us to earlier generations who were trying to cope with the same enduring existential questions that we and future generations will always need to face.

Terminology

Throughout I have used the word *cathedral* to refer to what are in fact different kinds of ecclesiastical buildings, some of them cathedrals, others not. I did so on the advice of readers and editors who felt that consistent usage of the strictly accurate terms for different types of buildings would prove cumbersome and confusing. Here I explain briefly the distinctions among the different types of ecclesiastical buildings that are mentioned in the text.

As indicated in Chapter 1, the cathedral is the seat of the bishop, who is charged with the care of souls within a designated territory termed a *diocese*. Originally, the Greek term *ecclesia* was used to denote all places of worship. It meant simply an "assembly of the faithful." As churches grew in size and power, it became necessary to find a term to distinguish the church that belonged to a bishop from other churches of the diocese. The Latin word *cathedra*, meaning "the bishop's throne," was used. *Cathedra* became *cathedralis*, and then *cathedral church*, and this phrase was ultimately shortened to the familiar *cathedral*.

Over the course of history, cathedrals grew in size from single buildings to whole complexes of buildings that included not only a great church but the bishop's palace *(domus episcopi)*, a place dedicated to charity, termed a *hospice*, and other buildings as well. This evolution occurred partly because, from the sixth century onward, monarchies grew weaker and thus less able to fulfill basic civic and administrative responsibilities. The only other municipal or regional force capable of fulfilling these duties was the bishopric. Consequently, bishops acquired more and more power over civic affairs, and as this happened the size and complexity of cathedral compounds grew.

Initially, a cathedral was served and administered by bishops and their entourages, or households, but over time this responsibility was delegated to a separate body of clergy, the *cathedral chapter*. In most cases, this body was headed by a *dean*, who in turn directed a body of resident *canons*. Cathedral chapters were of two types: some were *monastic* and others were *secular*. Members of monastic orders (examples were Canterbury and Winchester) were required to live within a closed community and follow a strict rule of daily worship. Secular orders (Salisbury for example), were organized differently. Most secular orders had two ranks of canons: "canons regular," who followed the same order of daily worship as members of monastic communities, and "secular canons," who were not obligated to follow the same strict rules of daily worship. Though responsible for the maintenance of cathedral services for certain periods of time during the year, secular canons often lived on estates associated with *prebends*, which were grants of land controlled by bishops and awarded to canons at the time of their appointment as members of the chapter.

Distinctions also arose among cathedral churches of different ranks, their standing dependent on whether they were home to a single diocesan *bishop* (as at Salisbury or Wells), an *archbishop* (as at York or Canterbury), or a *primate* (the pope). Additional distinctions, which we need not explore here, emerged among various kinds of religious units, which further cross-cut, subdivided, and differentiated the basic cathedral unit I have described.

In contrast to cathedrals, *parish churches* were places where ordinary people went to worship. Each parish was served by a pastor or *priest*, based at the local parish church, who served as the link between ordinary parishioners and the diocesan bishop. Though diocesan parishioners occasionally visited cathedrals to attend special services or to venerate shrines, they did not (indeed in some cases, were not permitted to) worship there regularly. Rather, cathedrals were meant to provide settings for the performance of liturgy by the resident canons. The program of liturgy included the daily office, celebration of masses, special feast days, and other occasions.

A second main type of ecclesiastical great church was the monastic church, or *abbey*. An abbey is a group of buildings housing a monastery or convent, centered on an abbey church and under the direction of an *abbot* or *abbess*. In effect, the abbey is the seat of an abbot, the title given to the leader of a religious house belonging to an established religious order. Familiar examples of monastic orders are the Cluniacs, the Benedictines, and the Cistercians, and familiar examples of monastic churches include Bath Abbey, Westminster Abbey, Fountains Abbey, Romsey Abbey, and Glastonbury Abbey in England, and Mont-Saint-Michel and the Abbey Church of St. Denis in France.

An abbey is the home of a religious community dedicated to a life of greater Christian perfection and set apart from the profane world. An *abbey mother church* is in effect the headquarters of a given monastic order, and an ordinary abbey church is an affiliate of the mother church. A *priory* is a spin-off of an abbey, on which it remains dependent, and is known as a *daughter church*. Some priories evolved into abbeys. The head of a priory is called a *prior* or *prioress*, that is, a monk or nun deputized by an abbot to head one of these smaller outposts. Cathedrals and abbey churches were designed, built, and used as settings for the enactment of *liturgy*, the formal worship of God through strict adherence to a daily round of prayers and meditations by duly ordained members of clergy.

Notes

INTRODUCTION: *A Personal Journey*

1. Clifford Geertz, *The Interpretation of Culture*, 50–53.
2. Samuel Johnson, *The Letters of Samuel Johnson*, ed. R. W. Chapman, vol. 3, *1783–1784, Letters 821.2–1174*, 892.
3. For details about the surviving records of Salisbury Cathedral, see Pamela Blum, "The Sequence of the Building Campaigns at Salisbury"; Thomas Cocke, "Historical Summary"; Kathleen Edwards, *Salisbury Cathedral: An Ecclesiastical History;* Peter Kidson, "The Historical Circumstances and the Principles of the Design"; Roy Spring, *Salisbury Cathedral: The New Bell's Cathedral Guides;* and Tim Tatton-Brown, *Great Cathedrals of Britain.*

CHAPTER 1: *What Is the Gothic Enterprise?*

1. Jean Gimpel, *The Cathedral Builders*, 1; Richard Morris, *Cathedrals and Abbeys of England and Wales: The Building Church, 600–1540*, 1.
2. See Christopher Wilson, *The Gothic Cathedral*, 13.
3. Regarding the reception of the new style, see Robert Branner, *Gothic Architecture;* Georges Duby, *The Age of the Cathedrals;* Morris, *Cathedrals and Abbeys of England and Wales;* Tim Tatton-Brown, *Great Cathedrals of Britain;* Wim Swaan, *The Gothic Cathedral;* Wilson, *Gothic Cathedral.*
4. For further information about cathedral-building in England, see Branner, *Gothic Architecture*, 31–35; Tatton-Brown, *Great Cathedrals of Britain;* Swann, *Gothic Cathedral*, 173–222; Wilson, *Gothic Cathedral*, 72–90, 160–88, 204–23.
5. For materials about cathedral-building in Germany, see Branner, *Gothic Architecture*, 35–38; Virginia Jansen, "Gothic Art and Architecture," 274–78; Norbert Nussbaum, *German Gothic Church Architecture;* Swaan, *Gothic Cathedral*, 225–56; Wilson, *Gothic Cathedral*, 145–56.

6. For materials about cathedral-building in Italy, see Branner, *Gothic Architecture*, 42–44; Swaan, *Gothic Cathedral*, 289–315; Wilson, *Gothic Cathedral*, 258–76.

7. For materials about cathedral-building in Spain, see Branner, *Gothic Architecture*, 38–42; Swaan, *Gothic Cathedral*, 259–86; Wilson, *Gothic Cathedral*, 157–59, 276–91.

8. See Paul Frankl, *Sources from the Gothic Period*, 217–25.

CHAPTER 2: *How Were the Cathedrals Built?*

1. Among several outstanding fictional accounts of cathedral-building that I recommend, a personal favorite is Ken Follett's *Pillars of the Earth* (1990), a highly readable account of a fictional project that reflects the author's superb technical knowledge. For an excellent fictional account of the building of Salisbury Cathedral, see Edmund Rutherford's *Sarum* (1988: 433–560). William Golding's *The Spire* (1964) is a novel about the Salisbury tower and spire.

2. For further details about the building of Salisbury Cathedral, see Pamela Blum, "The Sequence of the Building Campaigns at Salisbury"; Thomas Cocke, "Historical Summary"; Kathleen Edwards, *Salisbury Cathedral;* Peter Kidson, "The Historical Circumstances and the Principles of the Design"; Roy Spring, *Salisbury Cathedral;* and Tim Tatton-Brown, *Great Cathedrals of Britain.*

3. This comment is part of Roy Spring's lectures delivered to our travel-study groups in Salisbury (most recently in July, 2001).

4. See Spring, *Salisbury Cathedral*, 14.

5. L. F. Salzman, *Building in England Down to 1540*, 119.

6. Ibid., 119–20.

7. See Douglas Knoop and G. P. Jones, "The First Three Years of the Building of Vale Royal Abbey, 1278–1280."

8. See Jean Gimpel, *The Cathedral Builders*, 69; and Knoop and Jones, "Building of Vale Royal Abbey, 1278–1280."

9. See Spring, *Salisbury Cathedral*, 14.

10. This information is from Roy Spring's lectures delivered to our travel-study groups in Salisbury (July, 2001).

11. See Spring, *Salisbury Cathedral*, 14.

12. For an analysis of the workforce of a similar building site, Westminster Abbey in 1253, see Richard Jones, "Gleanings from the 1253 Building Accounts of Westminster Abbey," 19.

13. Richard Morris, *Cathedrals and Abbeys of England and Wales*, 113.

14. Robert Willis, *The architectural history of Chichester cathedral*, xvi.

15. Ibid., xvii–xviii.

16. See Jones, "Gleanings."

17. Ibid., 19, 23–24.

18. Knoop and Jones, "Building of Vale Royal Abbey, 1278–1280," 15.

19. Knoop and Jones, "The Impressment of Masons in the Middle Ages."

20. See Jones, "Gleanings," 19; Jean Gimpel, *The Cathedral Builders,* 59–75; Knoop and Jones, "Building of Vale Royal Abbey, 1278–1280," 37; Spring's lectures (July, 2001); Knoop and Jones, "The English Medieval Quarry."

21. Knoop and Jones, *The Medieval Mason,* 129–41.

22. Gimpel, *Cathedral Builders,* 66.

23. See Jones, "Gleanings," 17; Salzman, *Building in England,* 68–72; and Knoop and Jones, "Building of Vale Royal Abbey, 1278–1280," 18.

24. See Knoop and Jones, "Building of Vale Royal Abbey, 1278–1280," 27–29, and *Medieval Mason,* 142–44.

25. See Christopher Dyer, *Standards of Living in the Later Middle Ages,* 109–187.

26. Gimpel, *Cathedral Builders,* 41; and Jones, "Gleanings."

27. See Gimpel, *Cathedral Builders,* 54; Knoop and Jones, "Building of Vale Royal Abbey, 1278–1280," 23–25, 110–11, 235–37. For an exhaustive study of medieval currency, see Peter Spufford, *Money and Its Uses in Medieval Europe.* For additional details about the workforce, see H. M. Colvin, ed., *The History of the King's Works,* vol. 1, *The Middle Ages;* John Fitchen, *The Construction of Gothic Cathedrals;* Gimpel, *Cathedral Builders;* John James, *The Contractors of Chartres,* vol. 2; Knoop and Jones, "Building of Vale Royal Abbey, 1278–1280"; Stephen Murray, *Building Troyes Cathedral,* as well as his *Beauvais Cathedral,* and *Notre-Dame, Cathedral of Amiens;* Salzman, *Building in England;* Swaan, *Gothic Cathedral;* and Tatton-Brown, *Great Cathedrals of Britain.*

28. James Boyd, "Construction Dates for Gothic Cathedrals and Great Churches (1135–1550)."

29. For further information on the population of England during this period, see Dyer, *Standards of Living in the Later Middle Ages,* 4–6; Josiah Russell, *British Medieval Population,* 173–234, and "Population in Europe, 500–1500."

CHAPTER 3: *Kings, Feudal Lords, and Great Monasteries*

1. The quotation is from Georges Duby, *The Age of the Cathedrals,* 10. See also Malcolm Barber, *The Two Cities,* 24–25; Duby, *Early Growth of the European Economy,* 49, as well as *The Three Orders,* 17–18, and *The Age of the Cathedrals,* 11, 30.

2. Duby, *Early Growth of the European Economy*, 49.

3. The quotation is from Duby, *Age of the Cathedrals*, 12; see also pp. 50–51, and his *Three Orders*, 10–12.

4. See Duby, *Age of the Cathedrals*, 10–11, and *Three Orders*, 58.

5. See Duby, *Early Growth of the European Economy*, 52, and *Age of the Cathedrals*, 11, 22.

6. See Duby, *Early Growth of the European Economy*, 53–55, and *Three Orders*, 58; see also Keith Thomas, *Religion and the Decline of Magic*, 25–50.

7. Duby, *Early Growth of the European Economy*, 54.

8. Ibid., 110.

9. Duby, *Three Orders*, 150–51, and *Early Growth of the European Economy*, 161. For an account of France during this period, see Georges Duby, *France in the Middle Ages, 987–1460*, 43–152.

10. Duby, *Early Growth of the European Economy*, 162, and *Three Orders*, 141, 150–66.

11. Duby, *Early Growth of the European Economy*, 162, and *Three Orders*, 141, 150–66.

12. Duby, *Early Growth of the European Economy*, 162–64, and *Three Orders*, 21–43, 128, 134–39.

13. Jonathan Sumption, *The Albigensian Crusade*, 116; Stephen O'Shea, *The Perfect Heresy*, 112–13; Robert Bartlett, *The Making of Europe*, 60–64; Duby, *Early Growth of the European Economy*, 167.

14. Duby, *Early Growth of the European Economy*, 167.

15. Thomas Beaumont James, *The Palaces of Medieval England*, 85–86.

16. Duby, *Three Orders*, 59–60; Peter Speed, *Those Who Worked*.

17. For a discussion of the monastic movement, see Barber, *Two Cities*, 141–67; C. H. Lawrence, *Medieval Monasticism;* Brian Tierney, *The Crises of Church and State, 1050–1300*, 24–32; Gerd Tellenbach, *The Church in Western Europe from the Tenth to the Early Twelfth Century*, 101–21; and Stephen Tobin, *The Cistercians*. For a superb fictional account of the building of a Cistercian Abbey, see Fernand Pouillon, *The Stones of the Abbey*.

18. Duby, *Three Orders*, 174, and *Age of the Cathedrals*, 47.

19. Duby, *Three Orders*, 201–5, and *Age of the Cathedrals*, 66; see also Patrick Geary, *Living with the Dead in the Middle Ages*, 77–92.

20. Duby, *Early Growth of the European Economy*, 178–80, 222–23.

21. For information about one such innovation, the plow, see Bartlett, *Making of Europe*, 148–56.

22. Duby, *Early Growth of the European Economy*, 232–70.

23. Ibid., 216–17, 236–39.

24. Bartlett, *Making of Europe*, 280–88; Duby, *Early Growth of the European Economy*, 260–61; Edward Miller and John Hatcher, *Medieval England: Towns, Commerce and Crafts*, 255–322.

25. See Miller and Hatcher, *Medieval England: Towns, Commerce and Crafts*.

26. Duby, *Early Growth of the European Economy*, 244–88.

CHAPTER 4: *The Age of Cathedral-Building*

1. Georges Duby, *The Early Growth of the European Economy*, 216.

2. For materials about the various movements associated with monasticism, see Malcolm Barber, *The Two Cities*, 141–67; Robert Bartlett, *The Making of Europe*, 153–55, 227–29, 255–60; Duby, *Early Growth of the European Economy*, 166; Gerd Tellenbach, *The Church in Western Europe from the Tenth to the Early Twelfth Century*, 101–21.

3. Duby, *The Age of the Cathedrals*, 140–41.

4. Ibid., 157.

5. Barber, *Two Cities*, 183–89; Duby, *The Three Orders*, 130–33, 138, and *Age of the Cathedrals*, 96, 131–35; Stephen O'Shea, *The Perfect Heresy;* Jonathan Sumption, *The Albigensian Crusade*, 15–31.

6. For more about Eleanor of Aquitaine, see Alison Weir, *Eleanor of Aquitaine: By the Wrath of God, Queen of England;* and Duby, *Age of the Cathedrals*, 96.

7. Duby, *Age of the Cathedrals*, 137.

8. Sumption, *Albigensian Crusade*, 43–62; Duby, *Age of the Cathedrals*, 136–46.

9. See O'Shea, *Perfect Heresy*, 75–87 (quotation is on 84); see also Sumption, *Albigensian Crusade*, 90–93.

10. O'Shea, *Perfect Heresy*, 106; Sumption, *Albigensian Crusade*, 111.

11. O'Shea, *Perfect Heresy*, 191–200; Sumption, *Albigensian Crusade*, 226–43.

12. See especially Duby, *Age of the Cathedrals*, 144; see also Sumption, *Albigensian Crusade*, 226–43; and O'Shea, *Perfect Heresy*, 191–200.

13. Duby, *Three Orders*, 145–60; *Age of the Cathedrals*, 97–135.

14. Duby, *Age of the Cathedrals*, 135.

CHAPTER 5: *The Initial Vision*

1. For accounts that assign Suger a leading role in inventing Gothic architecture, see Otto von Simson, *The Gothic Cathedral: Origins of Gothic Architecture and the Medieval Concept of Order;* and Erwin Panofsky, *Abbot Suger: On the Abbey Church of St.-Denis and Its Art Treasures*. For an account that assigns him a more modest role, see Lindy Grant, *Abbot Suger of St.-Denis: Church and State in Early Twelfth-Century France*.

2. See *The New Encyclopedia Britannica*, 15th ed., s.v. "Denis, Saint."
3. See Sumner McKnight Crosby, *The Royal Abbey of Saint-Denis*, 113.
4. For a biography of Abbot Suger, see Grant, *Abbot Suger of St.-Denis*.
5. Ibid., 50.
6. See von Simson, *Gothic Cathedral*, 66.
7. See Uta-Renate Blumenthal, *The Investiture Controversy: Church and Monarchy from the Ninth to the Twelfth Century*.
8. For the history of this conflict, see von Simson, *Gothic Cathedral*, 61–90.
9. The two points of view are presented by von Simson and Panofsky, and by Grant (see note 1 above).
10. The quotation is from von Simson, *Gothic Cathedral*, 70; see also 71.
11. Again, the contrasting views are presented by von Simson and Panofsky, and by Grant (see note 1 above).
12. Quoted in Panofsky, *Abbot Suger*, 2.
13. See Gabrielle Spiegel, *The Chronicle Tradition of Saint-Denis*, 11.
14. Ibid., 45.
15. Von Simson, *Gothic Cathedral*, 133; see also Georges Duby, *The Age of the Cathedrals*, 99–135.
16. Von Simson, *Gothic Cathedral*, 79.
17. Suger is quoted in Panofsky, *Abbot Suger*, 6; see also Charles Radding and William Clark, *Medieval Architecture, Medieval Learning*, 64; Jean Gimpel, *The Cathedral Builders*, 17.
18. Von Simson, *Gothic Cathedral*, 136.
19. Duby, *Age of the Cathedrals*, 99.
20. Quoted in Panofsky, *Abbot Suger*, 113.
21. Quoted in von Simson, *Gothic Cathedral*, 139.

CHAPTER 6: *"The Cathedral Crusade"*

1. Christopher Wilson, *The Gothic Cathedral*, 44.
2. For details, see Robert Branner, *Gothic Architecture;* Georges Duby, *The Age of the Cathedrals;* Ian Dunlop, *The Cathedrals' Crusade: The Rise of the Gothic Style in France;* Paul Frankl, *Sources from the Gothic Period*, and *Gothic Architecture;* Wilson, *Gothic Cathedral*. For an excellent account of English cathedrals specifically, see Tim Tatton-Brown, *Great Cathedrals of Britain*.
3. Martin Warnke, *Bau und Überbau;* Dunlop, *Cathedrals' Crusade*.
4. Duby, *Age of the Cathedrals*, 111.
5. Quoted in Dunlop, *Cathedrals' Crusade*, 137.
6. Dunlop, *Cathedrals' Crusade*, 138.
7. Quoted in ibid., 6.

8. Quoted in Gimpel, *The Cathedral Builders*, 11.

9. Barbara Abou-El-Haj, *The Medieval Cult of Saints*, 20.

10. Ibid.

11. See John Scott and John Ward, *The Vézelay Chronicle*.

12. See Stephen Murray, *Beauvais Cathedral*, 25, 49–50, and *Building Troyes Cathedral: The Late Gothic Campaigns*, 11.

13. Jane Williams, *Bread, Wine, and Money*.

CHAPTER 7: *What Is the Gothic Look?*

1. Otto von Simson, *The Gothic Cathedral: Origins of Gothic Architecture and the Medieval Concept of Order*, 144.

2. Stephen Murray, *Notre-Dame, Cathedral of Amiens: The Power of Change in Gothic*, 40–41.

3. Victor Hugo, *Notre-Dame of Paris*, 124.

4. Erwin Panofsky, *Gothic Architecture and Scholasticism*, 48.

5. For information on different kinds of arches, see Jean Bony, *French Gothic Architecture of the Twelfth and Thirteenth Centuries*, 17–21; John Fitchen, *The Construction of Gothic Cathedrals*, 78–80; J. E. Gordon, *Structures*, 171–97; Mario Salvadori, *Why Buildings Stand Up*, 213.

6. Bony, *French Gothic Architecture*, 17.

7. Paul Frankl, *Gothic Architecture*, 3.

8. See Paul Frankl, *Sources from the Gothic Period*.

9. See Frankl, *Sources from the Gothic Period*, and *Gothic Architecture*, 218.

10. Von Simson, *Gothic Cathedral*, 5.

CHAPTER 8: *An Image of Heaven*

1. Otto von Simson, *The Gothic Cathedral*, xix.

2. Ibid., 8.

3. Ibid., cited at 28.

4. Ibid., cited at 24–26.

5. Ibid., quoted on 23.

6. Ibid., as explained at 23.

7. Ibid.

8. Christopher Wilson, *The Gothic Cathedral*, 268–76.

9. See von Simson, *Gothic Cathedral*, 21–22.

10. See Lindy Grant, *Abbot Suger of St.-Denis: Church and State in Early Twelfth-Century France;* Erwin Panofsky, *Gothic Architecture and Scholasticism;* Charles Radding and William Clark, *Medieval Architecture, Medieval Learning: Builders and Masters in the Age of Romanesque and Gothic*, 58–61.

11. Panofsky, *Gothic Architecture and Scholasticism*, 28–29.
12. Ibid.; see also Radding and Clark, *Medieval Architecture*.
13. Panofsky, *Gothic Architecture and Scholasticism*, 32.
14. Ibid., 44–45.
15. Ibid., 454–46.
16. Paul Frankl, *Gothic Architecture*, 220–25.
17. For information on Dionysius the Areopagite, see von Simson, *Gothic Cathedral*, 52–53.
18. Georges Duby, *The Age of the Cathedrals*, 99–100.

CHAPTER 9: *A Pragmatic View of Cathedral-Building*

1. A. Richard Jones, "Gleanings from the 1253 Building Accounts of Westminster Abbey," 17.
2. See L. F. Salzman, *Building in England Down to 1540: A Documentary History*, 303–44; Jean Gimpel, *The Cathedral Builders*, 77–78; John James, *The Contractors of Chartres*, 2 vols., and "An Investigation into the Uneven Distribution of Early Gothic Churches in the Paris Basin, 1140–1240."
3. Stephen Murray, *Building Troyes Cathedral*.
4. Cecil Roth, *A History of Jews in England;* see also David Nirenberg, *Communities of Violence*.
5. Douglas Knoop and G. P. Jones, "The First Three Years of the Building of Vale Royal Abbey, 1278–1280."
6. Herbert A. Simon, "The Architecture of Complexity."
7. Erwin Panofsky, *Gothic Architecture and Scholasticism*, 46–47.

CHAPTER 10: *Sacred Force and Sacred Space*

1. See *The Oxford English Dictionary*, 2d ed., s.v. "sacred." See also Pascal Boyer, *Religion Explained;* H. Knoblauch, "Phenomenology of Religion," 13093–96, esp. 13094; Mircea Eliade, *Patterns in Comparative Religion;* and Victor Turner and Edith Turner, *Image and Pilgrimage in Christian Culture*.
2. David Freedberg, *The Power of Images: Studies in the History and Theory of Response*, 85–86.
3. Ronald C. Finucane, *Miracles and Pilgrims: Popular Beliefs in Medieval England*, 1–38.
4. Émile Durkheim, *The Elementary Forms of Religious Life*, 418.
5. Ibid.
6. Ibid.
7. John Sallis, *Stone*, 26.
8. Quoted in Georges Duby, *The Age of the Cathedrals*, 98.

9. See Sallis, *Stone*, 32–79.

10. Quoted in Duby, *Age of the Cathedrals*, 122–23.

11. Ibid.; quotation at 98.

12. See Otto von Simson, *The Gothic Cathedral*, 109–15.

13. William Mahrt, unpublished lecture, "Sacred Space, Sacred Time, and Music in the Processions of the Sarum Rite," delivered to our seminars and travel study groups, most recently in July, 2001.

14. See von Simson, *Gothic Cathedral*, 160–64.

15. Patrick Geary, *Furta Sacra: Thefts of Relics in the Central Middle Ages*, xii–xiii, 14, 32–35, 44–45, 56–63, 65.

16. See John Harper, *The Forms and Orders of Western Liturgy from the Tenth to the Eighteenth Century*, 45–57.

17. Ibid., 5–17, 121–50.

18. For discussions of the *Ordinal* and the *Customary*, respectively, see Harper, *Forms and Orders of Western Liturgy*, 206–7, 227–29, 231–32; and 168, 197–98.

19. The description of this procession is provided by William Mahrt in his lectures on music and liturgy, and is based on his research into the *Sarum Use*, the medieval liturgy of Salisbury. See also Harper, *Forms and Orders of Western Liturgy*, 128, 139–140.

20. See Durkheim, *The Elementary Forms of Religious Life*.

CHAPTER 11: *Imagining the Cathedral*

1. Frances A. Yates, *The Art of Memory*, 1–2.

2. Ibid., 16.

3. Mary Carruthers, *The Book of Memory*, 3–6; Yates, *Art of Memory*, 82–101.

4. Carruthers, *Book of Memory*, 122, and *The Craft of Thought: Meditation, Rhetoric, and the Making of Images*, 7–24.

5. Yates, *Art of Memory*, 46–47.

6. The following discussion of Quintilian depends on the sources cited here: Carruthers, *Book of Memory*, 122–55, and *Craft of Thought*, 130–33; Yates, *Art of Memory*, 21–28, 35–43.

7. Yates, *Art of Memory*, 74, 80–81, and see also 82–104.

8. See Carruthers, *Craft of Thought*, 221–76; Yates, *Art of Memory*.

9. Carruthers, *Craft of Thought*, 4.

10. Ibid., 19–21 (condensed).

11. Ibid., 244.

12. Ibid., 221–76.

13. Ibid., 224–27. For a fuller examination of this thesis, see pages 221–76,

and especially pages 228–31 for Carruthers's discussion of the Plan of St. Gall.

CHAPTER 12: *Honoring the Dead*

1. Ronald C. Finucane, *Miracles and Pilgrims: Popular Beliefs in Medieval England*, 28–29.
2. Peter Brown, *The Cult of the Saints*, 90.
3. Ibid., 2.
4. Patrick Geary, *Living with the Dead in the Middle Ages*, 83; for a broader discussion of the obligations of the living to the dead and vice versa, see also 77–92.
5. Ibid., 78–79, 83–87.
6. Ibid., 89–90; see also Geary, *Phantoms of Remembrance*.
7. See Georges Duby, *The Three Orders*, 202; Geary, *Living with the Dead*, 89–92.
8. Geary, *Living with the Dead*, 95–124.
9. Ibid., 96–100.
10. Ibid.
11. Ibid., 96.
12. Ibid., 99–101.
13. Ibid., 106–107.
14. Ibid., 95–124.
15. Finucane, *Miracles and Pilgrims*, 13.
16. André Vauchez, *Sainthood in the Later Middle Ages*, 457.
17. W. H. Vroom, *De Financiering van de Katheldraalbouw in de Middeleeuwen*, 629–31.
18. Finucane, *Miracles and Pilgrims*, 29; see also Otto von Simson, *The Gothic Cathedral*.
19. See Finucane, *Miracles and Pilgrims*, 193; Jonathan Sumption, *Pilgrimage: An Image of Medieval Religion*, 160; and Benedicta Ward, *Miracles and the Medieval World: Theory, Record, and Event, 1000–1225*, 95.
20. Sumption, *Pilgrimage*, 161.
21. Donald Weinstein and Rudolph Bell, *Saints and Society*, 5.
22. Vauchez, *Sainthood in the Later Middle Ages*, 462–77; Ward, *Miracles and the Medieval World*, 34; Patrick Geary, *Furta Sacra: Thefts of Relics in the Central Middle Ages*, 57; Finucane, *Miracles and Pilgrims*, 13; Thomas Coffey, Linda Kay Davidson, and Maryanne Dunn, *The Miracles of Saint James*, xxi–lxiv.
23. Geary, *Furta Sacra*, 22.

24. Ward, *Miracles and the Medieval World*, 34.
25. Sumption, *Pilgrimage*, 78.
26. See Keith Thomas, *Religion and the Decline of Magic*, 27.
27. Von Simson, *Gothic Cathedral*, 161–62.
28. Vauchez, *Sainthood in the Later Middle Ages*, 461.
29. Ibid., 427–29.
30. Sumption, *Pilgrimage*, 24.
31. Barbara Abou-El-Haj, *The Medieval Cult of Saints*, 12; see also Geary, *Furta Sacra;* Sumption, *Pilgrimage*.
32. Finucane, *Miracles and Pilgrims*, 26.
33. See David Ewing Duncan's account of the continual struggle to determine a true and accurate year in his fascinating book, *Calendar*.
34. Thomas, *Religion and the Decline of Magic*, 28; Robert Gottfried, *The Black Death*, 87; Abou-El-Haj, *Medieval Cult of Saints*, 43.
35. William Melczer, *The Pilgrim's Guide to Santiago de Compostela*, 3–4.
36. Vauchez, *Sainthood in the Later Middle Ages*, 466–77; see also Finucane, *Miracles and Pilgrims*, 32; Geary, *Furta Sacra*, 22; and Sumption, *Pilgrimage*.
37. Finucane, *Miracles and Pilgrims*, 9.
38. Ward, *Miracles and the Medieval World*, 82–90.
39. Thomas, *Religion and the Decline of Magic*, 261.
40. Ward, *Miracles and the Medieval World*, 2.
41. Sumption, *Pilgrimage*, 14.
42. Finucane, *Miracles and Pilgrims*, 74.
43. Ibid.; see also Vauchez, *Sainthood in the Later Middle Ages*, 468.
44. See especially Finucane, 69, 73–82.
45. Finucane, *Miracles and Pilgrims*, 75–76.
46. Ward, *Miracles and the Medieval World*, 142.
47. See Thomas, *Religion and the Decline of Magic*, 211; Robert Ader, "The Placebo Effect as a Conditioned Response"; Robert Ader, D. L. Felton, and N. Cohen, *Psychoneuroimmunology;* and Jerome Frank, *Persuasion and Healing: A Comparative Study of Psychotherapy*.
48. Thomas, *Religion and the Decline of Magic*, 209–10, 211.
49. Finucane, *Miracles and Pilgrims*, 17–24, especially 21; Thomas, *Religion and the Decline of Magic*, 25–26.
50. Finucane, *Miracles and Pilgrims*, 22; Vauchez, *Sainthood in the Later Middle Ages*, 15.
51. Vauchez, *Sainthood in the Later Middle Ages*, 16.
52. Ibid., 153.
53. Sumption, *Pilgrimage*, 62.

54. Vauchez, *Sainthood in the Later Middle Ages*, 19; Sumption, *Pilgrimage*, 63–72.

55. Finucane, *Miracles and Pilgrims*, 31; Vauchez, *Sainthood in the Later Middle Ages*, 36–37.

56. Ward, *Miracles and the Medieval World*, 187; Michael E. Goodich, *Violence and Miracle in the Fourteenth Century*, 7–14.

57. Vauchez, *Sainthood in the Later Middle Ages*, 40–48; Goodich, *Violence and Miracle*, 12.

58. Vauchez, *Sainthood in the Later Middle Ages*, 45–48.

59. Ibid., 482.

60. Ibid., 61, 65, 71, 279–84.

61. Ibid., 81.

62. Ibid., 100.

63. Ibid., 64.

CHAPTER 13: *Medieval Living Conditions*

1. Max Weber, *The Sociology of Religion*, 399.

2. See Christopher Dyer, *Standards of Living in the Later Middle Ages*.

3. See Jacques LeGoff, *The Birth of Purgatory;* Robert Lacey and Danny Danziger, *The Year 1000: What Life Was Like at the Turn of the First Millennium.*

4. The demographic data for the Middle Ages are compiled from Dyer, *Standards of Living*, 4–6; Josiah Cox Russell, *British Medieval Population*, 173–74, and "Population in Europe, 500–1500."

5. Graunt is quoted in Keith Thomas, 5–6. See also Ronald C. Finucane, *Miracles and Pilgrims*, 71–73; William Manchester, *A World Lit Only by Fire*, 54–56; and Barbara Hanawalt, *The Ties That Bound: Peasant Families in Medieval England*, 45–63.

6. See H. E. Hallam, *The Agrarian History of England and Wales, 1042–1350*, 818–24.

7. William Chester Jordan, *The Great Famine.*

8. Jordan, *Great Famine*, 108–23; Manchester, *World Lit Only by Fire*, 54.

9. Hanawalt, *Ties That Bound*, 48–51.

10. Manchester, *World Lit Only by Fire*, 55; Thomas, 5–6.

11. For information about the Black Death, see Robert S. Gottfried, *The Black Death;* David Herlihy, *The Black Death and the Transformation of the West;* Colin Platt, *King Death;* and Philip Ziegler, *The Black Death.*

12. Thomas, *Religion and the Decline of Magic*, 15–17.

13. William G. Naphy and Penny Roberts, *Fear in Early Modern Society*, 1.

14. Vauchez, *Sainthood in the Later Middle Ages*, 444.
15. Jordan, *Great Famine*, 21–22.

CHAPTER 14: *The Spiritual Brokers—Priests and Monarchs*

1. For a discussion of this hierarchy, see Georges Duby, *The Three Orders*, 13–20, 56–60.
2. See Duby, *Three Orders*, 57–58; Keith Thomas, *Religion and the Decline of Magic*, 29; Max Weber, *The Sociology of Religion*, 20–31, esp. 28.
3. Duby, *Three Orders*, 31.
4. John Harper, *The Forms and Orders of Western Liturgy from the Tenth to the Eighteenth Century*, 121–50.
5. See Kathleen Basford, *The Green Man*.
6. Michael Camille, *Images on the Edge: The Margins of Medieval Art*, 9–10.
7. See Émile Durkheim, *The Elementary Forms of Religious Life;* Siri Dulaney and Alan Fiske, "Cultural Rituals and Obsessive-Compulsive Disorder: Is There a Common Psychological Mechanism?"; Victor Turner and Edith Turner, *Image and Pilgrimage in Christian Culture*.
8. Thomas, *Religion and the Decline of Magic*, 29.
9. Suzanne Lewis, "Henry III and the Gothic Rebuilding of Westminster Abbey: The Problematics of Context," 130, 159, quotations at 147 and 163.
10. Christopher Wilson, *The Gothic Cathedral*, 178; see also Beat Brenk, "The Sainte-Chapelle as a Capetian Political Program."
11. Wilson, *Gothic Cathedral*, 224.
12. Georges Duby, *The Age of the Cathedrals*, 23.
13. Marc Bloch, *The Royal Touch: Sacred Monarchy and Scrofula in England and France*, 56–57.

CONCLUSION: *Learning from Stonehenge*

1. See Colin Burgess, *The Age of Stonehenge;* Rodney Castleden, *The Stonehenge People*, and *The Making of Stonehenge;* Christopher Chippindale, *Stonehenge Complete;* Alex Gibson, *Stonehenge and Timber Circles;* Gerald Hawkins and J. White, *Stonehenge Decoded;* John David North, *Stonehenge: Neolithic Man and the Cosmos;* Mike Pitts, *Hengeworld;* Julian Richards, *Stonehenge;* Miles Russell, *Monuments of the British Neolithic*.
2. *Sarsen stones* are a special variety of naturally occurring sandstone. According to archeologist Christopher Chippindale, 70 million or more years ago, "much of the chalk deposit, still lying on the sea-bed where it had been laid down, was covered with sand. In places the sand became firmly concreted into irregular blocks, and these remained when the chalk was raised into hills,

and the looser sand eroded away. These boulders are sarsens. They lie on or just under the chalk surface; their upper and lower faces, corresponding to the top and bottom of the sand stratum from which they formed, tend towards being flat and parallel" (see Chippendale, *Stonehenge Complete*, 38). The following explains terms used in the subsequent discussion: *Bluestones* are igneous rocks that are bluish in color and flecked with pink spots (ibid., 14). A *trilithon* is a structure consisting of three stones, two of them upright and parallel to each another; the third, termed a *lintel*, rests atop the parallel uprights. The term *henge* is imprecise, but generally describes a monument that is surrounded by a circular earthen bank and ditch (see North, *Stonehenge*, 286–87).

3. Castleden, *Making of Stonehenge*, 48; Pitts, *Hengeworld*, 109.

4. Castleden, *Making of Stonehenge*, 50.

5. Ibid., 55–58.

6. Ibid., 50–62. For an explanation of Castleden's method for making this calculation, see 254–55.

7. Ibid., 112–24.

8. Ibid., 150–54.

9. Ibid., 44.

10. Ibid.

Bibliography

Abou-El-Haj, Barbara. "The Audiences for the Medieval Cult of Saints." *Gesta* 32 (1991): 3–15.

———. *The Medieval Cult of Saints: Formations and Transformations.* Cambridge: Cambridge University Press, 1994.

Acland, James H. *Medieval Structure: The Gothic Vault.* Toronto: University of Toronto Press, 1977.

Ader, Robert. "The Placebo Effect as a Conditioned Response." In *Experimental Foundations of Behavioral Medicine,* ed. R. Ader, H. Weiner, and A. Baum, 47–66. Hillsdale, NJ: Lawrence Erlbaum, 1988.

Ader, Robert, D. L. Felton, and N. Cohen, eds. *Psychoneuroimmunology.* 2d ed. New York: Academic Press, 1991.

Amundsen, Darrel. *Medicine, Society, and Faith in the Ancient and Medieval Worlds.* Baltimore, MD, and London: Johns Hopkins University Press, 1996.

Barber, Malcolm. *The Two Cities.* London and New York: Routledge, 1992.

Bartlett, Robert. *The Making of Europe.* Princeton, NJ: Princeton University Press, 1993.

Basford, Kathleen. *The Green Man.* 1978. Reprint, Cambridge, U.K.: D. S. Brewer, 1998.

Bloch, Marc. *Feudal Society.* Chicago: University of Chicago Press, 1961.

———. *The Royal Touch: Sacred Monarchy and Scrofula in England and France.* London: Routledge and Kegan Paul, 1973.

Blum, Pamela. "The Sequence of the Building Campaigns at Salisbury." *Art Bulletin* 72, no. 1 (March 1991): 6–38.

Blumenthal, Uta-Renate. *The Investiture Controversy: Church and Monarchy from the Ninth to the Twelfth Century.* Philadelphia: University of Pennsylvania Press, 1988.

Bony, Jean. *French Gothic Architecture of the Twelfth and Thirteenth Centuries.* Berkeley, Los Angeles, London: University of California Press, 1983.

Boyd, James. "Construction Dates for Gothic Cathedrals and Great Churches (1135–1550)." Mimeo. November 1996.

Boyer, Pascal. *Religion Explained.* London: William Heinemann, 2001.

Branner, Robert. *Gothic Architecture.* New York: George Braziller, 1991.

Brenk, Beat. "The Sainte-Chapelle as a Capetian Political Program." In *Artistic Integration in Gothic Buildings,* ed. Virginia Chieffo Raguin, Kathryn Brush, and Peter Draper, 195–213. Toronto: University of Toronto Press, 1995.

Brown, Peter. *The Cult of the Saints: Its Rise and Function in Latin Christianity.* Chicago: University of Chicago Press, 1981.

Burgess, Colin. *The Age of Stonehenge.* London: Phoenix Press, 2001.

Camille, Michael. *Image on the Edge: The Margins of Medieval Art.* Cambridge, MA: Harvard University Press, 1992.

Carruthers, Mary. *The Book of Memory: A Study of Memory in Medieval Culture.* Cambridge: Cambridge University Press, 1990.

———. *The Craft of Thought: Meditation, Rhetoric, and the Making of Images, 400–1200.* Cambridge: Cambridge University Press, 1998.

Castleden, Rodney. *The Stonehenge People.* London and New York: Routledge and Kegan Paul, 1987.

———. *The Making of Stonehenge.* London and New York: Routledge, 1993.

Chippindale, Christopher. *Stonehenge Complete.* Rev. ed. London and New York: Thames and Hudson, 1994.

Cocke, Thomas. "Historical Summary." In *Salisbury Cathedral: Perspectives on the Architectural History,* by Thomas Cocke and Peter Kidson, 1–34. Ed. Royal Commission on the Historical Monuments of England. London: HMSO, 1993.

Coffey, Thomas, Linda Kay Davidson, and Maryanne Dunn. *The Miracles of Saint James.* New York: Italica Press, 1996.

Colvin, H. M., ed. *The History of the King's Works.* Vol. 1. *The Middle Ages.* London: HMSO, 1963.

Crosby, Sumner McKnight. *The Royal Abbey of Saint-Denis.* New Haven, CT: Yale University Press, 1987.

Dissanayake, Ellen. *What Is Art For?* Seattle and London: University of Washington Press, 1988.

Douglas, Mary. *Purity and Danger: An Analysis of Concepts of Pollution and Taboo.* New York: Praeger, 1966.

Duby, Georges. *The Early Growth of the European Economy.* Ithaca, NY: Cornell University Press, 1974.

———. *The Three Orders.* Chicago: University of Chicago Press, 1980.

———. *The Age of the Cathedrals: Art and Society, 980–1420.* Chicago: University of Chicago Press, 1981.

———. *France in the Middle Ages, 987–1460.* Oxford, U.K., and Cambridge, MA: Blackwell, 1991.

Dulaney, Siri, and Alan Fiske. "Cultural Rituals and Obsessive-Compulsive Disorder: Is There a Common Psychological Mechanism?" *Ethos* 22, no. 3 (1994): 243–83.

Duncan, David Ewing. *Calendar.* New York: Avon Books, 1998.

Dunlop, Ian. *The Cathedrals' Crusade: The Rise of the Gothic Style in France.* New York: Taplinger, 1982.

Durkheim, Émile. *The Elementary Forms of Religious Life.* Tr. with an intro. by Karen E. Fields. New York: Free Press, 1995. (Originally published as *Les Formes élémentaires de la vie religieuse: Le système totémique en Australie.* Paris: F. Alcan, 1912.)

Dyer, Christopher. *Standards of Living in the Later Middle Ages: Social Change in England c. 1200–1520.* Cambridge: Cambridge University Press, 1989.

Edwards, Kathleen. *Salisbury Cathedral: An Ecclesiastical History.* Trowbridge, England: Wiltshire County Council Library and Museum Service, 1986.

Ekelund, Robert, Robert Hebert, Robert Tollison, Gary Anderson, and Audrey Davidson. *Sacred Trust: The Medieval Church as an Economic Firm.* New York and Oxford: Oxford University Press, 1996.

Eliade, Mircea. *Patterns in Comparative Religion.* New York: Sheed and Ward, 1958.

Finucane, Ronald C. *Miracles and Pilgrims: Popular Beliefs in Medieval England.* 1977. Reprint, with a new introduction, New York: St. Martin's Press, 1995.

Fitchen, John. *The Construction of Gothic Cathedrals.* Chicago: University of Chicago Press, 1961.

Flint, Valerie. *The Rise of Magic in Early Medieval Europe.* Princeton, NJ: Princeton University Press, 1991.

Follett, Ken. *Pillars of the Earth.* New York; London; Victoria, Australia; Toronto; Auckland: Penguin Group, 1990.

Frank, Jerome. *Persuasion and Healing: A Comparative Study of Psychotherapy.* Baltimore, MD: Johns Hopkins University Press, 1961.

Frank, Robert Worth, Jr. "Pilgrims and Sacred Powers." In *Journeys Toward God: Pilgrimage and Crusade,* ed. Barbara Sargent-Bauer. Kalamazoo, MI: Medieval Institute Publications of Western Michigan University, 1992.

Frankl, Paul. *Sources from the Gothic Period.* Princeton, NJ: Princeton University Press, 1960.

————. *Gothic Architecture.* Baltimore, MD: Pelican Books, 1962.

Freedberg, David. *The Power of Images: Studies in the History and Theory of Response.* Chicago: University of Chicago Press, 1989.

Geary, Patrick. *Furta Sacra: Thefts of Relics in the Central Middle Ages.* Princeton, NJ: Princeton University Press, 1978.

————. *Living with the Dead in the Middle Ages.* Ithaca, NY, and London: Cornell University Press, 1994.

————. *Phantoms of Remembrance.* Princeton, NJ: Princeton University Press, 1994.

Geertz, Clifford. *The Interpretation of Culture.* New York: Basic Books, 1973.

Getz, Faye. *Medicine in the Middle Ages.* Princeton, NJ: Princeton University Press, 1998.

Gibson, Alex. *Stonehenge and Timber Circles.* Stroud, Gloucestershire: Tempuse, 1998.

Gimpel, Jean. *The Cathedral Builders.* New York: Evergreen Books, 1984.

Golding, William. *The Spire.* New York: Harcourt, Brace and World, 1964.

Goodich, Michael E. *Violence and Miracle in the Fourteenth Century: Private Grief and Public Salvation.* Chicago: University of Chicago Press, 1995.

Gordon, J. E. *Structures.* 1978. Reprint, London: Penguin Books, 1991.

Gottfried, Robert. *The Black Death: Natural and Human Disaster in Medieval Europe.* New York: Free Press, 1983.

Grant, Lindy. *Abbot Suger of St.-Denis: Church and State in Early Twelfth-Century France.* London and New York: Longman, 1998.

Hallam, H. E., ed. *The Agrarian History of England and Wales, 1042–1350.* Cambridge: Cambridge University Press, 1988.

Hanawalt, Barbara. *The Ties That Bound: Peasant Families in Medieval England.* New York and Oxford: Oxford University Press, 1986.

Harper, John. *The Forms and Orders of Western Liturgy from the Tenth to the Eighteenth Century: A Historical Introduction and Guide for Students and Musicians.* Oxford: Clarendon Press, 1991.

Hawkins, Gerald, and J. White. *Stonehenge Decoded.* London: Souvenir Press, 1965.

Herlihy, David. *The Black Death and the Transformation of the West.* Cambridge, MA: Harvard University Press, 1997.

Hindle, Brian Paul. *Medieval Town Plans.* Princes Riseborough, Buckinghamshire: Shire Publications, 1990.

Hugo, Victor. *Notre-Dame of Paris.* Tr. John Sturrocki. 1831. Reprint, London: Penguin Books, 1978.

Icher, François. *Building the Great Cathedrals.* Tr. Anthony Zielenka. New York: Henry N. Abrams, 1998.

James, John. *The Contractors of Chartres.* 2 vols. Dooralong, New South Wales: Mandorla Publications, 1979 and 1981.

—————. "An Investigation into the Uneven Distribution of Early Gothic Churches in the Paris Basin, 1140–1240." *Art Bulletin* 66, no. 1 (March 1984): 15–46.

James, Thomas Beaumont. *The Palaces of Medieval England.* London: Seaby, 1990.

Jansen, Virginia. "Gothic Art and Architecture." In *Medieval Germany: An Encyclopedia,* ed. John M. Jeep, 274–78. New York and London: Garland Publishing, 2001.

Johnson, Samuel. *The Letters of Samuel Johnson, with Mrs. Thrale's Genuine Letters to Him.* Ed. R. W. Chapman. Vol. 3. *1783–1784, Letters 821.2–1174.* Oxford, England: Clarendon Press, 1952.

Jones, A. Richard. "Gleanings from the 1253 Building Accounts of Westminster Abbey." *Avista Forum Journal* 2, no. 2 (fall 1998/winter 1999): 13–32.

Jordan, William Chester. *The Great Famine.* Princeton, NJ: Princeton University Press, 1996.

Kantorowicz, Norman. *The King's Two Bodies: A Study in Medieval Political Theology.* Princeton, NJ: Princeton University Press, 1957.

Kidson, Peter. "The Historical Circumstances and the Principles of the Design." In *Salisbury Cathedral: Perspectives on the Architectural History,* by Thomas Cocke and Peter Kidson, 35–91. Ed. Royal Commission on the Historical Monuments of England. London: HMSO, 1993.

Kienzle, Beverly Mayne, and Pamela J. Walker, eds. *Women Preachers and Prophets through Two Millennia of Christianity.* Berkeley, Los Angeles, London: University of California Press, 1998.

Knoblauch, H. "Phenomenology of Religion." *International Encyclopedia of the Social and Behavioral Sciences.* Ed. Neil J. Smelser and Paul B. Baltes, 13093–96. Amsterdam, Paris, New York, Oxford, Shannon, Singapore, Tokyo: Elsevier, 2001.

Knoop, Douglas, and G. P Jones. *The Medieval Mason: An Economic History of English Stone Buildings in the Later Middle Ages and Early Modern Times*. Manchester: Manchester University Press, 1933.

———."The Impressment of Masons in the Middle Ages." *Economic History Review* 8 (1937–38): 57–67.

———."The English Medieval Quarry." *Economic History Review* 9 (1938–39): 17–37.

———."The First Three Years of the Building of Vale Royal Abbey, 1278–1280." *Transactions of the Quatour Coronati Lodge* 46 (n.d.): 5–31.

Kusaba, Yoshio. "Is There a Relationship between Geometry and Construction Sequence at Salisbury Cathedral?" Thirty-third International Congress on Medieval Studies. Mimeo. Kalamazoo, MI: The Medieval Institute, May, 1998.

Lacey, Robert, and Danny Danziger. *The Year 1000: What Life Was Like at the Turn of the First Millennium*. London: Little, Brown, 1999.

Lawrence, C. H. *Medieval Monasticism*. 2d ed. Harlow, Essex, England: Longman Group, 1989.

LeGoff, Jacques. *The Birth of Purgatory*. Chicago: University of Chicago Press, 1981.

Lewis, Suzanne. "Henry III and the Gothic Rebuilding of Westminster Abbey: The Problematics of Context." In *Traditio: Studies in Ancient and Medieval History, Thought, and Religion*, 129–72. New York: Fordham University Press, 1995.

Manchester, William. *A World Lit Only by Fire*. Boston, New York, Toronto, London: Little, Brown, 1992.

Martin, Henri-Jean. *The History and Power of Writing*. Chicago: University of Chicago Press, 1988.

McKitterick, Rosamond, ed. *The Use of Literacy in Early Medieval Europe*. Cambridge: Cambridge University Press, 1990.

Melczer, William. *The Pilgrim's Guide to Santiago de Compostela*. New York: Italica Press, 1993.

Miller, Edward, and John Hatcher. *Medieval England: Rural Society and Economic Change, 1086–1348*. London: Longman, 1978.

———. *Medieval England: Towns, Commerce and Crafts, 1086–1348*, London and New York: Longman, 1995.

Mollat, Michel. *The Poor in the Middle Ages*. New Haven, CT: Yale University Press, 1986.

Morris, Richard. *Cathedrals and Abbeys of England and Wales: The Building Church, 600–1540*. New York: W. W. Norton, 1979.

Murray, Stephen. *Building Troyes Cathedral: The Late Gothic Campaigns.* Bloomington and Indianapolis: Indiana University Press, 1987.

————. *Beauvais Cathedral: Architecture of Transcendence.* Princeton, NJ: Princeton University Press, 1989.

————. *Notre-Dame, Cathedral of Amiens: The Power of Change in Gothic.* Cambridge: Cambridge University Press, 1996.

Naphy, William G., and Penny Roberts, eds. *Fear in Early Modern Society.* Manchester and New York: Manchester University Press, 1997.

Nirenberg, David. *Communities of Violence.* Princeton, NJ: Princeton University Press, 1996.

North, John David. *Stonehenge: Neolithic Man and the Cosmos.* London: HarperCollins, 1996.

Nussbaum, Norbert. *German Gothic Church Architecture.* New Haven, CT: Yale University Press, 2000.

O'Shea, Stephen. *The Perfect Heresy.* New York: Walker, 2000.

Panofsky, Erwin. *Abbot Suger: On the Abbey Church of St.-Denis and Its Art Treasures.* Princeton, NJ: Princeton University Press, 1946.

————. *Gothic Architecture and Scholasticism.* New York: Penguin Books, 1957.

Pitts, Mike. *Hengeworld.* London: Arrow Books, 2001.

Platt, Colin. *King Death: The Black Death and Its Aftermath in Late-Medieval England.* Toronto and Buffalo: University of Toronto Press, 1966.

Pouillon, Fernand. *The Stones of the Abbey.* Tr. Edward Gillott. Orlando, FL: Harcourt Brace Jovanovich, 1985.

Radding, Charles, and William Clark. *Medieval Architecture, Medieval Learning: Builders and Masters in the Age of Romanesque and Gothic.* New Haven, CT: Yale University Press, 1992.

Richards, Julian. *Stonehenge.* London: B. T. Batsford/English Heritage, 1991.

Risebero, Bill. *The Story of Western Architecture.* Rev. ed. Cambridge, MA: MIT Press, 1997.

Roth, Cecil. *A History of Jews in England.* Oxford: Clarendon Press, 1941.

Rubin, Miri. *Corpus Christi: The Eucharist in Late Medieval Culture.* Cambridge: Cambridge University Press, 1991.

Russell, Josiah Cox. *British Medieval Population.* Albuquerque: University of New Mexico Press, 1948.

———— "Population in Europe, 500–1500." [1966]. In *Fontana Economic*

History of Europe. Vol. 1. *The Middle Ages*, ed. Carlo M. Cipolla, 25–71. Glasgow: Collins/Fontana, 1972.

Russell, Miles. *Monuments of the British Neolithic*. Stround, Gloucestershire, U.K.: Tempus, 2002.

Rutherford, Edward. *Sarum*. New York: Ballantine Books, 1988.

Sallis, John. *Stone*. Bloomington and Indianapolis: Indiana University Press, 1994.

Salvadori, Mario. *Why Buildings Stand Up*. New York and London: W. W. Norton, 1980.

Salzman, L. F. *Building in England Down to 1540: A Documentary History*. 1952. Reprint, Oxford: Clarendon Press, 1992.

Sargent-Baur, Barbara, ed. *Journeys toward God: Pilgrimage and Crusade*. Kalamazoo, MI: Medieval Institute Publications of Western Michigan University, 1992.

Scott, John, and John O. Ward. *The Vézelay Chronicle*. Binghamton, NY: Center for Medieval and Renaissance Studies, 1992.

Simon, Herbert. "The Architecture of Complexity." *Proceedings of the American Philosophical Society* 106 (December 1962): 467–82.

Siraisi, Nancy G. *Medieval and Early Renaissance Medicine: An Introduction to Knowledge and Practice*. Chicago: University of Chicago Press, 1990.

Speed, Peter, ed. *Those Who Worked*. New York: Italica Press, 1997.

Spiegel, Gabrielle. *The Chronicle Tradition of Saint-Denis: A Survey*. Brookline, MA and Leyden, Netherlands: Classical Folio Editions, 1978.

Spring, Roy. *Salisbury Cathedral: The New Bell's Cathedral Guides*. London: Unwin Hyman, 1987.

Spufford, Peter. *Money and Its Uses in Medieval Europe*. Cambridge: Cambridge University Press, 1988.

Strayer, Joseph. *On the Medieval Origins of the Modern State*. Princeton, NJ: Princeton University Press, 1973.

Sumption, Jonathan. *Pilgrimage: An Image of Medieval Religion*. London: Faber and Faber, 1975.

———. *The Albigensian Crusade*. London and New York: Faber and Faber, 1978.

Swaan, Wim. *The Gothic Cathedral*. 1969. Reprint, Ware, Hertfordshire: Omega Books, 1984.

Tatton-Brown, Tim. *Great Cathedrals of Britain*. London: BBC Books, 1989.

Tellenbach, Gerd. *The Church in Western Europe from the Tenth to the Early Twelfth Century*. Cambridge: Cambridge University Press, 1993.

Thomas, Keith. *Religion and the Decline of Magic*. New York: Charles Scribner's Sons, 1971.

Tierney, Brian. *The Crises of Church and State 1050–1300.* Toronto, Buffalo, NY, and London: University of Toronto Press in association with the Medieval Academy of America, 1988.

Tobin, Stephen. *The Cistercians.* Woodstock, NY: Overlook Press, 1996.

Turner, Victor, and Edith Turner. *Image and Pilgrimage in Christian Culture.* New York: Columbia University Press, 1978.

VanDam, Raymond. *Saints and Their Miracles in Late Antique Gaul.* Princeton, NJ: Princeton University Press, 1993.

Vauchez, André. *Sainthood in the Later Middle Ages.* Tr. Jean Birrell. Cambridge: Cambridge University Press, 1997.

von Simson, Otto. *The Gothic Cathedral: Origins of Gothic Architecture and the Medieval Concept of Order.* Bollingen Series 48. 1956. Reprint, Princeton, NJ: Princeton University Press, 1988.

Vroom, W. H. *De Financiering van de Katheldraalbouw in de Middeleeuwen.* Maarssen, Netherlands: Gary Schwartz, 1981.

Ward, Benedicta. *Miracles and the Medieval World: Theory, Record, and Event, 1000–1225.* Rev. ed. Philadelphia: University of Pennsylvania Press, 1987.

Warnke, Martin. *Bau und Überbau.* Frankfurt am Main: Syndikat, 1976.

Weber, Max. *The Sociology of Religion.* Tr. Talcott Parsons. 1922. Reprint, Boston: Beacon Press, 1993 .

Weinstein, Donald, and Rudolph Bell. *Saints and Society.* Chicago: University of Chicago Press, 1982.

Weir, Alison. *Eleanor of Aquitaine: By the Wrath of God, Queen of England.* London: Pimlico, 2000.

Williams, Jane Welch. *Bread, Wine, and Money: The Windows of the Trades at Chartres Cathedral.* Chicago and London: University of Chicago Press, 1993.

Willis, Robert. *The architectural history of Chichester cathedral, with an introductory essay on the fall of the tower and spire, by the Rev. R. Willis; of Boxgrove priory, by the Rev. J. L. Petit; and of Shoreham collegiate church, together with the collective architectural history of the foregoing buildings, as indicated by their mouldings, by Edmund Sharpe.* Chichester: W. H. Mason, 1861.

Wilson, Christopher. *The Gothic Cathedral.* London: Thames and Hudson, 1990.

Yates, Frances A. *The Art of Memory.* Chicago: University of Chicago Press, 1966.

Ziegler, Philip. *The Black Death.* Stroud, Gloucestershire, U.K.: Sutton, 1969.

Illustrations and Credits

All grotesques on chapter openings were drawn by Cindy Davis. Those on the openings for chapters 1, 4, 7, and 10, as well as the Green Man in lower left of figure 50 (page 226), are based on photographs from *The Green Man* by Kathleen Basford, by kind permission of Common Ground. All Crown copyright material is reproduced by permission of English Heritage acting under license from the Controller of Her Majesty's Stationery Office.

FRONT MATTER

Lantern tower of Rouen Cathedral. Photograph © Robert Scott. / ii

Salisbury Cathedral from water meadow. Photograph © Vicki Fox. / vi

PART OPENERS

FIGURES

in William G. C. Backinsell's "Medieval Engineering in Salisbury Cathedral," Historical Monograph 10, South Wiltshire Industrial Archeology Society (August 1986). / 26

7. Capstone of Salisbury Cathedral's spire. Drawing by Cindy Davis. / 27

8. Wooden scaffolding inside Salisbury Cathedral's spire. Photograph © Robert Nyden. / 28

9. Windlass for lifting building materials. Drawing by Cindy Davis, based on an artist's rendering in William G. C. Backinsell's "Medieval Windlasses at Salisbury, Peterborough and Tewkesbury," Historical Monograph 7, South Wiltshire Industrial Archeology Society (June 1980). / 29

10. *The Interior of Salisbury Cathedral Looking Towards the North Transept*, by J. M. W. Turner, c. 1802. Photograph © Salisbury and South Wiltshire Museum. / 30

11. Westminster Abbey. Photograph © John Wilkes. / 37

12. Canterbury Cathedral as it appeared in 1799. Painting by James Malton in the collection of The King's School, Canterbury; photograph Crown Copyright, NMR. / 41

13. Romsey Abbey. Photograph © Lois Gerber. / 59

14. Burgos Cathedral and city. Photograph © John Wilkes. / 69

15. West front of Abbey Church of St. Denis. Photograph © Virginia Jansen. / 83

16. Nave of Abbey Church of St. Denis. Photograph © Virginia Jansen. / 87

17. Cathedral of Notre Dame, Paris. Photograph © John Wilkes. / 93

18. Cathedral of Santiago de Compostela. © John Wilkes. / 96

19. Design of Salisbury Cathedral as geometrically derived from 39-foot square. Drawing by Cindy Davis. / 104

20. Plan of Amiens Cathedral, "unfolding" from center. Drawing by Cindy Davis, after and by permission of Stephen Murray. / 105

21. Amiens Cathedral interior. Photograph © Virginia Jansen. / 107

22. Gothic ceiling vaults inside Amiens Cathedral. Photograph © Virginia Jansen. / 108

23. Side aisle of Canterbury Cathedral. Photograph © John Wilkes. / 109

24. Barrel vault and ribbed vault. Drawing by Cindy Davis, after James H. Acland's *Medieval Structure: The Gothic Vault*, by permission of University of Toronto Press. / 111

25. Nave of Christchurch Priory. Photograph © Lois Gerber. / 112

26. Transformation of Winchester Cathedral from Romanesque to Gothic. Drawing by John Hardacre after Robert Willis, by permission of the Dean and Chapter, Winchester Cathedral. / 114

Index

Page numbers in italics refer to illustrations.

Text: 11.5/15 Fournier
Display: Fournier
Designer: Nola Burger
Indexer: Carol Roberts
Compositor: Integrated Composition Systems
Printer + binder: Edwards Brothers